HISTORY ON THE MOVE

Credits:
Cover Illustration: Mrs. Seeroon Yeretzian - Glendale, California
Cover Design: Mr. Harry Mesrobian, Gemini Designs - Glendale, California
Back Cover Photo: Tchamsarian - Aleppo, Syria

HISTORY
ON THE MOVE

VIEWS, INTERVIEWS AND ESSAYS
ON ARMENIAN ISSUES

BY

Edmond Y. Azadian

Edited, with an Introduction

by

Agop J. Hacikyan and Edward S. Franchuk

1999

RECOGNITION

The author of this book owes a deep debt of gratitude to the writer and scholar Agop J. Hacikyan for initiating the project of this book, for selecting the texts and editing them along with Prof. Edward S. Franchuk.

Also, sentiments of gratitude are in order to Harout Yeretzian of Abril Printing for volunteering his time and exquisite taste to the lay-out and pagination of the book.

Finally, sincere thanks to Judy and Michael Cheteyan Educational Foundation, for undertaking and underwriting the publication of this book.

The Author

ACKNOWLEDGEMENTS

We wish to thank Edmond Y. Azadian for letting us edit and select freely from the many essays, articles and commentaries he has written over the past ten years.

We also acknowledge with gratitude the editors of The Armenian Mirror Spectator *and* Abaka *who first published the major bulk of the essays and articles included in this book.*

The Editors

CONTENTS

Introduction

Edmond Yervant Azadian has been contributing essays, reviews, editorials, commentaries, and letters, both in Armenian and in English, to the Armenian press for the last four decades. As a journalist and essayist he keeps constant watch over every crucial event related to Armenia and the Armenian diaspora and reports the results of his observations with remarkable reliability.

Azadian has always demonstrated a fiercely focused energy that complements his impressive intelligence and versatility. He has been a tireless advocate for Armenian cultural, religious, and political affairs. He has served as Chairman of the Armenian General Benevolent Union's Alex and Marie Manoogian Cultural Fund for more than twenty years, and is a member of the governing boards of several Armenian community schools from Los Angeles to Detroit, the producer of Armenian cultural radio programs aired throughout the United States, an active member on an international level of the Armenian Democratic Liberal Organization, a member and one time president of the Tekeyan Cultural Association Central Board of Directors, a member of the editorial boards of several Armenian journals and newspapers, and a member of the Writers Union of Armenia. Such involvements keep him well informed of developments that might have a direct or indirect bearing on Armenian political, economic, and cultural aspirations. His numerous missions have taken him all over the globe, especially to Armenia, on countless occasions; this has given him the opportunity to witness many of the events which have changed Armenian destiny over the last decade.

Edmond Yervant Azadian was born in Lebanon and graduated from the American University of Beirut, assuming a full-time position as assistant editor of *Zartonk*. Then, at the age of 23, he agreed to take over the Arev daily newspaper in Cairo, the past editors of which included Vahan Tekeyan, Mikael Giurjian, and Mihran Damadian. In this environment of intellectual stimulation, Azadian replenished his creative strength and developed an extraordinary consciousness of the Armenian social, cultural, and political past. This experience has been constantly reflected in his work, whether written in Armenian or English.

After a fruitful literary and journalistic career and public life in Egypt, he was asked to direct the Baikar Association in Boston, which published *Baikar* and *The Armenian Mirror-Spectator*, a function he filled until his appointment as personal assistant to Alex Manoogian, the prominent Armenian benefactor, and to the position of Chairman of the Manoogian Cultural Fund. Azadian's new duties did not, however, put an end to his contributions to the Armenian press: his editorials and commentaries appear regularly in North America, the Middle East, South America, and Armenia.

History on the Move is a collection of Azadian's English-language essays and articles on a wide range of contemporary issues: politics, religion, social questions, and community affairs, as well as interviews with well-known contemporary figures. The tone of these pieces is mostly personal, and they are written in a consistently graceful and accessible style. But the clarity and elegance are deceptive: each piece exhibits considerable subtlety in its awareness of meanings and distinctions and even a certain measure of complexity in its development of underlying meanings through occasional figures of speech and other devices.

Azadian is an incomparable commentator on complex situations, political stalemates, and ironic developments, regardless of the context. He is an observer and explorer, who allows the reader to share in his observations and accompany him on his explorations. Like all accomplished essayists and journalists, he has constructed a persona: although he seldom writes about himself or personal matters, his ideas, scenarios, and suggestions are direct reflections of his personality and principles. The reader is always aware of the presence of the author as a human being, a thinker, and an analyzer, with human feelings and convictions. Observations based on his own experiences underline his points and draw connections between his suggestions or solutions and the subjects being examined. His very personal engagement with the subjects he writes about in fact gives his essays their deepest dimension, so that even when he is being self-effacing the reader senses the significance his carefully chosen topics have for him. This personal quality raises his writing above mere political or social commentary.

Azadian bolsters his ideas and opinions by ensuring that they are presented in articulated and effective forms: a sense of movement and climax, a placing of arguments so that they are cumulative in effect, a contrasting of points-of-view that produces irony and surprise. His frequent attention to detail fleshes out the subjects and the people he is writing about, lending them extra persuasiveness. On the other hand, his essays are often filled with cross-references: parenthetical sign-posts that help the reader make thematic connections to other articles and essays.

The practice probably stems from his background as a man of letters, journalist, cultural administrator, and political activist: a man endowed with a flexible mind in pursuit of novel solutions and new horizons.

Having said all this, one must point out that Azadian is not overly dependent on any one literary or stylistic technique. Many prolific essayists have characteristic stylistic strategies, pet phrases, or even quotations, which get them going. Azadian, on the other hand, tackles his diverse subjects with a variety of approaches and techniques. His way of handling a debate is to yoke disparate elements successfully together. His writing proceeds from a deep core of concern, outrage, grief, passion, and above all national centrality--the Armenian nation, the diaspora, Etchmiadzin, national events--seasoned with equilibrium and punctuated with up-to-date information.

History on the Move reveals Azadian as above all a chronicler of the Armenian national consciousness, the unearther of those rare but fascinating moments that build the historic pageant of a nation. He chronicles the fortunes and misfortunes both of Armenia and of the Armenian diaspora against the backdrop of changing international political realities. The pieces in this book have a cumulative effect, forming what is in effect an extended essay, united by controlling metaphors and resonant motifs. The writer tours his homeland, looking through the eyes of a concerned citizen, and he takes the reader with him, pointing out along the way what we urgently need to know or feel before we can properly assess the issues he examines. He believes firmly that an issue can only be understood in its historical, social, and cultural context and he considers the providing of this context to be a major function of journalism. Indeed, the bulk of Azadian's carefully examined expositions in English consists of precisely this placing of issues in their historical context. His frequent references to the events of Armenian and world history demonstrate the relevance of his subjects to the human history in progress and project his vision into the course of future developments. Historical information and similar details help us visualize and comprehend the unfolding and development of the issues he examines. This is why all of his articles, whether on political, social, or religious issues, can be said to deal, at least analogically and subtly, with the shaping of post-Soviet Armenia and the diaspora.

In his political articles, what might appear to be weaknesses in an essayist are in fact his greatest strengths, as he always uses them to his own advantage, to underline his arguments. His extraordinary eye for ordinary details stimulates him to come up with fresh and telling observations. For him physical details, which might perhaps seem insignificant or even irrelevant, can clarify and reinforce abstract arguments, and he always knows which details to emphasize, as though through some kind of journalistic epiphany. The prime example included in this collection is the essay "Destination Deir Zor." Furthermore, some of his essays and commentaries might seem to lack tightness of construction or polish; some might even be thought to lack inner tension. But in most instances this seems to be a deliberate ploy, in order to allow the reader the opportunity to think the issue through for himself; Azadian's hints on the side, though, his lucidity of analysis, make sure that the reader does not stray from the issue at hand. His habitual stance is that of a conciliator between conflicting parties or issues. While this approach is undeniably positive and constructive, it may occasionally risk sweeping the substantial differences between the two sides of an argument under the carpet.

Azadian is a rare polemicist: he analyzes the conditions and circumstances surrounding his topics and subjects his ideas to rigorous examination, in an attempt to discover the concepts central to understanding the issue under discussion. This process ensures that his discussions are infused with rigor and clarity, as well as maintaining the insights requisite to the task at hand.

In his hundreds of political articles, essays, and letters, Azadian has written on all of the contemporary national questions: the Karabagh conflict, American foreign policy regarding Armenia and Azerbaijan, the Turkish blockade, the Armenian elections, the collapse of Communism, etc. A good political commentary requires a psychologist's eye, a historian's nose, and an essayist's feel for narrative. It is a highly organized form of international gossip, and the more controversial corners the commentator can wriggle into--and the more sensitive--the better (and more interesting) the resulting article. In these respects Azadian excels. He writes with a sharply defined "take" on his subject, which determines how he views the evidence and what construction he places on it. The result is often an essay--usually a short one--that brings the issue before the reader in vivid detail.

The political essays are written by the public Azadian, the thinker and activist responsible for an extraordinary output of commentaries, analyses, and reviews, and the tireless laborer for truth and freedom. His essays on community affairs and religious questions are more personal, often revealing much about his feelings; indeed, reading these essays in conjunction with the political pieces leads one to conclude that for Azadian to think and to feel is to write. In less capable hands, many of his remarks in these emotional pieces would be dismissed as muttered asides or hyperbolic utterances proceeding from the bitterness or rancor of private debate: his opposition to the election of Karekin II as Catholicos of All Armenians is so deeply felt as to be almost tangible, for example. In his straightforward prose, however, these emotional outbursts are usually transformed into incisive comments on contemporary issues of burning interest to the entire community. This is not to say that his emotional involvement with a topic does not sometimes lead him to overstatement and diatribe--his inability to see Turks and Turkey in any light but that of the Genocide is an obvious example--but the intelligent reader will soon recognize these sensitive areas (and they are not many) and perhaps make allowances for them: they proceed from very devastating and bitter personal and family experiences. Furthermore, they are unintentional: as Azadian himself writes, "viewing ... events in their historic perspective, we do not have the right to allow our biases to color our objective judgments" ("Armenia's Independence Day").

It is impossible to write about Azadian's essays without mentioning his long years as a public worker devoted to his political principles, the political aspirations of his homeland, and the Armenian Apostolic Church. Even when he is conducting an interview, the rudiments of his major beliefs may sometimes interject themselves into the process of the interview, putting the person interviewed under the obligation of starting an unexpected polemic with him: the provocative interview with Dr. Jack Kevorkian is a prime example. The result is almost always both interesting and informative.

History on the Move does not include any of Azadian's extensive reviews, which reveal him also to be a perceptive literary critic and scholar. The essays included here do, however, expose another of his literary facets: that of craftsman. His essays are often more like short stories: well-rounded, self-contained, and resonant, written with a distinctive sensitivity that draws the reader in. Again, the essay "Destination Deir Zor" springs most readily to mind.

Despite his predilection for analysis and detail, Azadian is not a laborious writer. One cannot help being impressed by his ability to write under pressure, his tact which is nevertheless combined with total honesty, and indeed his very persistence as a writer. His work reflects his talent for cutting through complicated circumstances, digging out the important facts, and serving them up in intelligent, convincing, and at times controversial ways. He is at his best when confronting situations of conflict head-on, asking and arguing the questions that we would all love to put directly to the people involved.

Among the most lucid of Azadian's expositions are those written after the collapse of Soviet Armenia. They comprise overwhelming criticisms of religious affairs and the Karabagh conflict. They expose the evasions, muddle-headedness, self-deception, and bad faith that to an alarming degree currently shape the Armenian destiny. In his essays as well as in public life, Azadian argues an impassioned case for self-determination for the Armenians of Nagorno Karabagh, but he never ignores the devastating emotional turmoil and physical ravages that all the people of that mountainous region have suffered. He points out that the position of the international community regarding this long-standing conflict is ravaging both the region and the nation. His work continues a long line of polemics that use examples to illustrate and decry the ugliness that pervades the war-stricken zone, emphasizing what everybody interested in the subject knows to be true: that too much of what masquerades as Turkish or American aid intervention in fact degrades the situation and enhances hostilities between the Azeris and the Armenians. As a journalist, Azadian is eager to understand the forces that shape Armenian destiny and to explain convincingly the reasons behind so much long-lasting suffering and cruelty, which have taken heavy tolls and ruined the chances of a sustained peace. He emphasizes, among a variety of other causes, the rich Azerbaijani oil deposits and their influence on American foreign policy in the region.

In his ecclesiastical essays, especially in those concerning the election of Catholicos Karekin II in April 1995, Azadian's journalism generally favors assertion over argumentation. In other instances, he probes the logical roots of his topic, providing concise references and historical summaries before arriving at his conclusion. Such varied information is brought together and coheres through the essays' highly personal organization. After all, Azadian's perceptions of issues inherent to the Armenian Church and his outspoken views on other topics have been amplified and sharpened by forty years of journalism. He renders judgments in a style that is distinctively cadenced and weighty: sometimes stentorian but always morally commanding and always ready to make a leap of the imagination.

A journalist's strength lies not only in his ability to report accurately what he sees, but also in his ability to pose pertinent questions before he even begins writing. Such questions have a sort of nagging power, creating at times a feverish desire that the writer delve more deeply into his subject and expand his analysis. Azadian is a master at exploring his topic before he puts pen to paper, and the impact is immediate and gratifying.

Azadian is an informed writer. He is fully aware that contemporary world politics and the economic evolution of Armenia are sometimes in conflict. Perhaps the situation can be expected to worsen, as the full effect of contradictions between Armenia's transition to a new economy and the harsh measures of international policies hit home. Despite this disheartening possibility, Azadian remains confident that, whatever else may change and no matter what the obstacles, the nation will attain its goal. Such confidence is a luxury that many journalists do not permit themselves--but Azadian always gives the impression that the dangers he expresses in blunt and passionate warnings to his readers lie precisely in those areas where he most passionately desires a successful outcome. His anxieties naturally have to do with economics, in particular with the present confused state of Armenia's budding market economy. An even stronger concern is the outside partisan forces which are eroding Armenia's control over its own internal affairs. Because of his confidence in the outcome, however, he is able to write about these matters without letting prevailing conditions reduce his ideas and articles to mere reactionary twaddle.

In a nutshell, to read Azadian is to find a path through a terrain littered with countless day-to-day issues, obstacles, intrigues, aspirations, advice, and warnings. His essays and even his interviews reflect his opinions and observations on various matters. They are the work of an empirical critic, who does not scruple to contradict himself whenever he feels the urge to declare his feelings honestly. Although often relentless and provocative, they are always systematic, persuasive vignettes, of inestimable value to those who would feel the temper and tenor of the Armenian nation. What it comes down to is that what distinguishes Azadian's writing is its essential claim to truth. Even though his essays are sometimes ironic or even playful, each of them sets forth a serious thesis, which the reader is invited to accept.

Although concise and disparate, these essays create a continuum, a web of connections and relationships. However critical or relentless some of them may be, the larger effect is one of great gusto and good advice, even more, of wisdom and veracity. Few writers know more about Armenia and can express what they know better than Edmond Y. Azadian has done in these insightful and informative pieces.

Agop J. Hacikyan
Edward S. Franchuk

Part One

ARTZAKH (KARABAGH) & ARMENIA

Opposite page, the author with:
1. Former President Levon Ter Petrossian.
2. President Robert Kocharian.
3. Zori Balayan.
4. Baroness Caroline Cox.
5. Mascot of Independence Movement (middle),
   Vasken Sarksian, Prime Minister and former
   Minister of Defense (right).

ADDRESS TO THE PARLIAMENT OF ARMENIA:

On Independence and the Future of the Republic

The Republic of Armenia declared independence on September 23, 1991, following a referendum which took place on September 21, 1991. Edmond Azadian was present in Parliament to witness the historic event.

A year earlier, Armenia's Parliament had debated a draft resolution on its intention to declare independence from the Soviet Union. That Resolution of Intent was adopted by Parliament on August 23, 1990.

During the debate preceding the adoption of that Resolution, Edmond Azadian was one of the few Armenian leaders from the diaspora to address Parliament. His address was delivered on behalf of the diaspora leadership of the ADL[1] on August 20, 1990. He was introduced to Parliament by Levon Ter Petrossian, at that time the Speaker of Parliament.

Below is a translation of Azadian's speech.

After many long centuries during which our ancestors were denied their freedom, for me it is like a long-cherished dream come true to stand on this land, now free, to rise to the podium of Armenia's Parliament, and share my thoughts and feelings in my own native language with an august group of people who hold in their hands the responsibility of determining the destiny of this land and consequently the destiny of the entire Armenian nation. It is indeed a historic dream, for me as well as for the Armenian Democratic Liberal Organization, on whose behalf I have the distinct pleasure and honor to address this legislative body.

---

1. Armenian Democratic Liberal Organization.

Both as an individual and as a representative of my organization, I have always had the highest esteem for the legendary heroes of the Armenian liberation movement, whose blood and struggle are about to be vindicated today. Our organization, through its roots in the Armenakan Party of Van and the Reformed Hunchak Party, has reared a group of fine patriots among the ranks of those legendary heroes. Our organization has also already celebrated the rebirth of statehood in this land through very tangible support. On August 4, 1920, during the French occupation, one of our patriotic leaders, Mihran Damadian, the hero of Mush, declared Armenian home rule in Cilicia, raising the tri-color flag on Government Headquarters in Adana.

Our leaders and founders supported the first Republic of Armenia,[2] despite their ideological differences with and reservations about the ruling party of the day.

Our organization also supported the Soviet Republic of Armenia, while expressing our opposition to its totalitarian and socialistic regime.

Our organization provided a squadron of military aircraft to the first Republic of Armenia, as well as funds for the creation of a tank division, named after David of Sassoun, during World War II. And it extended that support to the Soviet Republic with the same patriotic fervor, despite the fact that the first Republic was the ideological antithesis of the latter.

That consistently patriotic approach was born out of concern for the people of this land, who had survived the Genocide: an approach over and above ideological considerations and positions.

And today, at the birth of this new Republic, I come to extend my hand to its new leadership, with the same belief, dedication, and commitment that our founding fathers harbored during the earlier days of the First Republic of Armenia and the Soviet Republic of Armenia. I extend my hand to the freely elected leadership which has been called to the sacred task of leading our country into the future.

The Armenian people have many noble traits of character which we recognize and of which we feel proud. But at this moment of truth, only self-analysis and the recognition of our inadequacy to face these historic times with wisdom will help us arrive at the right answers. Because of the unfortunate plight of our people in the past, we have not been able

---

2. 1918-20.

to rise to the challenge of building state authority and paying due respect to our national heroes and leaders, and for that reason we have lost many opportunities to restore our statehood, thereby losing our freedom. Indeed, at heart every individual Armenian is still a subject, which hampers our collective will to build our own statehood and run our own country.

It is now high time to subjugate all of our individual egos to the collective ego of the homeland. The history of the past 72 years serves well to demonstrate that no single group possesses a monopoly on the wisdom needed to save our homeland.

Today we have a freely elected Parliament and a Speaker of that Parliament in the person of Levon Ter Petrossian. Therefore, no matter what reservations, preferences, and grievances we may harbor in our hearts, we must postpone their expression to a later date, and rally around our newly-created statehood. That is the logic of these momentous events. Once our independence is restored and a stable government has emerged, we will have ample time to indulge in the luxury of democratic debate and discourse.

The ADL has already announced its whole-hearted support to the new government, pledging to contribute towards its stability and towards the reconstruction of the entire country. Do we not, then, have criticisms and reservations, as moral citizens of this Republic and as representatives of an organization which stands for democracy? Of course we have: just as many as the members of this body or groups outside of Parliament have. But the internal stability of the homeland is at stake, and as the country faces a siege from outside, how patriotic would it be for us to give first priority to our right to express disagreement, thereby consigning to second place more urgent issues, which might jeopardize the very existence of the homeland?

Let us be aware of the danger that the present Republic might become history's last gift to us if we fail to demonstrate the wisdom to preserve it through unconditional and broad-based support.

The new developments in Armenia allow us to promote many issues. Already our history is being revised and our past values are being re-appraised. The focus of this re-evaluation is on our history: on the leaders of our liberation movement, and on the glorious battles we have fought in the past. Of course, we must show some understanding for the overzealous exaggerations that inevitably arise in these days of euphoria. As time passes, judicious and well-balanced evaluations will replace the lavish enthusiasm of the present.

I am convinced that in the process of carrying out its agenda of re-evaluating our past, the new Parliament will restore our classical orthography, consigning to history the current orthography—created by Abeghian —which caused a schism between the people of Armenia and the diaspora, while disfiguring our language and alienating our people from its history and ancient culture.

Today, many divided nations are seeking re-unification. Armenians need unity more than any other nation. It is our fervent hope that this Parliament, in its wisdom and through its actions, will restore unity among Armenians, not only in orthography, but in all other spheres of our life. The declaration which is being debated at this time can play a crucial role in this mission.

We have followed the debates in which this legislative body has been engaged with undivided attention. All the results of your deliberations are not only being communicated to our leadership abroad, but are also being exposed to the general public through our news media.

Like most Armenians in the diaspora, we are familiar with the various drafts of the declaration currently being debated in Parliament. One of those drafts, or perhaps a composite of all of them, will soon be adopted, and will chart the course for the independence of our Republic.

It would not be proper for me to comment on any one of those drafts. But I feel duty-bound to propose here certain issues of vital importance to our people, which the final draft of the declaration must address:

A. Independence is an absolute necessity for a country operating under democratic rule, as well as the inalienable right of our people. We support independence wholeheartedly and unequivocally.

B. Independent national statehood is not simply a declaration on paper. It is action and achievement. Therefore, the entire nation must take those actions which will lead our homeland, in successive stages, to the achievement of full independence, politically and economically.

C. As an organization which cultivates realism and pragmatism, we believe that we can neither move in advance of historic events nor lag behind. Any steps that are taken must reflect the political realities which exist in our homeland today. There is no need to run ahead of the train, if that will hurt our cause; nor should we postpone getting off the train until it crashes. We have to gauge the proper moment to leave the train in a timely fashion, without any undue losses.

D. Based on our analysis of political developments, we believe that the new government must arrive at security arrangements within a defense system which will build up the confidence of our people. Those security arrangements may also translate into new markets, with which the new Republic may engage in mutually advantageous economic relations. In addition to taking all due precautions, we must heed the lessons of our bloody history. Indeed, our history demonstrates that freedom and independence may be achieved and maintained only by creating our own defense system.

E. The newly independent state must simply be called the Republic of Armenia, which does not necessarily imply that it is the continuation either of the First Republic of Armenia, which lasted from 1918 to 1920, or of the Soviet Republic which followed it.

In this context, it is understandable that we may wish to revive some of the symbols of the past, without feeling ourselves obliged to do so. If we are to keep pace with modern times, our symbols and our anthem must reflect the current aspirations of the Armenian people.

F. We have always maintained that the territory of this Republic is the nucleus of tomorrow's Greater Armenia. In this respect, we expect the newly-formed government to commit itself to the restoration of our historic rights. More specifically, the new Republic must include in its on-going agenda the recognition of the Armenian Genocide and our historic territorial claims by the international community. But the ways, means, and the opportune time to pursue those goals must be left to the best judgment of our far-sighted leader.

The momentous events which have plagued Armenia during the past two years have united the entire diaspora behind Armenia. Each and every diaspora organization, while maintaining its own methods of operation, has made assistance to Armenia its main priority, especially in the wake of the earthquake and the painful struggle in Karabagh.

As a democratic national government solidifies its position, we believe that relations between Armenia and the diaspora will enter a new phase. We believe that the new government will realize the true potential of the diaspora and adopt a new approach towards diaspora Armenians.

The diaspora and the Western Armenian community begin here, within the borders of Armenia, which has absorbed successive waves of immigrants: in the early days from Vaspurakan,[3] and later from various countries around the world. But, unfortunately, those immigrants have not always enjoyed equal opportunities, and have been treated as second-

---

3. An historic Armenian region. Present-day Van region in Turkey.

class citizens, not necessarily as a result of the policies of the former regime.

In this respect, we notice a symbolic departure from the past with the election of Levon Ter Petrossian, who comes from an immigrant family. That departure will lead Armenia towards a healthier and more broadly based political vision.

By mobilizing the diaspora around Armenia, we empower the entire nation. But we must not overlook the caveat that the diaspora is not a country in itself, nor is it a government: it is a collection of disparate groups which only Armenia's magnetic field can pull together into a cohesive force.

The historic sittings of this Parliament have witnessed the declarations of diaspora political groups, pledging their return to the political life of Armenia. That places the ADL in a dilemma. Many people are asking when the ADL will officially return to Armenia. Our organization has already signaled its symbolic return to Armenia through its business ventures and through the establishment of its press in Yerevan. We believe that the time has come for this legislative body to promulgate laws which would allow the diaspora political parties to participate officially in Armenia's political life. When that happens, the ADL will be the first organization to announce the lawful resumption of its activities in the homeland. At this very complex and sensitive time, Armenia needs all of the political factions.

In conclusion, I wish to appeal once more to all factions to rally around the government of the new Republic in order that it may lead Armenia to a safe haven.

At this historic moment I believe that our ancestors have been watching us from Heaven, wishing us the wisdom and determination to choose the right course and to place Armenia on the road to true and eternal salvation.

I wish you success in your noble cause.

August 20, 1990

The Ravages of Pollution in Armenia

After almost two years of controversy in the Soviet Armenian press and the press in Moscow, it was announced that the Nayirit Synthetic Rubber Factory in Yerevan would be shut down permanently. The closure of the above mentioned factory is only symbolic, and Armenia has been driven to the verge of panic, with its rampant ecological problem ruining and damaging the lives of its population. Scientific writer Varoujan Vassilyan indicates in a recent article that abnormal births in Armenia during 1982 were 8.5 times greater than the average in the entire Soviet Union during 1986.

At this point no questions must be raised about whether it is patriotic to point to these troubling phenomena: in the hope of seeing them corrected, with a little help from glasnost, intellectuals, scientists, and government officials have been openly discussing the issue, which concerns all Armenians. The facts and figures presented in this article have been compiled from the Soviet Armenian press and provided to this writer by Dr. Garabed Kassakian. Nothing appears in this article which has not been publicly expressed in the news media or in scholarly articles by writers in Armenia. Therefore, it is incumbent upon any individual who has love and respect for the population of Armenia to address these issues, share their concerns and, if possible, try to help remedy the present situation.

It is very difficult to obtain statistical data from the Soviets. At best, a few percentages are given out, which sometimes hide the hard figures, by creating more confusion than clarification.

The average life expectancy for men is believed to have dropped to age 53. Infant mortality and birth defects are rampant. Heart attacks and cancer have attained epidemic proportions.

Major ecological blunders are: the depletion of the Lake Sevan Water Reservoir; the construction of the nuclear power plant at Metzamor; and the location of the Nayirit Synthetic Rubber Plant in the heart of Yerevan.

The construction of hydroelectric power plants on Lake Sevan has contributed to the depletion of its water reservoir and as a result the

Ishkhan fish, a species of mountain trout peculiar to that lake, has been listed as an endangered species. It has almost drained another river, the Arpa, which became a tributary of Sevan through the construction of a 48-kilometer-long tunnel. The negligent planning of the diversion of the Arpa River has had irreversible and tragic consequences on the Sevan ecosystem.

Two entire years after water from the Arpa river started flowing into Lake Sevan, it was "discovered" that the fresh water of the latter was thoroughly incompatible with the highly saline waters of the Arpa. As the salinity of Lake Sevan increased, its indigenous fish species started vanishing. The mountain trout Ishkhan has already been eradicated. Its rival, "siga," which was taking over the lake habitat, suddenly started dying in tens of thousands in the spring of 1984, as a result of a major radioactive spill into the lake. The origin of this spill was not disclosed officially, but it was speculated in knowledgeable academic and governmental circles that the cause was tailings at the Arpa head waters. The Arpa-Sevan Tunnel transported the contamination to Lake Sevan.

The domestic and industrial sewage of the surrounding communities is dumped into the lake untreated. Besides the customary pollutants, huge amounts of unused but highly toxic pesticides and herbicides are discharged into the lake by neighboring state and private farms.

All these factors combined to devastate the "siga" fish harvest. The stricken fish (young and old) had both eyes covered with cataracts, and exhibited multiple body lesions and tumors of various sizes.

When environmental scientists decide to test the toxicity of an unknown substance, various doses are introduced to aquariums, and the substance is declared toxic at a dosage which results in a 50% kill ratio of the fish in the aquarium.

Based upon the foregoing, for all practical purposes Lake Sevan, Soviet Armenia's huge and sole reservoir of fresh water, has become unusable.

Before the construction of the Metzamor Nuclear Power Plant, 38 sites were studied geologically as potential locations for construction. The power plant was built in the Ararat Valley, the only agricultural area in Armenia after only a cursory geological study (the 39th site!). It was built, without adequate safeguards, on the crossing of two geological faults. The spent radioactive waste from the uranium-enriched fuel was supposed to have been shipped in lead-lined armored containers to Siberia, to be disposed of in subterranean mines. Upon the refusal of the Azerbaijan SSR to permit the radioactive waste cargo to be transported through its territory for fear of actively contaminating its countryside and irradiating the population along the route, the nuclear waste was quarantined in artificial ponds in the Ararat Valley to cool for a period of 10 to 15 years, and then it was placed in 100-meter-deep holes, contaminating the artesian well waters of the Valley. These waters are the sole source for the irrigation of Armenia's "bread and fruit basket," the Arpa Valley. The water table in the Artashat region of the Valley is less than four feet (or 1.2 meters) below the surface.

The half-life of the nuclear waste is 250,000 years.

Ever since the construction of the nuclear power plant, 100 accidents or close calls have been reported, killing and/or injuring an undisclosed number of people.

The current reactors are to be dismantled in 10 years, whereby the radioactive concrete and building materials surrounding the core of the reactors themselves will become an insurmountable nuclear disposal problem. Their burial in an artesian well-laden ground water area, such as the Ararat Valley, would doom the region forever, quickly depleting it of both population and vegetation.

The Nayirit Rubber Factory, on the other hand, was considered so dangerous that the central government in Moscow decided to shut it down in 1982, but it did not receive support from government leaders and the Academy of Sciences in Armenia and, consequently, the plant continues to this date to pollute the air, dumping 60 tons of toxic waste into the air and 100 tons into the soil and water every day from its 25 production facilities. Recently it was reported that the plant might shut down by December 30, 1987. A safety zone of one square kilometer is required for any facility which stores one railroad tanker (about 20,000 gallons) of chlorine. Nayirit receives 30 tanks at a time, one month's supply, and does not have that safety zone. In 1983, five twenty-story high rise apartment buildings were constructed in the immediate vicinity of this rubber factory, exposing the inhabitants to a very real danger. A chlorine explosion in Kemerovo, Russia killed 330 people and injured many more in 1983.

Smog is a real problem in Yerevan: it has destroyed agricultural land and endangered the population's health, causing serious eye diseases. The exhaust fumes from cars contribute to 30% of the air pollution, and yet a mandatory system of catalytic converters is not in place; cars continue to emit toxic fumes five times above the limit of tolerable standards. Unleaded fuel is unheard of.

Official inspection by the Environmental Department of the Armenian Council of Ministers (headed by Deputy Prime Minister Yuri Y. Khodjamirian and chief investigator Suren Vharian) yielded incontrovertible evidence of willful, widespread mixing of diesel fuel with high octane leaded gasoline, thus reducing the octane rating of the gasoline sold (still marketed to the population at the same high octane prices) and increasing the emissions of hydrocarbons not burned in the engine.

The factories and the chemical plants contribute their share of air pollution. There are 79 chemical plants in one region of Yerevan alone: the Lenin Region. The major polluters of the atmosphere remain the Nayirit Rubber Plant, the Polyvinylacetate plant, and the Aluminum factory. No factory has a safety zone and many of them are surrounded by densely populated areas, schools, kindergartens, and sports facilities. As a result of measures taken in 1980, one of the factories was shut down, thereby eliminating the daily emission of 30 tons of calcium carbide. Also, a chlorobenzol factory, which used to emit 100,000 kilograms of toxic fumes daily, was closed. Pollution control devices have reduced the emission of toxic fumes by 12% at the Polyvinylacetate factory, which nevertheless continues to emit 25 different kinds of poisonous gases into the atmosphere. Ten per cent of the cement produced in the experimental Factory No. 5 is released into the air.

Kirovakan, Razdan, Ararat, and Alaverdi, where huge chemical plants operate, are considered the most dangerous areas ecologically. For the last 50 years the cement factory at Ararat has been covering the orchards and vineyards with cement and asbestos dust.

The Armenian Ministry of Health has not recognized asbestos as an occupational health hazard. Tiles, roofing material, insulation, fireproofing material, and water pipes made of cement and asbestos compounds abound in the country. No health warning is issued to the populace or the factory workers. As described in 1984 by Yuri Abovian, head of the Environmental Department of the State Planning Commission (Gosplan ArmSSR), the workers at the Ararat Cement Factory asbestos division "were covered with asbestos dust from head to toe, as if it were simply wheat flour at a mill. They wore no masks and no protective coveralls, gloves, or headgear."[1]

There are 1,500 pollution control devices in various factories. A 1983 inspection revealed that two-thirds of these devices, over 1,000 of them, were either defective or non-operational.

A second inspection, one year later, indicated no improvement, and in fact deliberate acts of disconnecting the air filters were noted by

1. Annual meeting of the Yerevan City Society for the Protection of Nature, May 1984.

the Director of the Air Pollution Control Devices Commission, Sergei Vassilyan. Evidence was also gathered that money allocated for air pollution control devices had been misappropriated by the factory personnel.

At the time Mr. Vassilyan, a tireless crusader for air and water pollution control, was also vice-president of the Yerevan City Society for the Protection of Nature, and a contributor to the Russian-language party newspaper, *Kommunist*, on the environment. After uncovering two "boiler room" operations in February and April 1984, in which several dozen experts were engaged in conjuring up daily clean-up statistics for nonexisting waste water treatment plants, he was summarily fired from his high position, and in a highly uncharacteristic move in a society where full employment is mandated and guaranteed by the constitution, Mr. Vassilyan was left unemployed. He currently survives by selling honey from his ancestral land plot in Kanaker.

Water pollution has become a very serious problem and is affecting the ecological balance of Armenia. Waste water treatment plants need to purify sewer water ten times in order to render it reusable, whereas water released from the Nayirit Factory needs to be diluted 200 times in order to cease being a health hazard. It is estimated that the entire reservoir of clean water in Armenia is not sufficient to dilute the water released from industrial plants to a degree that the pollutant levels might attain acceptable international discharge limits.

There are 20 small and medium-sized rivers in Armenia. They are all polluted. The Razdan River serves as a collector for untreated sewage at 18 different points in Yerevan. The Hydroelectric factory, Nayirit, and the Polyvinylacetate and Aluminum factories dump their toxic wastes into the Razdan, which eventually reaches the Ararat Valley, where it irrigates the agricultural land. Thus irrigated, the agricultural produce is unfit for human or animal consumption.

It is estimated that every year acid rain releases 2,500 metric tons of lead, oil derivatives, salts, and other dangerous compounds over the city of Yerevan.

The River Tepet is poisoned right at its source in Lori, where a sugar factory releases large quantities of citric acid. An attempt to correct the situation has failed. A judge who ordered restrictions on this pollution has been removed from the bench.

To treat the polluted waters released by the factories, the government has built 73 water treatment plants, with a capacity of 1,330,000 cubic meters. But some of the plants are not in operation and the treatment efficiency levels of the rest are below tolerable standards.

Together the factories of Armenia use 529 million cubic meters of water, of which 219 million cubic meters is released into the rivers, affecting their ecological balance.

Water resources are scarce in Armenia. They are seven times less than in any other Republic, yet the waste of valuable water supplies is alarming.

Pollution has also affected the soil, by eroding large agricultural areas. Two hundred plant and 105 animal species have been placed on the endangered list.

The city of Yerevan suffers from perennial water shortages. Instead of using their own recycled and treated waste water, the Nayirit, Polyvinylacetate, and Aluminum factories, the Yerevan thermoelectric generating stations, and many smaller chemical and industrial factories find it cheaper and more convenient to use Yerevan city water for their technical needs. The city water is supplied by deep mountain springs, so pure that it needs no pretreatment or chlorination. The 1.3 million populace of Yerevan is supplied with water at odd hours and only for very short periods of time, such as 4-6AM or 11PM-12AM, causing flooding, ceiling and floor damage, and untold hygienic miseries. The water is collected in bathtubs for use during the rest of the day. Since 1984, hot water (literally boiling hot water) from the thermoelectric generating station is supplied at odd hours, as a substitute for cold domestic water. The hot water leaches out from the piping system a toxic chemical soup containing lead, copper, zinc, nickel, asbestos, etc., which the population drinks and bathes with.

All these violations take place while waste water treatment plants all over the city are left deliberately idle by officials. The $5.2 million dollar ion-exchange water treatment and purification plant at Nayirit Synthetic Rubber Factory has been idle since its construction in 1980. The plant was purchased--lock, stock and barrel--from France, and erected under the supervision of French engineers. It is now manned by an irresponsible skeleton crew.

Another water treatment plant at Kapuyt Lidj (Blue Lake) on the Soviet side of the River Arax, was intended to supply fresh water to Yerevan. It was completely misplanned by the Leningrad Water Planning Institute, because none of the people involved in the project bothered to make a site visit. After sitting idle for 2.5 years (a very long planning period indeed), the drawings of a Central Asian plant were relabeled and sent to Yerevan Planning Institute (Project Manager Hrant Kirishdjian). When the Armenian planners protested, the Moscow authorities reconsidered, and shelved the construction of the purification plant until the year 1995, thus leaving Yerevan with no domestic water supply once more.

Over 2,000 tons of hazardous and highly toxic wastes are produced daily in Yerevan alone. Since the city does not have a hazardous waste landfill, the toxic wastes are mixed with domestic wastes and dumped at the Yerevan Garbage Dump. Contrary to the claims of officials that this procedure dilutes and renders the toxic wastes harmless, it was found that all of the domestic garbage has now become contaminated, thus increasing the complexity of the solution tenfold. The Yerevan dump was erroneously situated on calcium-bearing deposits, which, since 1982, have started to collapse, thus releasing the highly toxic wastes into the shallow ground water table underlying Yerevan, and poisoning the natural water reservoirs of the capital.

The Yerevan Domestic Waste Incinerator has not been completed, and was delayed for 11 years. Only a cracked and sinking concrete pad indicates the site of the future incinerator. The plans for the incinerator do not contain any air pollution equipment to capture or neutralize suspended particles, ash, and health-threatening dioxins, phosgene, hydrogen chloride gas, and other pollutants.

The project manager for the City of Yerevan was Mrs. Svetlana Parkhudarova. After 6 years of inaction on the incinerator project, she was rewarded with the presidency of the Republic Lottery Commission, and the project was shelved until the year 2000.

Mining has also taken its toll on the land, as no plan exists to restore any mining site after the depletion of the ores. Mining is very intensive in Armenia. Per capita, Armenia's mining interests are 30 times the average in the USSR, and 230 times the average per square kilometer.

No matter how serious the pollution problem in Armenia may be, there certainly is a solution, and coordinated efforts, without panic, will help correct the sorry state of affairs, which seems to have gotten out of hand. Armenians in the diaspora may help, especially by providing medical assistance and know-how not readily available in Armenia. They may also help by providing Armenia with such technical help as is permitted to be exported from Western countries.

This is a national emergency, and emotions should not play a role; only positive and effective work will prove our patriotism, and will help Armenians pull through this calamity.

January 9, 1988

Dateline Karabagh
A Magic Date: March 26

Armenian history had never moved so fast. Indeed, within a few weeks masses of Armenians moved, millions of them marched in the streets of Yerevan and other major cities of the world, and the issue of Karabagh hit the headlines of the international news media.

The last time Armenia was brought to the focus of international diplomacy was in 1923, when its fate was sealed by the Treaty of Lausanne, which buried the pledges of European allies (to give Armenians a homeland in Cilicia) and the treaty obligations of Sèvres (expanding the boundaries of the Republic of Armenia).

For over 65 years, Armenians in Karabagh had endured the oppressive rule of their Azeri "brothers," who had unjustly taken over the fate of that autonomous region. The Baku[1] government, which had only given lip service to the Leninist principle of "internationalist brotherhood," had successfully harassed Armenians out of the Autonomous Republic of Nakhichevan, which similarly had come under the rule of Azerbaijan, even though the latter did not have a common border with Nakhichevan.

Despite the Baku government's misrule, the Karabagh Armenians had resisted all attempts to depopulate the region. Mr. Gorbachev's glasnost served notice to the Karabagh Armenians to rise and to blow the lid off their boiling resentment. The spill-over filled the streets of Yerevan and reverberated the world over. In an unusual step, the Karabagh Parliament almost unanimously voted to join Armenia. The legislature of Soviet Armenia cautiously supported the move and the tremors reached Moscow and Baku, touching off a series of massacres in major Azerbaijani cities.

Armenians, who are criticized for their political and factional divisions, this time around exercised statesmanlike restraint, political maturity, circumspection, and unity. It must be stated that in no place

---

1. Capital of Azerbaijan Soviet Socialist Republic,
   since August 30, 1991 the Republic of Azerbaijan.

were the demonstrations directed against Moscow, whose troops were ordered to protect the unarmed Armenians in Azerbaijani cities. So the traditional role of the Armenian Church was highlighted once more. The Communist party chief's call for calm was complemented by an appeal from His Holiness Vazken I, which had a positive impact in cooling off tempers and mobilizing the world community of Armenians in support of the Karabagh plea.

Armenians had never entertained illusions about the Azerbaijani rhetoric extolling "internationalist brotherhood," which was supposed to characterize the relations of the two neighboring republics. Recent events brought painfully home to Mr. Gorbachev and the authorities that "internationalism" had been but a thin coat or luster over Azerbaijan's Pan-Turanian[2] designs.

In view of the recent massacres in Sumgait, Stepanakert, and other Azerbaijani cities, I cannot help but remember the warning whispered in my ears in 1962 by the late poet Paruyr Sevak, who said: "Our master poet Avetik Issahakian used to warn us that the Communist Turk is more dangerous than the Muslim Turk." The recent massacres were only the tip of the iceberg of a philosophy of nationalism nurtured and developed under the very nose of the central authorities. During his recent visit to Yugoslavia, Mr. Gorbachev himself admitted that the republics in the south had been lost to central party control.

The nationalist philosophy of Azerbaijan is the essential component of the Pan-Turanian designs harbored by Ankara. That philosophy also sits well with their Shiite co-religionists in neighboring Iran.

Even if historic Armenian claims carry no weight in Moscow, the Gorbachev government has its hands full in dealing with the fundamentalist unrest fermenting on its southern borders and in central Asia, which threatens to tip the ethnographic balance of the entire Soviet Union by the turn of the century.

After repeated disappointments over the course of the last century, Armenians are hoping against hope that a historic watershed is in the making for March 26, when the Central Committee will discuss the Karabagh issue, within the framework of the nationalities problem in the Soviet Union.

These disappointments should have warned us to be more realistic and more cautious in our expectations. Despite expressions of sym-

---

2. Pan-Turkic.

pathy from Mr. Gorbachev, and despite the admission of past mistakes by his spokesman, Mr. Gerasimov, no official promises or guarantees have been given to solve the problem on that magic date. At this point there is room neither for excitement nor for pessimism, because neither is warranted. Barring outright refusal by the Central Committee to study the case, any solution must be taken positively, because only that will make March 26 the beginning of a long-drawn-out process, and not necessarily an end. At this point there are three possibilities in prospect: (a) Moscow may decide to table the issue to avoid aggravating Iran, Turkey, and the Muslim population of the Soviet Union, which has already suffered several setbacks since Gorbachev's emergence; (b) in the most fortunate turn of events, the Central Government may return Karabagh to Soviet Armenia, which is easier said than done, given the complex set of problems surrounding the nationalities issue in the Soviet Union; (c) the most plausible avenue seems to be to grant Karabagh more freedom and closer cultural and economic ties with Armenia, and to entrust the issue of territorial dispute to the study of a team of experts, hopefully within a designated timeframe. In the first instance the shock would be devastating to the Armenians. But even in that case a restrained, disciplined, sophisticated, and united response will have a stronger impact than an outburst of mob psychology (which characterized recent Azerbaijani actions).

The second case would of course bring boundless joy to the Armenians, who would finally witness a favorable step in the history of the Armenian cause. But it also should bring extreme caution. The prospect of returning Mountainous Karabagh[3] to Armenia touched raw nerves with the Azerbaijanis, triggering murderous rampage in Azerbaijani cities. That should be warning enough of the extremes Azeris might resort to if Karabagh is actually taken from their control. We must not forget that outside Karabagh, 400,000 Armenians still live in various Azerbaijani cities. It may prove to be a Pyrrhic victory for Armenia, if Soviet Army units are not deployed in the regions populated by Armenians.

We Armenians are disheartened when we are told that the Karabagh issue warrants further study. The conclusion that such a study must reach is very clear for us. It is equally crystal clear for the Azerbaijanis, but in the opposite direction. Therefore, even in the most favorable political climate, Moscow has to weigh the two opposing views

---

3. I.e., Nagorno Karabagh.

against each other and draw its own conclusion, consonant with overall Soviet interests.

The problems which the team of experts will face are many:

(a) Under Haidar Aliev, Azerbaijani scholars have developed a whole new historiography, similar to the one developed in Ankara. Zia Bouniatov has been the most outspoken proponent of that ersatz historiography, which denies the fact that the Azeris are the descendants of Tartars who invaded the Caucasus from Central Asia in the 10th or 11th centuries AD. This new theory claims that the Azeris are descended from the Caucasian Albanians, a people indigenous to the area. As for the people of Karabagh, they are labeled ethnic Azeris who have been forcefully converted to Christianity by "Armenian imperialists" (a claim also expressed by the Turkish paper *Cumhuriyet* only two weeks ago).

While Dinmuhammed Konayev of Kazakhstan held an influential position in the central party apparatus and Aliev served as a full voting member of the Politburo, this theory enjoyed a certain degree of credibility in Moscow. After the disgraceful disappearance of these two leaders, their theory will be more vulnerable to critical analysis, and much scholarly work needs to be done to discredit it completely.

(b) The Karabagh issue will be subject to further constitutional interpretation, including the one promulgated by Brezhnev in 1978, which denotes the names of the constituent republics and autonomous regions by the names of the people actually inhabiting those particular territories: for example, the Armenian SSR, the Georgian SSR, etc., as opposed to the Soviet Socialist Republic of Armenia, Georgia, etc. (which could in fact be inhabited by a majority of another ethnic group, not necessarily Armenians, Georgians, etc.). This seems, in essence, to be Lenin's principle of self-determination for Soviet nationalities.

However, there are two exceptions to this general rule and those exceptions happen to be the Nakhichevan Autonomous Republic and the Autonomous Region of Mountainous Karabagh. These are the only regions which are not named after the people inhabiting them. There is no such people as the Nakhichevani or the Karabaghi. Had these regions been named after their populations, they would have created a contradiction in the Constitution itself, because autonomous regions are republics created for ethnic minorities whose population does not warrant full republic status yet enjoys a large enough number to entitle it to the status of autonomy, under the tutelage of another republic populated by a different ethnic group. Had any of the autonomous regions been named after the people already inhabiting a full-fledged republic, a contradiction in terms would ensue and the necessity of incorporating the region with the republic would arise, in order to rid the Constitution of that contradiction.

Therefore, the authorities drafting the Constitution have resolved (or so they believe) that contradiction by avoiding to identify the Karabagh and Nakhichevan regions by their inhabitants. This unique status equally helps and defies both the Armenian and Azerbaijani positions. If the Karabagh population is defined as Armenian, a constitutional amendment will be in order, subsequently qualifying Karabagh to become an integral part of the Armenian SSR. If, on the contrary, the central authorities adopt the Bouniatov-Aliev theory, the same sequence of events will ensue in favor of Azerbaijan.

Our case, therefore, is not so simple as we believe. It is part of a very complex situation, compounded by almost 20 similar cases on the Central Committee agenda. To demonstrate how complex the nationality problem may get, it is worth remembering the appeal by the Autonomous Republic of Abkhazia (Muslim) requesting that they be transferred from Georgian to Russian rule. Their appeal was turned down, despite the fact that the adjustment might have enhanced the long-standing policy of russification favored by the central authorities.

In the light of the above problems, March 26 loses all its magic, leaving us with the gravity of the situation, which requires sober political calculation, unity of purpose, and determination to carry on the struggle for as long as it takes.

March 26, 1988

UNDER GORBACHEV'S PROPOSED UNION TREATY:

Armenia the Lesser Sovereign Among Sovereigns

After giving up so much power and allowing the old Soviet system to disintegrate, in a last-ditch effort, Mikhail S. Gorbachev is now trying desperately to salvage the Union and solidify his position as the most powerful ruler in Russian history. He has come up with a new Union pact and has demanded that the 15 constituent republics ratify it, leaving no alternative for those seeking secession from the Union.

Until recently, Gorbachev ostensibly used a double standard in dealing with unrest in the country. He applied a European approach to the Baltic states and an Asian one to the Caucasian republics. Indeed, while he coerced Baltic republics to the negotiating table to discuss their secessionist demands, he dispatched Red Army units to quell dissent or civil disobedience in the Caucasus: Armenia, Georgia, and Azerbaijan each experienced its share of bloodshed at the hands of the Red Army.

Although the proposed treaty seems directed mostly to the Baltics, it will unquestionably affect all the republics. Perhaps the winner in this case will be the Russian Federative Republic, by the sheer weight of its size. The imbalance thus created will endow Gorbachev with all the trappings of a Russian czar, especially after the deletion of the word socialist from the country's name.

It is understandable, therefore, why the mildest reaction comes from Russians, whereas the Baltic republics have become most vocal in opposing Gorbachev's new measures. Indeed, the Lithuanian President announced that "in the Baltic countries, the President will be able to exercise the powers given to him by the Soviet Parliament only with the help of brute military force," and then concluded: "The Baltic countries will defend themselves."

Gorbachev's proposed treaty is virtually an ultimatum to the republics to fall back in line, after three years of confusion and chaos created in the name of most celebrated perestroika.

That ultimatum is further underlined by the stern statements of the Minister of Defense, Marshal Dmitri Yazov, who, in no uncertain terms, warned of military measures against those republics, threatening denial of supplies to the military units stationed in their respective territories. The Defense Minister also went to great lengths to announce that "under no circumstances will nuclear weapons be scattered throughout the republics," and then added: "They were, are, and will remain in the hands of the united Soviet armed forces."

The propaganda machine seems to continue its course inexorably, churning out misinformation about the situation in Armenia. The Soviet central news media have long been engaged in portraying Armenia as an aggressor, and the Western press seems to take its cue from that propaganda machine. *The New York Times'* Moscow bureau chief, Bill Keller, long known for his pro-Azerbaijani bias, writes in the paper's November 28th issue: "Attacks on the military have taken many forms, from raids on military arsenals by vigilante militia in Armenia, to pervasive draft dodging in all republics."

Anyone who has seen the antiquated weapons in the hands of the Armenian militia will be easily convinced that those weapons have been deliberately given to the Armenians to compromise their safety. This writer has discussed the nature of military confrontation with the Soviet forces with several militia leaders who defend Armenia's borders against Azerbaijani incursions. Their contention is that Azerbaijanis attack border villages in Armenia and immediately withdraw behind Soviet Army lines, leaving the Soviet soldiers to confront Armenian retaliation. At the very moment, the Soviet central mass media broadcast to the world and to the Soviet people that Armenians have attacked the Soviet army. That seems to be Mr. Keller's news source.

In theory, Mr. Gorbachev allows the republics to secede, but only after a lengthy and impossible process of holding first one referendum then another, following a waiting period of five years. This "voluntary" severance is not very different from the "rights" prescribed in the previous constitution.

The proposed treaty concentrates all power in the hands of the Union President. Indeed, the Union government will remain in charge of defense, the protection of borders, the organization of the armed forces, foreign and economic policies, and customs. Financial credit and monetary policy, based on a single currency, will also be controlled by the central government. On the other hand, local laws will have priority, except when they affect control of natural resources and raw materials deemed important by the Union government.

This new treaty is intended to serve as a replacement for the one signed in December 1922, which established the Union of Soviet Socialist Republics.

The republics have not much to cheer about. Perhaps the only difference between Gorbachev and his predecessors is that he has deleted from this new treaty the element of delusion: the republics are being told bluntly about the limitations of their sovereignty.

Armenia is in a difficult situation, and given the tribulations of the last two years, it does not even possess any leverage to put forth terms to moderate the suffocating conditions of this new treaty, such as those proposed by the other republics. That is why the President of the Armenian Parliament, Levon Ter Petrossian, has chosen most careful terms to enunciate his reaction to the treaty, announcing to *Pravda* on November 23: "Some people believe that if power is strengthened and law and order are secured, everything will be alright. It is an illusion. In such a case, the center will face a serious resistance by the republics, because sovereignty is a reality for us."

The new treaty will definitely dampen hopes for an early reconstruction or a speedy economic recovery of Armenia.

In matters of foreign policy, Armenia cannot espouse our historic claims against Turkey, although the present government does not seem to be very sanguine to identify itself with those claims in any case.

On the other hand, its attempts to bluff Moscow by restoring normal ties with Turkey have backfired, as evidenced by a scornful article published in the influential Turkish daily *Milliyet* on November 19, because the Turks have already resumed cozy relations with Moscow and have very little to gain by restoring normal relations with Armenia, except to wrest from her a renunciation of our territorial claims, which the present government has virtually and voluntarily done even before any negotiations could be initiated. Political calculations in Ankara are that they should not bother dealing with Yerevan, since Moscow can deliver Armenia any time and in any shape they want.

The need to survive has also rendered Armenia less assertive in her demand for the reunification of Artzakh,[1] which, after a hopeful beginning, has completely reverted to ruthless Azerbaijani rule.

---

1. I.e., Nagorno Karabagh.

Following the Artzakh movement, ethnic and territorial tensions spread throughout the Soviet Union, from Tajikistan to the Crimea, where displaced Tartars claimed their homeland, and from Moldavia to the Black Sea, where Moslem Abkhaz residents demanded cessation from Georgia. In this context, the treaty promises a dim hope for a legal formula to allow the disputing parties to settle their differences, either in court or through the mediation of the central government. Based on the principle of human rights, that formula can perhaps help resolve the Artzakh issue, which seems to be safely buried at the present time.

Armenia cannot, and must not, hope for any sympathy from the central government, whose interests overtly lie with Azerbaijan, because of that republic's oil industry, and also because the occupation of Baku by the Red Army early this year assured the Communist Party's victory in the recent elections, thereby establishing a concurrence of interests between Moscow and Baku. On the other hand, Armenia and Georgia opted for a more independent and nationalist course, thus alienating Moscow. Unfortunately, relations between these two Christian nations have been unstable, and are characterized at best as a love-hate situation, whereas the formation of a confederation between them could have created a power base to counterbalance the Moscow-Baku axis. That would be a way to partially revive the Transcaucasian Seym,[2] formed prior to the declaration of independence by these republics. The central government still possesses the power to undermine any move in the republics which runs counter to its designs. The Army, the secret police, and economic planning are still in Moscow's hands. It is indeed revealing to note that after complete demoralization and chaos and some talk of weaning the nation away from Moscow, the conservatives carried the day at the recent party congress in Yerevan, and decided to remain in Moscow's fold and continue receiving a 45-million-ruble subsidy, which will buy a lot of influence in Armenia.

The shortage of food and fuel, compounded by border skirmishes with Azerbaijan, leaves no alternative for Armenia but to concentrate energies to develop self-sufficiency and a realpolitik to the swiftly shifting trends of Soviet and world politics.

December 15, 1990

---

2. In 1917, in an effort to maintain their freedom, Armenia, Georgia and Azerbaijan united and formed a Council in Tiflis, known as the Seym. This Council declared the Trans-Caucasus a Federal Republic, without severing its ties to Bolshevik Russia.

LEVON TER PETROSSIAN:

From Scholar to Statesman

At the age of 46, a scholar with a solid background in Armenian-Syriac relations and six major volumes to his credit, Levon Ter Petrossian today dominates the political scene in Armenia, as our homeland proceeds on its perilous path to independence.

Events in Levon Ter Petrossian's life--as well as in that of Armenia--have moved at a dizzying pace, propelling him from the obscure back rooms of the Matenadaran[1] to the center stage of political action--with two brief stops in jail.

The one-time ponderous scholar has been transformed into a charismatic leader to guide Armenia to independence in these most complex and dangerous times.

Although his political activities date back to his student days, when he was arrested for attempting to gain recognition of the Armenian Genocide, his actual political education evolved on the job, after he joined the Armenian National Movement and especially after he was elected President of the Supreme Soviet of the Republic of Armenia. His learning process has been amazing, and his political maturity has developed before our very eyes, in a matter of several months. One can but admire his ability to learn from his own, as well as other people's, mistakes.

As one of the leaders of the Karabagh Committee--which was later renamed the Armenian National Movement, the political group presently in power--he took Armenia by storm and heated rhetoric: slogans inundated the streets and Freedom Square, where Ter Petrossian and his revolutionary group felt most at home. Suddenly, to their surprise, and to the surprise of all political observers, these young men found themselves at the helm of the government, with little practical experience but superbly trained in fiery oratory.

---

1. The repository of ancient illuminated manuscripts in Yerevan.

No observer, in his wildest conjecture, could have imagined that this group of intellectual revolutionaries could acquire enough political acumen in such a brief period of time to hold Armenia's fate confidently in their hands.

Levon Ter Petrossian, among others, emerged as a visionary statesman, with his finger on the political pulse of historic developments in and around Armenia.

As a prudent strategist, he shifted from political slogans to bread-and-butter issues when he was faced with the specter of starvation in Armenia. He weathered the political storm with admirable courage when he backed down on the very issues which had brought his group to power; indeed, political realism prevailed when he advocated negotiation rather than confrontation in the Artzakh[2] issue. He was also decisive in reopening the Nayirit[3]--an ecological disaster--which was destined to maintain Armenia's beleaguered economy, and he was equally determined on the issue of reopening the nuclear power plant--considered by many the potential cause of a nuclear holocaust. The resolution of these thorny issues--albeit temporary--would have ruined the reputation and career of any politician in the West. The determination of Ter Petrossian, on the contrary, enhanced his position, as he drove home to the Armenian public that rhetoric alone cannot build democracy or a viable economy when people are faced with the imminent danger of famine.

In all his ventures, Ter Petrossian proved to have a sure hand in his gamble. As a result of the earthquake and subsequent Azerbaijani blockade, Armenia was facing one of its most severe winters. During a visit to Ter Petrossian's office early this January, this writer warned him that unless he came up with a realistic economic plan to feed Armenia's population--long fed up with demonstrations or speeches--his administration would face a serious crisis, allowing other groups to step in. Ter Petrossian answered with a grin: "Any group which can feed Armenia is welcome and deserves the leadership of this country."

His policies at home and abroad have proved very resourceful.

He took a serious chance when he convinced the Central Government to allow Baruyr Hayrikian to return to Armenia, because the latter, with a long record as a dissident and political prisoner, enjoyed

2. I.e., Nagorno-Karabagh.
3. A synthetic rubber factory in Yerevan;
   see the first article in this section, "The Ravages of Pollution."

a considerable degree of popularity, and in a moment of emotional outburst the people could have elected him President. But Hayrikian's
return demystified him and reduced him to his actual size. His irresponsible and adventurous activities also contributed to the public disillusionment. Today Hayrikian and his dwindling group are viewed as a
bunch of troublemakers or, at best, political irritants.

The other domestic measure which had a direct bearing on the
citizens' everyday life was the integration of disparate militias into government military units, a step that averted bloodshed, which Armenia
faced following Gorbachev's ultimatum, in August 1990, to curb the
activities of the militias. During that period, the militias ruled the streets
and threatened ordinary citizens. They were also engaged in internecine
warfare for turf control. Ter Petrossian was able to convince militia leaders to disband or be integrated into local police forces. He was also firm
with dissenters in implementing the government's policy on the issue.
His success not only brought internal peace to Armenia, but also protected his image throughout the Union as a peacemaker on the political
scene. It was that stature which Ter Petrossian utilized later, when he
acted as a mediator between the Central Government and Lithuania,
averting yet another imminent bloodbath in a different troubled region
of the USSR.

Armenia was among the first republics to privatize land, while
Moscow and other republics debated the issue for months. That successful program did not go unnoticed in the West, as *The New York
Times* and *The Christian Science Monitor* dedicated columns of commendations and recommended that the Center and the other republics
emulate Armenia's lead.

The program resulted in more tangible rewards to the ordinary
citizens, who today are enjoying a bumper crop.

Ter Petrossian's foreign ventures were not without hurdles or
setbacks. His first trip abroad brought him to the United States. That
was a poorly planned visit, the failure of which was compounded when
he was snubbed by the White House while in the US. Ter Petrossian
himself failed to act like a statesman, and his statements ruffled some
feathers. But he was quick to recognize his failure, and he was not too
embarrassed to learn the exigencies of his role as a head of state.

Later, trips to France and Italy and his meetings with President
Mitterrand and the Pope enhanced his international stature. President
Bush's invitation to attend the state dinner at the US Embassy in
Moscow symbolized Ter Petrossian's growing role in Union affairs. His

public evaluation of Gorbachev and other leaders, as well as his predictions on the prospect of glasnost, proved to be true, especially after the aborted coup in August. He also became one of the republican leaders most quoted by the Soviet and foreign press.

Ter Petrossian is a proud, confident--perhaps overconfident--leader, whose actions are bold yet well planned; his analyses are precise, based on solid facts. With the passage of time, his policies have emerged from earlier assumptions which are being proven realistic in the whirlwind of political events.

"It is a foregone conclusion that the empire is doomed," he stated at his first press conference after his election last August, when many political pundits would have affixed a big question mark to that statement. But Ter Petrossian was vindicated by the attempted coup and by his brief statement in the Soviet Parliament in the aftermath of that failed coup: "The Center is dead and the Union has committed suicide."

Early in the political game his bet was on Boris Yeltsin, when the latter was still being portrayed in the West as a political buffoon. But the dramatic events thrust Yeltsin into the limelight and reduced Gorbachev to the status of a symbolic figurehead. Since Ter Petrossian has strengthened his ties with the Yeltsin camp from the beginning, that will certainly yield dividends to him and to Armenia in general.

Today Ter Petrossian remains the most popular political figure in Armenia. He is definitely the front runner in the presidential race. He is articulate and charismatic, and the achievements of his very brief tenure testify to his ability to read the historic consequences of every event. The hopes of the Armenian people are focusing more and more on him as the leader who can guide the country safely in these turbulent times.

Ter Petrossian is a towering figure in Armenian politics. He remains the most "presidential" among nine contenders for the October 16 presidential election.

September 14, 1991

The Presidential Election in Armenia

Today Armenia is reliving its history, and the situation which existed between 1918 and 1920 is back on the horizon. During those years, political events precipitated border wars with Azerbaijan and Georgia; and Armenia's confrontation with Turkey sounded the death-knell, especially after Turkish commander Kazim Karabekir's forces occupied Alexandrapol (Leninakan) in November 1920 and imposed one of the most humiliating treaties in Armenian history. Catastrophe was averted when Armenia chose the lesser of two evils and accepted Soviet rule.

As a historian, President Levon Ter Petrossian had learned the hard lessons of the past and he had to avoid repeating them at all costs. That would, of course, entail some unpalatable decisions and unpopular steps. One of such steps was the disassociation of Armenia's historic claims against Turkey from the desirability of doing business with that country. That would ensure peace on Armenian-Turkish borders, and secure an outlet for a small republic under siege. This policy did not sit well with some groups alien to cool political calculation. It was also exploited by his political foes. But it remains a fact that direly needed goods are now arriving in Armenia through Turkish territory, and the Republic has been invited to be a trading partner in the Black Sea economic system.

On the other hand, when frictions were intensifying on the Armenia-Georgia border Georgia was wooed by Azerbaijan into signing a treaty. Over half a million Armenians in Georgia have been reduced to the status of second-class citizens, Armenian churches have been taken over--common Christian faith notwithstanding--and clashes between Georgians and Armenians were reported in the Javakhk region, which borders Armenia. But when ethnic clashes flared up in Georgia itself, and when southern Ossetians and Abkhaz rebelled, Ter Petrossian seized the opportunity to signal Georgia's President Zviad Gamsakhurdia that his country needed border peace as much as Armenia. Armenia had to give in or risk war on an issue which had been a Georgian demand all along: respect of each other's territorial integrity, which meant that Armenia would not fuel the aspirations of Armenians living in Javakhk. Ter Petrossian convinced Georgian Armenians that at this juncture their demands stand no better chance than those of Karabagh Armenians.

On August 14, Ter Petrossian flew to Vilnius to sign a treaty with Lithuania before that republic became independent. And the events of these last few days render that treaty more significant and more valuable.

At these most critical times, Ter Petrossian faced his most serious crisis when Parliament debated two different and opposing bills on Karabagh. The first bill, supported by the Armenian Revolutionary Federation members in Parliament, proposed all-out war in Karabagh and recognition of the struggle there as a "national liberation war." The second bill sought more conciliatory avenues: it advocated negotiations by Karabagh leaders with the Azerbaijani government to freeze the status quo and to save lives. The debate ended in a showdown, and Ter Petrossian's bill was approved overwhelmingly.

Today he faces the toughest test of his short but eventful political career. He is the prime contender in the upcoming October 16 presidential elections. Seven other candidates have thrown their hats into the ring, but only one poses a real threat to him. Until recently, it was assumed that the leadership of the governing Armenian National Movement would preserve its unity, and Ter Petrossian was regarded as the obvious and natural candidate. But the break-up in the ranks of its leadership created disarray, encouraging other groups to propose their own candidates and pin their hopes on second-round run-off elections, when they could enter into political bargaining with the major contenders.

Vazken Manoukian, the Prime Minister, quit the ANM and formed his own political party.

It would have been very unusual and out of character with historical pattern, had that revolutionary group kept its unity. It is an axiom that all revolutions devour their own revolutionary children--Danton, Robespierre, Marat, and others bloodied the French revolution with their infighting, as did the Bolshevik leaders when they eliminated Trotzky, Kirov, and others. Modern times have followed the same pattern: Mohammed Naguib was eliminated by Gamal Abdel Nasser after the Egyptian revolution succeeded in 1952. Abdul Kerim Kassem was assassinated by his cronies a few years after he overthrew the monarchy in Iraq in 1958, and Ben Bella was jailed by Boumédienne soon after he negotiated Algeria's independence following a decade of revolutionary war.

It seems that ANM unity, which was once proclaimed unshakable, is currently developing along the historic pattern of all revolutions. We may, perhaps, be gratified that it has not yet taken an ugly bloody turn.

There seems to be no major political or philosophical difference between Ter Petrossian and Manoukian; it is more a contest of personalities and ambitions. Manoukian claims that he has been Ter Petrossian's political mentor, and must therefore automatically enjoy primacy over all the other ANM members. Soon after he severed his affiliation with the ANM, he announced in a press conference that it was he who had ushered Ter Petrossian into the revolutionary movement.

The other announced or unannounced candidates are Rafayel Ghazarian, Souren Haroutunian, Sos Sarkesian, Zori Balayan, Baruyr Hayrikian, and Haroutune Aristakessian (the last is the leader of the home-grown ARF).

The abundance of candidates will certainly dilute the votes and will not allow Ter Petrossian to be elected on the first ballot, forcing him to realign himself to accommodate the terms of minor groups in order to attain the required majority.

The failed coup in Moscow dissolved the ARF-Communist coalition which was in the works, by further humiliating the Communists. The Communist Party has taken Gorbachev's suggestion seriously, and has dissolved itself.

The ARF made some strides following the election of the democratic government, and developed some inroads in the masses, with the help of enduring historic myths. But its recent flirtation with Communists in Yerevan and Moscow and its antagonism to and vicious attacks against the democratically elected government have cost the party its popularity. The disillusionment continues as people in Armenia find out that ARF rule during the first Republic of Armenia[1] was not much different from the totalitarian regime that took over the government in 1920, and that the ARF has employed the same undemocratic style in the diaspora, by using terror against fellow Armenians.

The ARF has proposed actor Sos Sarkesian, who enjoys genuine popularity for his uncompromising nationalistic activities. But he lacks political experience, and it looks as if it is already too late for him to attain that experience.

Baruyr Hayrikian, the leader of the National Self-Determination

---

1. 28 May, 1918 to 29 November, 1920.

Union, enjoyed some measure of popularity in the past. But his adventurism and his suspicious political ties have reduced him to a diminutive political figure who poses a threat to no candidate.

The campaign will be between Ter Petrossian and Manoukian. The first enjoys vast popularity, which has given him a dangerous overconfidence. Vazken Manoukian would come nowhere near the President in a popularity contest, but as Prime Minister he is in a position to dispense favors for political commitments. We must be mindful that old infrastructures are still intact and old political relations are still in force. All ministers, heads of lucrative manufacturing concerns, and directors of institutes are appointed by the Prime Minister's office. Therefore, the old Communist mafia, which pledged allegiance to the new order overnight, is still in power, operating in the old Communist style but under a new guise. Even under the best of conditions, the transition will take a long time, until new and more democratic processes become functional.

The movement towards democracy has reached a stage where no major catastrophe will take place, no matter which candidate wins the election. We are at the point of no return, and totalitarian rule cannot make a comeback. That is the result and beauty of democracy.

Should Ter Petrossian wage his presidential campaign more cautiously and mend political fences more skillfully, he will enlist the support of the majority of Armenians, and will therefore stand a very good chance of winning the presidency.

But it seems that success intoxicates leaders, and that overconfidence has been a major flaw for many successful rulers of Armenia. The first and last empire builder in Armenian history, Dikran II, remarked sarcastically from his hilltop fortification, upon noticing the advancing Roman army: "If these are delegates, they are too many. If they are soldiers, they are too few!" He had hardly uttered his famous remarks when the Romans moved in and overthrew him, with the help of his own son, who served the enemy as a guide!

With further fine tuning of his political realism, I hope Ter Petrossian enjoys better luck than our first and last emperor did!

September 21, 1991

IN THE AFTERMATH OF ARMENIA'S PRESIDENTIAL ELECTION

No Room
for Mistakes

It was too good to be true! Five years of stability, internal unity, and national determination to win against all odds--earthquake, war, blockade, economic depression, and many other setbacks--were all important factors in helping Armenia to survive. Indeed, Armenia boasted of being the most stable nation among the former Soviet Republics, to the chagrin of her enemies.

The dream has been shattered, as this tiny republic plunges into the sea of instability and social unrest.

What seemed a peaceful exercise in democracy turned sour overnight. The presidential elections were proceeding normally, with the opposition enjoying media freedom, using and abusing it to the extreme. But still the predictions were that President Ter Petrossian would win the race by a wide margin.

But as the elections drew closer, the opposition gained momentum when the minor party candidates dropped from the political scene in favor of Vazken Manoukian one by one, except for former presidential adviser Ashot Manoucharian and Communist candidate Sergei Badalian. It was obvious that the margin was growing narrower, with the prospect of a run-off election, in which case the Communist candidate promised to withdraw in favor of one of the front runners. He certainly would not have sided with the incumbent.

With Armenian democracy in its infancy, it was predictable that traditional democratic processes could not be applied in full force. But it was at least expected of candidates to come up with well defined platforms. The opposition came up with a platform of sorts, playing up to the dire needs of the economically strapped populace. Indeed, Vazken Manoukian promised to increase wages and pensions tenfold, which did not make much economic sense. Ter Petrossian, on the other hand, refused to give promises that he knew he could not keep. He also criticized the opposition for its generous offer, which could bankrupt the country in three months and send home the army, which is credited with so many valiant deeds.

The election took place on Sunday, September 23, on the fifth anniversary of independence. As of this writing, the Central Election Committee has declared Ter Petrossian the winner, with 52%, and his closest rival, Vazken Manoukian, the loser, with 41%. The latter refused to accept the election results, declared himself the winner, and marched on Parliament, vowing to unseat Ter Petrossian. Tempers boiled over and demonstrators began storming the parliament building. The security forces intervened to establish order. The arrest of some opposition leaders further heightened the tension.

After the first waves of huge demonstrations which hastened the fall of the Soviet empire five years ago, Armenia fared much better politically when the national debate moved from the streets to the parliament.

The return to street politics is fraught with many dangers, the outcome of which no one can predict at this time.

If we are to believe the CSCE[1] observers' report, it cites many "serious irregularities," without challenging the legitimacy of the elections. Since the CSCE was the only major neutral observer, we have no reason to put its findings in doubt. One thing can be said: that had the tables been turned, the Manoukian camp would surely have done the same in the imperfect world of democracy.

The opposition has the right to challenge the election results, especially when the "irregularities" are substantiated by reliable independent sources. They even have the right to appeal to the Constitutional Court. But pushing the fight to the streets may lead the country into turmoil, with unpredictable results.

As we follow the unfolding of bloody events with much trepidation, we hope that the government and the opposition can rise to the occasion and move the debate from the streets to a more civilized forum. Armenia can ill afford any instability.

It is obvious that Ter Petrossian and his camp have not been able to attain a clear mandate from the electorate. This will force them to adopt a more conciliatory policy towards the opposition.

On the other hand, Manoukian's 41% vote does not signify genuine support for his policies, which are familiar to the electorate from the days when he ran the day-to-day affairs of the government as Prime

---

1. Conference on Security and Cooperation in Europe.

Minister. Most of his votes, rather, are votes against Ter Petrossian, by people drawn to desperation by economic hardship.

What to make of the estimated one million Armenians who have left the country temporarily or for good, in a way voting with their feet?

By denying a mandate to Ter Petrossian, the voters have sent a clear message that certain things in the country have to be corrected. Ter Petrossian inherited a government plagued with corruption and nepotism, which means that the old story continued, with new actors in the roles. In particular, the members of the Armenian National Movement--the party in power--became conspicuous elements in corrupting the government, sometimes acting as a government within the government. Their demonstrative opulence, arrogance, and utter insensitivity towards a deprived society turned them into a political liability for the president. Vano Siradeglian, the Minister of the Interior, who is credited with the country's stability, distanced himself from ANM operatives early on, although he himself was being criticized for certain excesses.

During the past year or so, the President also started shifting his allegiance from the ANM towards the business elite, which had just begun to firm up a power base for him. But the distancing was too late and too little to rid the President completely of that political liability. He can certainly do much more during his second term to tame the ANM's arrogance and appetite for corruption.

In the estimate of close political observers, foreign influences also cannot be dismissed as important factors in the recent developments. There must certainly be an outside influence to embolden Vazken Manoukian and his camp to the point of resorting to bloodshed.

Some believe that Russia may have played a major role behind the scenes. Yeltsin, who was believed to be a solid ally, has been forced out of the political arena because of ill health, and there is no love lost between the Armenian leadership and General Lebed, Russia's rising star and heir-apparent to Yeltsin. Indeed, the Armenian leadership had been too cozy with Lebed's archenemy, General Grachov, the former Defense Minister of Russia who was ousted at Lebed's bidding.

As Lebed becomes more critical of the west for NATO's expansion towards Russia's borders, Armenia may seem too friendly towards the West for a number of reasons, with economic aid topping the list.

There are also those who believe that the US may have played a behind-the-scenes role, in an attempt to break Armenia's so-called "intransigence" on the Karabagh issue, to force her to a more conciliatory position, hastening the flow of oil from Baku to the West.

It is hard to verify if any foreign powers are involved at this stage. Should the parties renounce violence and resort to compromises, that will indicate that the present crisis has a limited scope and can be contained rather easily. But should the confrontation continue at the present level of tension, with all parties firmly entrenched in their positions, that could be a clear sign of outside intervention.

Economic hardships are not the fault of the present government which, on the contrary, should be credited with many positive developments in the social and economic spheres.

Levon Ter Petrossian charted a rational course, took up difficult challenges, and refused to make false promises which would make his electors happy for a short period of time but cause more bitter resentment later. That course yielded many tangible results, by enhancing Armenia's military might and international political stature. It also helped ease some of the economic problems, increased the availability of electric power, and placed Armenia on the path to recovery. No one claims that Armenia's ills have been remedied or could be remedied overnight. The opposition's impatience and intolerance could prove detrimental to the country. They may deceive people for a short while with catchy slogans which can lead nowhere.

Ter Petrossian has learned from his mistakes over the past five years, and can now steer the country on a more experienced course. Should the opposition take over, it would have to commit new mistakes in order to learn from those mistakes.

Today's historic circumstances leave no room for mistakes.

The Presidential Visit

It is hard to break away from old habits. All these years we have become used to thinking of Armenian affairs in terms of community standards, whereas today we have the fact of an emerging independent Armenia, which requires rethinking our old ways and introducing some statesmanship into our conduct.

We must certainly use different standards to assess the historic significance of the present Republic of Armenia, and especially its President. Those differences are reflected in the Armenian news media in the homeland and in the diaspora. They are also reflected in the parliamentary debates, sometimes rather vociferously. This may be considered normal and healthy, within certain limits.

Today President Ter Petrossian will visit the United States as a White House guest, and much depends on his skills and strength, if he is to secure maximum support from his hosts. Therefore, it is incumbent upon the Armenian-American community not to let President Ter Petrossian down. He must find a united community behind him. Dissenters and indifferent Armenians cannot harm him personally as much as they will harm Armenia's vital interests.

Armenia's President comes from a beleaguered country, which is still recovering from the ravages of a devastating earthquake, its borders still insecure and its economy at a standstill because of a crippling blockade by Turkey and Azerbaijan, but its people still resilient and hopeful of a better life. It is easy to hold the President and his administration responsible for some of these problems, and perhaps with good reason. But to point an accusing finger at this stage will get us nowhere, other than promoting dissension and division, which we can ill afford at this time.

We are entitled to our ideological and political philosophies, but today, over and above that right, what we need to demonstrate is unity and support for the President.

Credit is also due to Mr. Ter Petrossian, who emerged from the back halls of the Matenadaran[1] and was propelled onto the world polit-

---

1. The repository of manuscripts in Yerevan.

ical scene, where he performed successfully, winning the respect of world leaders. Thanks to his prudent policies, Turkey was kept at bay, victories were scored in Karabagh, and above all, social and political stability was maintained at home, while the neighboring republics of Georgia and Azerbaijan were torn by civil strife. Armenia's foreign policy, has thus far steered clear of pitfalls in one of the most dangerous tinderboxes of the world. One could say that the president has learned diplomacy on the job, and he has not fared badly either.

Nations struggling for their survival cannot afford all the luxuries that fully developed democracies can enjoy because security and national interests are at stake, and sometimes even abuses of power may be experienced in attaining those goals.

Relations between communities require certain criteria, but it is an entirely different ball game when communities deal with a sovereign country.

Therefore, all group interests and partisan politics aside, the only way we may attain self respect is by demonstrating our unity and statesmanship in welcoming President Ter Petrossian to the US. That much we owe to ourselves and to Armenia.

August, 1991

Armenia in the Family of Nations

After being a nebulous entity in the Soviet hinterland for seven decades, Armenia has been propelled by historic events to the forefront of the international scene. Together with Armenia, many former Soviet republics have joined the United Nations, but few, if any, of their leaders can claim full support from their respective nations, such as President Ter Petrossian enjoys at home and abroad. The republics in the Caucasus in particular are fragmented and their leaders at best represent the powerful elite of their respective countries.

This statement does not intend to whitewash or ignore the differences and grievances that some groups and individuals still maintain, but in no way can that chip away the prestige that the President enjoys nationally and internationally.

This is not the first time that Armenia's President will be visiting the United States and the UN forum, but this visit will prove to have deeper and farther-reaching ramifications than the previous ones, for a number of reasons. This is the visit during which President Ter Petrossian will cash in on his five-year investment in international politics.

When the Soviet empire collapsed and its constituent republics declared independence, Armenia was perhaps the most disadvantaged country among them, having suffered one of the most devastating natural calamities, compounded by the flow of Armenian refugees expelled from Azerbaijan.

Despite all those drawbacks--and perhaps because of them--the government of Armenia had to risk the boldest of economic and political reforms, in order to survive and to keep pace with the international community. Armenia pioneered land reform and initiated privatization of industry in order to deserve the confidence of international funding agencies. The majority of Armenia's population survives under the poverty line and will be hard pressed to understand the austerity measures--painful as they are--to curb inflation and to place Armenia's economy on a healthy footing; but down the road, as they reap the benefits of that economic policy, they may come to tolerate or condone it, even if they do not accept it now.

Conversion from a controlled to a free-market economy has never been easy, and only economists can see the light at the end of the tunnel. The general populace will continue struggling for survival and yes, corruption, organized crime, and racketeering will still continue to be the unpleasant companions of Armenia's growing pains.

It is difficult for the man in the street to comprehend the significance of the loans and economic assistance pouring in from the International Monetary Fund, the European Union, the United States, Germany, and other major countries, when the price of daily bread jumps eleven-fold overnight. But at least he must understand that Armenia has gained the confidence of the agencies and nations who hold the purse strings of the money supply.

Any nation's foreign policy is the extension of its domestic policy. The recent parliamentary election, and especially the adoption of a new constitution, have steered Armenia towards the rule of law. The election may not measure up to the standards of Western democracies and the constitution may put too much power in the hands of the President, but they have proven to be historic necessities, sometimes at the expense of being unpalatable. We have to measure the ideals of democracy against the reality of survival. A fragmented nation, with very little experience in true democracy, needs a strong hand to guide her through difficult times. Who knows, had Antranik[1] been as ruthless towards his own kind as he was towards the Turkish enemy, had he dared to topple the democratically elected government of the first republic,[2] and had he ruled the country as Mustapha Kemal did in his nation-building drive, after the collapse of the Ottoman Empire, we would certainly have a larger Armenia, with over seventy years of experience in democracy, or at least be free of Soviet domination. A centralized power is, then, a historic necessity, with the full understanding that people on different levels of the power structure will take advantage of the situation for their own selfish ends. In the end, Armenia will survive and hopefully thrive. And in the final analysis that is what counts for posterity.

The strengthening of the internal power structure and the strong national army at home have helped President Ter Petrossian develop a very successful foreign policy, which has earned him the highest marks.

---

1. Armenian general and national hero (1865-1927).
2. 1918-20.

Karabagh proved to be the pinnacle of that policy, because, while retaining the captured territories, the Armenian side engineered a cease-fire, which has been in force now for more than a year and a half. On the other hand, thanks to Yerevan's international maneuvers, coupled with the diaspora's political activism, Turkey was convinced that it was no longer to her advantage to make her relations with Armenia conditional on progress in the Karabagh conflict. As a result, the air corridor over Turkey was opened and even regular Yerevan-Istanbul flights have begun, without any significant concessions, so far, from Armenia. The passage of the recent corridor act in the US Congress leaves Turkey with no alternative but to open the land corridor also.

The Turkish press, which takes its cue from Ankara, has been advocating the establishment of diplomatic relations and resumption of trade with Armenia. We should not underestimate the significance of the delegation which visited the Martyrs' Memorial in Yerevan and placed a wreath with official government sanction. Many people discounted that act as an insignificant gesture by the mayor of an Istanbul borough. But it was more than that. We should not be surprised if that were to prove a major breakthrough in Turkish-Armenian relations.

The Armenian leadership enjoys respect--if not always affection--from all parties which have conflicting interests in the region. Iran and Turkey on the one hand, and the US and Russia on the other, have all become rivals in their attempts to capture the hearts and natural resources of the region. Armenia has correct--if not always cordial--relations with all those nations and their representatives, except, understandably, for Azerbaijan.

Diaspora-Armenia relations have changed dramatically and will never be the same. All centers of power in the diaspora will gradually understand that interfactional community relations and relations with a government are, of necessity, on different levels. Whereas factions in the diaspora may strive to please the Armenian government by certain undertakings or policies, the reverse is no longer true. The government, by definition, has a different agenda, and it has to base its actions on Armenia's national interests. This sudden change may take a certain time to sink in, but eventually it will become a fact of life which we have to deal with.

We may disagree with certain policies and actions of the government in Yerevan. We may resent or even criticize those actions in the press. That has to be understood and tolerated by the government. What cannot be understood and tolerated is driving the conflict to the extreme and inviting foreign powers to meddle in Armenia's internal affairs, or trying to solve some problems in favor of a certain faction, whether or not it happens to be justified in its criticism. No foreign power will meddle for purely altruistic reasons; it will try to take advantage, in order to promote its own selfish agenda.

Also, extending our internal quarrels to the international arena may hamper Armenia's ability to receive foreign aid, which in turn will hurt the people, already suffering under insurmountable duress and deprivations. Unified public support will strengthen the President's hand, solidifying Armenia's international gains and further enhancing its international stature and prestige.

These are some of the considerations and thoughts to be borne in mind on welcoming President Ter Petrossian, who will soon be joining other world leaders to celebrate the 50th anniversary of the UN in New York City. Ter Petrossian has already proven to be a seasoned statesman, as he demonstrated recently when he visited the European capitals during the celebrations commemorating the end of World War II.

Armenia's President basked in the attention of the international media as he proudly represented Armenia and stood next to the most powerful leaders on the earth.

This visit will afford Armenian-Americans the opportunity to meet with the President at the dedication of the new Embassy building in Washington, which, along with its diplomatic mission, will showcase Armenian pride, because there is so much emotional and financial investment from the growing Armenian-American community.

Ter Petrossian will be bringing Armenia's case and her pain to the world forum of the UN, and he will also be bringing her pride at finally joining the family of free nations.

October 25, 1991

What Price Armenian-Turkish Relations!

It would be an understatement to say that events in the Soviet Union--or what remains of that former Union--are proceeding at an exhilarating pace, and Armenia is caught in the whirlwind.

The leaders who brought democracy to Armenia are seriously concerned that historically, every time an empire has collapsed in the region, our homeland has become a loser. That happened with the disintegration of the Byzantine, Ottoman, and Czarist empires, and it threatens to happen again with the breakup of the Soviet empire. Armenia intended to jump the train before it was too late. But, as it is becoming apparent, there can be no escape from geography, nor from the inexorable course of history.

In addition to the breakup--and because of it--Armenian leaders have their hands full. They have to get an accurate reading of the trends in the Soviet Union and make hasty but precise political decisions, while containing a bellicose neighbor across the Armenia-Azerbaijan border. Thus far, the Armenian leadership has fared remarkably well. Levon Ter Petrossian weathered the August coup in Moscow courageously and intelligently. Following the formation of the Slavic commonwealth, Armenia and Kirghizia were the first non-Slavic republics to apply for membership. In fact, Ter Petrossian gained his international stature as a statesman through his perceptive and prophetic predictions about the turn of events in the Soviet Union.

There is an intense soul-searching debate, both inside and outside Armenia, on how to find a viable policy towards Turkey. Our history and collective memory would instinctively suggest to us that we refrain from any contact with a country still unrepentant 76 years after committing the Genocide. But nations have to be guided by the logic of realpolitik to assure their survival. Once the political equation between Armenia's survival and her prerequisite of dealing with Turkey is formulated, every Armenian with survival instincts will opt for the obvious choice, and painfully but realistically prescribe negotiations.

Turkey entertains long-term and short-term goals. As a long-term goal, Turkey would gleefully like to wipe Armenia off the map, as it tried to do during World War I. Other political solutions may also serve Turkish interests, depending on the situations in the region. The most astute Armenian political genius, General Antranik, warned the Armenian political leadership of long-term Turkish goals right after the 1908 Young Turk revolution and throughout World War I, but he was not heeded. His premonitions remain as valid today as they were at that time. Turkey may promote good-neighborly relations with Armenia, but when the opportunity arises, she will not fail to strike and destroy Armenia. No one should have any illusions about that prospect.

A short-term Turkish goal is admission into the European Community. Poor human rights records, atrocities against Kurds, the illegal occupation of Cyprus, and denial of the Armenian Genocide remain the European Community's stated objections to Turkey's admission, unstated reasons being Turkey's third-world economy and incompatible Islamic culture. The European Parliament cited the Armenian Genocide as an obstacle to admission which Turkey cannot circumvent.

Skillful Turkish diplomacy is set out to resolve these problems one by one in order to be eligible for membership in the European Community.

Armenia's short-term goals are: finding an outlet through the economic blockade, rebuilding the earthquake-ravaged country, and developing trade relations with the West. Long-term goals include basic survival, recognition of the Genocide, retribution, and the settlement of territorial claims.

While Armenia is faced with mere survival, Turkish diplomacy is convinced that a weak country has no choice but to trade its long-term goals against Turkey's short-term objectives. The trade-off for Armenian access to the Black Sea seems to be renunciation of territorial claims and a pledge to discontinue the struggle for recognition of the Genocide.

Recently there has been an intense flurry of diplomatic activity between Armenia and Turkey, and the United States is emerging as godfather of that rapprochement. It is in the interest of United States policy to score a few low-cost points with the million-strong Armenian community in the US, and on the other hand to ease the admission of an ally into the European Community.

A prominent Jewish businessman from Turkey, Ishak Alaton, has undertaken trips to the US and Armenia as an unofficial goodwill ambassador. A trade delegation from Armenia has visited Turkey to transmit a personal message from Deputy Premier Hrant Bagratian to newly appointed Premier Suleyman Demirel of Turkey, expressing the desire to initiate trade relations and to have access to a free-trade zone at the Turkish Black Sea port of Trebizond.

Thus far, there is no official word from the Turkish government, but the press has had mixed reactions. Some newspapers have advocated development of commercial and political relations, others have proposed strict terms for those relations, and right-wing extremist papers have even insisted that Armenia must first apologize for the Armenian massacre of Turks (sic!) during World War I.

The official Turkish position may be somewhere between the extremes. Turkey may expect a vague statement that Armenia no longer entertains any territorial claims.

Political expediency in this case may prove detrimental to long-term Armenian interests. The Genocide issue cannot be tabled without a national debate. Although, in the long run, only the Republic of Armenia will be Turkey's negotiating partner, yet the diaspora has as much say as Armenia on the issues of Genocide and territorial claims. The Armenian government does not need to rush into hasty decisions and unnecessary disclaimers, when the treaties of Alexandropol, Moscow, Kars, and Lausanne, which determined the boundaries between Armenia and Turkey and the status of Armenians in Turkey, speak for themselves. Those treaties certainly do not favor Armenia, but they are internationally recognized agreements which, in this case, serve as grounds for the Armenian government to refrain from any new public pronouncement.

Turkey has been skillfully attempting to pit Armenia against the diaspora by trying to wrest a statement from any government official in Armenia alleging that Genocide claims are the work of Armenian extremists in the US or the diaspora. One such statement has been attributed to Mr. Bagratian; hopefully the allegation will prove untrue, just as earlier statements were also found to be untrue and were courageously refuted by the Armenian government.

These are extremely volatile and explosive times, and caution must be exercised both within and outside Armenia every time an outrageous statement appears in the Turkish media.

No Armenian can forget the Genocide issue, nor can we forgive until it is internationally recognized. Similarly, not an inch of historic Armenian territory can be sold short or bartered for temporary interests.

Granted, realism and objectivity must serve as our guides in dealing with Turkey. Claims can be achieved and settlements reached only through power. Armenia does not now possess that political power, nor will it possess it in the foreseeable future. Therefore, Armenia has to weigh its priorities, and for the time being the survival issue must top her political agenda. Survival today and political power tomorrow may lead Armenia to a point where, one day, it may be feasible and realistic to raise those issues and guarantee their success. Governments do not raise issues unless they assume that their success is guaranteed.

Diaspora Armenians are realistic enough to accept the pragmatic policy of the Armenian government to avoid confrontation with Turkey over the Genocide and territorial issues. But it will be hard for any Armenian to forgive leaders or groups who deny the Genocide or forfeit all territorial claims in exchange for Turkish concessions of questionable and temporary value.

It is also in the best interest of modern-day Turkey to come to terms with her history, because she cannot be admitted into the family of civilized nations without voluntarily absolving herself of past crimes, as the US did recently and unilaterally in the case of Japanese nationals interned in concentration camps during World War II.

Diaspora Armenians are not bound by any policy that Armenia chooses to pursue at this juncture of its history. For more than seventy years, Armenia had no foreign policy of her own. The Soviet central government did not recognize the Genocide, nor did it allow the Armenian Republic to recognize it officially. Moscow unsuccessfully claimed Kars and Ardahan in 1948, with the aim of turning them over to Georgia.

With the demise of the central government, the burden is on Yerevan again.

While Armenia was denied her own voice on matters concerning her historic rights for seventy years, the Armenians and political parties of the diaspora continued the struggle to keep the spirit alive among Armenians and the campaign going to educate the general public.

It may sound ironic, but those policies may have to continue well into the next century, with Armenia continuing to avoid a confrontation and the diaspora doing its best to keep our claims alive, but with one difference: a tacit understanding and coordination of policies between the homeland and the diaspora.

December 21, 1991

Should Fate
Strike Once Again

President Levon Ter Petrossian is endowed with strong political instinct and keen insight. For a man who lacks the traditional training in diplomacy, he has shown a remarkable proficiency at gauging political trends in this period of transition from the collapse of the Soviet Union to the shaping of the new Commonwealth. He is ahead of the game, and he has become one of the most visible leaders in this transformation.

Those who feared that Ter Petrossian could lead Armenia onto a collision course with Moscow have come to realize that his combative and confrontational style was directed against the person of Gorbachev, a proven foe of the Armenians, and not necessarily against the Russian people or any other form of central authority.

Ter Petrossian deserves credit for having foreseen Gorbachev's eventual failure and subsequent exit from the political arena (when it was still early enough to devise a strategy), and for having consequently allied himself with Yeltsin's camp and its rising power.

Today, in its most trying times, Armenia is reaping the dividends of this prudent policy.

Indeed, as the situation in Artzakh deteriorated alarmingly, Yeltsin came to Ter Petrossian's rescue by signing the first cooperation treaty between Russia and Armenia on the eve of the Minsk meeting of Republic Presidents, who were charged with defining the parameters and the role of the new Commonwealth.

That was a timely warning to Azerbaijan and her leader, Ayaz Mutalibov, who have been hastily alternating their hats, as Communists, Islamic fundamentalists, and democrats.

It is still too early, while Azerbaijan continues massing its forces on the Armenian border and bombarding Stepanakert, to expect any outcome of this timely warning. But Yeltsin's sympathies have been demonstrably directed towards Armenia, signalling Azerbaijan that it should think twice about its policy of brinkmanship. It would be politically naive to believe that all of these developments in the region's politics were brought about solely through the fine skills of Armenia's president. Those skills only yield results when conditions are ripe and other factors are at play. No matter how democratic the rule in Armenia, our tiny republic, with its crumbling economy and the devastation left behind by the earthquake, can only become a burden to Yeltsin's Russia or to the new Commonwealth. Yet it is obvious that Yeltsin's geopolitical concerns and strategic interests have played an important role in defining his southern policy. Yeltsin seems determined to extend Russia's strategic land mass to the Turkish border. Since the East-West honeymoon may not last very long, new power blocks may soon emerge. US Secretary of Defense Dick Cheney has already warned that Russia has not stopped producing nuclear warheads and continues to aim them against United States targets. This announcement may dampen hopes for an early thaw and permanent peace in the world. There may still be turbulent times ahead, and maintaining turfs may remain a serious political priority for Moscow.

Ter Petrossian's diplomatic skills have scored important points with the Bush Administration as well. His last visit to Washington, feared by many to be premature, has also been yielding positive results. In the first place, he was able to sensitize the White House and the Congress to Armenia's dire and immediate needs. As a consequence to this visit, we have been relieved to witness the flow of food and medical supplies directly to Yerevan.

Armenia scored a decisive diplomatic victory when the US officially announced its intention to open a consulate in Yerevan to serve the three Caucasian republics. That was a tacit acknowledgement by the White House that Armenia is the only republic in the region that meets US standards of democracy and political stability.

Ter Petrossian has yet to win new converts in domestic politics, but many opposition groups have come to realize that one cannot argue with success. As the realignment process takes its course on the home front in this post-election period, the opposition groups--with the rare exception of some extremists--have been rethinking their policies and repositioning themselves in Parliament.

No political group with a minimal concern for Armenia's future can upset the cart during this sensitive period. Even the ARF,[1] which thus far has been the most vocal and belligerent faction in the opposi-

---

1. Armenian Revolutionary Federation.

tion ranks, seems to have moderated its stand, for its own good and for that of Armenia. Indeed, following its confrontation with Ter Petrossian--and its subsequent humiliating electoral defeat--the ARF has been facing a serious internal crisis and loss of credibility in Armenia. That, of course, relieves the government from internal pressure and allows it to pursue its daily chores, which have become increasingly difficult. Additionally, the ARF has sent a few conciliatory signals and made overtures to the government, moving its policy to a more realistic course and at the same time stifling the discontent brewing in the restive ranks.

The situation in and around Armenia is extremely volatile, and precarious enough to scare any leadership into blunders. Thus far, the leadership has fared reasonably well, by carefully calculating its moves.

Armenia experienced a similar fate in the 1918-1920 period. It was phenomenal that, after living under foreign domination for 600 years, Armenia was able to form a national government and hold quasi-democratic elections. Mistakes were committed, of course, and controversy over the political moves undertaken during that period still persists. Then, as today, independence was thrust upon Armenia, at a time when she was not ready to accept and to implement it fully. The political odds were overwhelming, and our first independent republic was short-lived.

Today our leadership in Armenia has made the best of the situation that has evolved since the demise of the Soviet Union. Should the tides of the times prove overwhelming again, history may once more point a blaming finger at the actors on the political stage, but at least their prudent performance under most trying circumstances is now on record.

January 11, 1992

Democracy in Its Infancy

It is a demonstrable truism of psychology that brutalized and abused children tend to become abusers themselves when they grow up. This theory seems to apply, in general terms, to nations and special groups as well as to individuals. A lack of democratic institutions will produce bruised generations for a long time. Democracy can be fully exercised only after a long and often arduous evolution towards fully developed traditions and institutions.

The Bolsheviks rose against the Czar's repressive rule in the name of freedom and democracy, but they ended up building the most ferocious totalitarian regime in the history of mankind. Another good case in point is Armenia's neighbor Georgia, where, after the collapse of the Communist regime, Zviad Gamsakhurdia's Round Table coalition took over, only to replace one violent regime with another. Political instability ensued, and Gamsakhurdia, who was accused of human rights violations, was forcibly removed from power. The militant opposition which replaced him in the name of democracy has been engaged in a witchhunt and has been chasing its opponents in the streets, at gun point.

Armenia's President Levon Ter Petrossian warned early in his term of office that we are no more intelligent than the Georgians, and that any wrong move could result in deterioration of the situation in our homeland into civil war. In making that statement, he probably also had in mind our experience early this century when, one year after independence, the fledgling republic came under one-party rule. The demise of that republic is mostly attributable to outside forces, but internal repression also took its toll by disrupting the unity of the Armenian people, thus exacerbating the fall of the republic.

Today Armenia is fortunate to have a functioning parliament, in which democratically elected representatives of the people try to put democracy into action for the first time in 70 years. The tragic demise of the first republic[1] may serve as a useful lesson to the present leaders, if

---

1. May 28, 1918 to November 29, 1920.

they are ready and willing to learn from history.

All the Republics of the former Soviet Union are scrambling to learn from Western experience how to develop functioning democracies in their countries. Armenia is fortunate to have an organized diaspora, which is all too willing to pass on its experience to the homeland, in order to see democracy institutionalized in that country.

But some trends which have surfaced recently indicate that democracy is still in its infancy, and any demagogue or group of demagogues may easily subvert it before it has the opportunity to develop into full bloom.

It was the Armenian National Movement which brought freedom to Armenia. The Movement was a coalition of various groups rather than a cohesive political party with a defined ideology. Each constituent group had its own agenda. Once the parliament was elected, many dissenting groups gradually dropped out, the last being that of former Prime Minister Vazken Manoukian.

At one point, the ANM looked as if it were on the verge of complete collapse. Many groups seriously considered merging with the newly formed ADL.[2] Others sought a coalition with that party. But the ADL leadership bent over backwards to prevent the collapse of the ANM. Finally, a memorandum of understanding was published in the press, vowing close cooperation between the two organizations during the referendum of September 21, 1991 and the presidential election on October 16 of the same year.

Following its recent shake-up, the ANM is looking and acting more and more like a political party rather than a coalition movement.

The ANM counts among its ranks many respected intellectuals, statesmen, political activists, and professionals, along with some opportunists who have joined the organization to pursue their own hidden personal agendas, all the while giving lip service to the Movement. President Ter Petrossian and the leadership are cognizant of this fact and early in the game they expressed their hope that in time the ANM would undergo a cleansing process, eliminating these opportunists. That process does not seem to have completed its course, since those elements, who were also the parasites of society during the former regime, continue to enjoy their cozy corners within the organization, bringing discredit on its stature as the ruling power.

---

2. Armenian Democratic Liberal Organization.

During the presidential election, Ter Petrossian's affiliation with the organization cost him a few votes, because many ANM regional representatives have been using the same tactics as the mafia used during the Communist era. In the rural areas, the relationship between the government and the governed still remains on an archaic level.

If a healthy democracy is to be established in Armenia, these aberrations must be criticized and corrected. After being on the receiving end of the abuse of power for so long, people will not change and reform overnight. Some may even think that now that the tables have turned, it is their chance to abuse the beneficiaries of the previous regime.

We have to be realistic and expect such reprehensible behavior to continue for some time to come, until affluence is achieved and more civilized conduct becomes the norm. It is possible that such development may have to wait for a new generation to be born and raised in freedom.

What is more serious is the provincialism which is all too familiar in that part of the world. Every Armenian believes in, or at least gives lip service to, the unity of the Armenian people, beginning with the poet Yeghishé Charentz. We all consider the diaspora to be complementary to Armenia. Only the defunct regime tried to use the diaspora for ulterior ends, which were not necessarily derived from Armenia's best interests. Those designs caused disruptions and disunity in the diaspora.

But as some leaders get the taste of power, it seems that they cannot avoid the temptation to abuse that power once again and are unable to break away from their old acquired habits. Indeed, some of the ANM leaders have recently extended their arrogance all the way to the diaspora, reminding us of the dictum attributed to Louis XIV: "L'État c'est moi" ("I am the State").

This is indeed a dangerous development, and if a democratic press is as vital as we earnestly believe it to be, that press has a serious task to accomplish: to address these issues before they get out of hand.

One of the prominent leaders of the ANM, and a member of parliament at that, recently made a revealing statement in the official organ of the ANM, *Hayk*. "The only goal of Armenian diaspora organizations," he said, "should consist of the development and strengthening of the statehood of Armenia and the development of its international relations. These are the only guarantees of the unity of the Armenian people. It would also be beneficial if once and for all diaspora Armenians could rid themselves of tendencies to develop political spheres of influence in Armenia."

We have no quarrel with the first part of the above statement, provided that our conduct is not prescribed by novices in politics; but the last segment of that statement could be taken as a prescription for dictatorship, if it did not sound so excessively provincial. Indeed, it is the very institutionalization of provincialism. This mentality is in stark contrast to the official statement made when Raffi Hovannisian was appointed as Foreign Minister of Armenia. Indeed, it was said that there was no one in Armenia of Hovannisian's caliber to fill that position. The truth of the matter is that the statement may be extended to cover even broader areas.

Granted, no political group must entertain presumptions of running Armenia's affairs from abroad; at the same time, the same new and inexperienced leaders in Armenia must not pontificate to diaspora Armenians by demanding that they support certain policies or define their patriotism. We all have to join forces, learn from each other, and share our individual experiences, since the situation in Armenia is too fragile to allow any group or individual to get carried away with long-distance disputes which may cause us to lose sight of our main priorities. The world is too dangerous a place to gamble with Armenia's destiny.

Provincialism was one of the major internal reasons which destroyed the first Republic. We should not allow that to happen again, while democracy in Armenia is still in its infancy.

January 18, 1992

AN IMMINENT THREAT TO ARMENIA:

The Brain Drain

We are rightfully concerned about dangers threatening Armenia's future and very survival: namely, economic strangulation and conflict with Azerbaijan. We seldom realize, however, the danger posed by the brain drain, which may have a lasting and irreversible impact on Armenia's economy and destiny. It may seem invisible at this stage, but it is very real.

News emanating from various corners of the former Soviet Union reveals that weapons experts in the former Soviet Union   are up for grabs by countries eager to develop modern and sophisticated weaponry of their own. And these experts are being offered top dollars for their expertise. In view of this proliferation of technology, the West is up in arms, alarmed by the prospect that dangerous weapons may fall into the wrong hands.

A similar alarm has to be sounded to the world Armenian community, although for other reasons: because Armenia faces the very same prospect as the other Republics. With the break-up of the Soviet Union, a free-for-all situation has emerged, and by the time the dust settles, Armenia may prove to have been the prime loser.

Something strange has happened to Armenia: it is unusual for any country of Armenia's size and economic infrastructure to be in possession of such advanced technology, which is normally only available to economic superpowers. As an integral part of such a superpower, over the years, Armenia has been the recipient of that technology. Today, with the break-up of the Soviet Union, Armenia finds herself with an important chunk of that technology, not commensurate with the resources and services available to sustain that level of technological set-up. The space and weapons industries have left behind an enormous technological base and know-how. Armenia is hardly able to convert the military-industrial complex to civilian industries on her own. A case in point is the Nayirit conglomerate of chemical plants, one of the largest and most advanced of its kind. Earlier, its operation was halted because of ecological concerns, but today it has become a white elephant which cannot be revived, even if those problems are properly addressed, because of shortages of raw materials and fuel, and because of the complete lack of distribution and marketing systems. An enterprising businessman from England, namely Vartan Ouzounian, who also happens to be a chemist by training, has taken up the challenge to convert one of the plants to consumer use, for the manufacture of detergents, soaps, and similar products.

But what is more appalling than the potential loss of the major industries which remain in Armenia is the potential loss of the institutions and brains that have developed those industries. Armenia boasts of her Academy of Sciences, Institutes of Physics and Chemistry, the Polytechnic Institute, and other scientific and research centers, which have advanced our tiny Republic to the cutting edge of such sophisticated fields as laser technology and the mathematical sciences.

This dramatic situation may also prove a blessing in disguise. On the one hand, if the current situation continues, we stand to lose precious technology developed over decades and, on the other hand, our newly-independent Republic does not begin its development from the footing of a third-world country. As soon as a trade outlet is worked out and reliable energy supplies are restored, Armenia will be in a position to develop its economy from an advanced industrial base: that is, if the brain drain does not become irreversible before that.

Thus far, all these institutes and their staffs have been on Moscow's payroll. As of January 1st of the current year, the budgets of these institutes have been cut off, leaving them hanging in limbo. The government of Armenia is in no position to substitute for Moscow's financial base. Therefore, Armenia's most coveted talents have become its most underprivileged class overnight. With an aggressive international head-hunt in progress, it is not very difficult to figure out that all of these scientists will sell their expertise to the highest bidder; already a brain drain has ensued, with catastrophic results in prospect.

Another tragedy is the case of Armenian historians, writers, scholars, researchers, and academics, whose work is mostly confined to Armenia and has extremely limited value outside the Armenian world community. Complete chaos and confusion have already emerged there. All these writers and scholars have been knocked off their economic base. The entire system has collapsed, and they cannot figure out who to turn to to finance their projects, much less who will show an interest in their work and pay for it after its completion.

Armenians around the world have their hands full of trying to help Armenia recover from the ravages of the earthquake and to feed

300,000 refugees deported from Azerbaijan. With these tragedies over-
taxing our resources, one might think that the issue of the brain drain
can be placed on the back burner until the country recovers and can handle the situation locally. But unfortunately, this burning issue cannot
wait that long. An international rescue effort must be undertaken today,
to try to save those institutions and maintain their staffs. If we cannot
afford to save those talents for Armenia today, tomorrow we will be
worse off, because when we are ready and in need of the technology, its
developers will be elsewhere, and the technology they are capable of
developing will be far beyond our means.

8 February, 1992

ARMENIA:

Focus on National and International Politics

Despite traditional fragmentations in the Armenian diaspora, suddenly all parties and groups have begun to work towards the same goals; namely, assisting Armenia to overcome its present economic problems and survive as a democratic state, and assisting Artzakh[1] politically, to avoid a bloodbath and to preserve its Armenian identity. Had this spontaneous support been more carefully coordinated, it would have a far-reaching political and historical impact on our future.

The US Secretary of State's warnings to Azerbaijan, Baroness Cox's relentless lobbying for human rights in Artzakh, Yelena Bonner's public appeals, Senator Dole's letter to President Yeltsin, and the European Community's cold shoulder to Azerbaijan have amplified the prospects of internationalizing the conflict, thereby rendering its solution in Armenia's favor more likely.

Even Turkey, currently engaged in a race against time to win over six Moslem republics of the former Soviet Union before Iran conflagrates the area with Islamic fundamentalism, has been soft-peddling its support of Azerbaijan, in an effort to disguise its long-term Pan-Touranistic[2] designs. Nonetheless, Western political analysts point out that the die is already cast and the area is on a collision course with the West. In an article published recently in the *International Herald Tribune*, John Cooley advises major Western powers to strengthen their Christian allies in the area--Armenia is one of them--against the rising tide of Islamic fundamentalism .

For the first time in seventy years, it seems that Russia's interests in the area converge with the West's. As these newly independent and

---

1. Nagorno Karabagh (Armenian).
2. Pan-Turkic.

impoverished republics seek assistance for development, Russia will be forced grudgingly to cede that role to her erstwhile adversaries--China, the Gulf states, Turkey, and Iran--who are already vying for a foothold in the region.

With the awakening of the West to the needs of the threatened Christian nations in the area, the tide has suddenly taken a positive turn for the Armenians in Artzakh in their four-year old struggle, and it has forced the Azeris into a defensive posture, especially in the Shushi region. The Azeris have been appealing to the Islamic nations to mediate a negotiated settlement, and Armenia's defense minister, Vazken Sarksian, has confidently announced that eventually Azerbaijan has to come to terms with the reality of the newly-independent Republic of Artzakh.

Recent Azeri losses have fueled Azerbaijani National Front rhetoric with calls for President Ayaz Mutalibov's resignation and accusations that he failed to take decisive action in the current crisis.

Just now, an equitable solution seems a far-off possibility, but should a peace treaty be signed, caution must be exercised to avoid any potential irritants because, since Armenia has been seeking neighborly relations with Turkey, Armenians will have more at stake than Azerbaijanis, especially when one considers the potential Islamization of the entire region.

Inevitably, developments in Artzakh will also shape domestic politics at home, and there are already early indications of that impact in recent occurrences.

Thanks to Levon Ter Petrossian's popularity, the Armenian National Movement was able to defeat its opponents soundly. But the overconfidence stemming from that victory has made the ANM leaders extremely unrealistic, and their neo-Communist style of operation has allowed their most dreaded enemies to score political points against them. Indeed, much of the credit for success in the Artzakh war has been given to the ARF,[3] although the majority of the fighters have no affiliation with that organization.

In a recent stand-off, the ANM's refusal to settle for a compromise candidate for the presidency of the Artzakh Parliament has led to Arthur Mekertichian's victory against the ANM candidate, whereas former Artzakh leader and compromise candidate Leonard Bedrosian could have saved all faces and kept the Artzakh struggle an all-Armenian

---

3. Armenian Revolutionary Federation.

endeavor. Therefore, it is no surprise that ARF leader Hrair Maroukhian's arrival in Yerevan coincides with Mekertichian's election, in a way vindicating the party's defeat in Armenia's presidential elections in October 1991.

If ARF history and past totalitarian tendencies are any indication, that organization will use an eventual Artzakh victory--to be won by the combined forces of all Armenians--as leverage to gain influence in Armenia or force concessions by the government, regardless of their ramifications. Should that happen, the blame must be shared equally with the ANM leadership, which has been losing its popularity at home. That decline is caused in particular by increasingly concentrating power in fewer hands, in a situation of economic chaos and social instability. For example, very recently Vano Siradeghian assumed his fourth position, this time as Minister of the Interior.

That prospect must not erode diaspora support for Armenia and Artzakh in these most difficult times. The hedge against the emergence of a totalitarian regime--in any shape or form--is strengthening democratic institutions in the Parliament and throughout Armenia. And indeed a realignment of power has become evident in the Parliament, where the democratic vote has resulted in an impressive increase in the ADL block of deputies.

Until recently, Azerbaijan and Georgia were denied Western aid because of the social unrest and hard-line rule which plagued those republics. Any resurgence of socialism--whether of the Marxist or the Scandinavian brand--may drive Armenia into the category of its neighbors.

And that we cannot afford in these crucial times.

February 22, 1992

Crying Wolf on the Turkish Border

It seems that Armenians are losing the propaganda war on the issue of Artzakh (Nagorno Karabagh). Today, when Azeris are able to hit the *New York Times* front page headlines in their propaganda war, after conducting a ruthless policy of extermination for four years in that tiny Armenian enclave, there is something very ominous in the making for Armenians, not only in Artzakh but also in Armenia itself. The organizers of the Baku, Sumgait, and Shahumian pogroms have been successfully playing victim, while portraying Armenians as victimizers. The Azeris have not yet developed enough sophistication to play the international game of politics. They are just emerging from the dark ages. But their Big Brothers across the border have projected their case into the international political forum and the press.

Most of the major papers, including the *New York Times* and the *London Times*, have given extensive coverage to the Khodjalu battle, which finally was able to silence the bombing over Stepanakert. Those papers have given only scant coverage to the fact that Armenians have also been dying in Stepanakert for the last four years, as if they were less human. Now that Armenians have successfully defended themselves against overwhelming Azeri forces, they are being portrayed as the aggressors.

An eye-witness to the Khodjalu incident, news reporter Florence David of Channel 5 in Paris, told an entirely different story; she reports that Armenian and Azeri warring factions exchange bodies from time to time. That is exactly what was happening in Khodjalu, when suddenly an Azeri helicopter appeared, overflew Khodjalu, and broadcast to the world that all the bodies were those of Azeris killed by Armenians!

Indeed, the Turks have mounted a massive propaganda campaign to portray earthquake-ravaged and blockade-weary Armenia as the aggressor. With Defense Minister Yevgeny Shaposhnikov's withdrawal of Commonwealth forces from Artzakh and Secretary of State James Baker's "winking at aggression in Baku" (as characterized by a *New York Times* editorial), the stage seems to have been set by the combined Turkish-Azeri forces for the "final solution" for Armenia, especially when, on the other hand, appeals fall on deaf ears at the UN and at

NATO headquarters in Brussels.

In an obvious attempt to bully and intimidate Armenia, the Turkish Third Army has been maneuvering on its eastern borders with live ammunition, while Azeris intensify their bombardment of Stepanakert, the capital city of Artzakh.

Turkey has thrown away its "mediator's" mask and has been looking for excuses to justify its aggression against Armenia. During last week's Senate hearing, Henry Kissinger's statement that today Ankara has more influence than Moscow in Azerbaijan, corroborates the Turkish intention to invade across the border and justifies fears of an imminent attack.

The emerging scenario is very similar to that which existed on the eve of the 1974 Turkish occupation of 38% of Cyprus. On his return from Washington, Turkish Prime Minister Suleyman Demirel warned that his country would not stay idle in the event of a conflict between Armenia and Azerbaijan. Mass hysteria in the Turkish news media has been increasing, to prepare public opinion for and justify an eventual incursion across the border.

It is no coincidence that, after a long period of silence, former Prime Minister Bülent Ecevit, who led the Turkish occupational forces into Cyprus, should emerge from the woodwork at this juncture to demand border "corrections" between Armenia and Artzakh.

There is very serious cause for concern and I do not think that pointing to the possibility of Turkish invasion is being alarmist. In 1974 Turkey and its allies concocted a so-called "coup" in Cyprus to justify Turkish intervention in that independent island. Turkey violated the sovereignty of a UN member state in broad daylight, and the civilized world has yet to force Turkish troops out of Cyprus. The Soviet Union has collapsed and the Berlin Wall has been knocked down, but the green line dividing the peaceful island of Cyprus is still in place.

All that Turkish-Azeri combined forces need at this point is a pretext, a big lie, such as that "Armenians are massacring thousands of Azerbaijanis," and the unwitting complicity of the Western press, to repeat the Cyprus scenario and move into Armenia as the great "defenders of threatened minorities."

The international news media have been taking their cue from Baku and Ankara, presenting their version of events, which is far removed from the truth. The escalation of this news campaign serves a hidden agenda which Ankara and Baku have been harboring for quite some time.

On the other hand, the unsubstantiated boasting of some

Armenian groups about the fighting in Artzakh has been directly playing into the hands of the Azerbaijanis.

At this grave moment the prospects of a Turkish aggression
seems less dangerous than the complacency and relative indifference of
the Armenians around the world.

March 14, 1992

ARTZAKH IS BURNING:

Is a Breakthrough in Sight?

Following the Turkish news blitz in the Western media, which portrayed Artzakh Armenians, fighting for their lives, as murderers, the conflict has been amplified into an issue of international magnitude that has triggered a flurry of diplomatic initiatives involving UN envoy Cyrus Vance, Iranian Foreign Minister Ali Akbar Velayati, the fact-finding mission of the Conference on Security and Cooperation in Europe (CSCE) and, most significant of all, Turkish Ambassador Vulkan Vural's visit to Yerevan to convey a special message from Prime Minister Demirel indicating Turkey's willingness to play a constructive mediating role, while resisting public pressure to take military action against Armenia. Turkey has been exercising unusual restraint under the current circumstances. Ordinarily, incendiary public pronouncements in the Turkish news media, coupled with military maneuvers on Armenia's borders, would have been translated into military action against that republic, as evidenced by the precedent of Cyprus in 1974. Two important factors seem to underlie the uncharacteristic restraint:

1. Now that NATO has almost lost its raison d'être in Europe, the center of gravity of its military structure has shifted eastward, mainly to Turkey. As the representative of Western military force in the area, Turkey seems to have been constrained not to use that force unilaterally and for the fulfillment of selfish goals. There is ample evidence that the US State Department has been twisting Turkey's arm to persuade it to use its newly enhanced military posture more responsibly.

2. Currently, Turkey has its hands full with the Kurdish insurrection, which is still simmering in its eastern provinces. The Turkish press has been openly discussing a spring military operation to crush the Kurdish independence movement. Therefore, the timing does not seem right for Turkey to add another military venture to its agenda. On the other hand, the Russian government has been observing with a degree of

alarm the possibility of introducing NATO forces at its southern flank and the growing influence of the Islamic countries in the south.

Turkish Prime Minister Suleyman Demirel has been critical of the political struggle to push the government into a military venture. "All we could do was to commit Armenia to respect Azerbaijan's territorial integrity," he said, referring to the joint declaration which was signed by all the members of the CSCE. That document is as much to Armenia's advantage as to Azerbaijan's, because it also commits Azerbaijan and Turkey to respect Armenia's territorial integrity, which is in danger at this time. Armenia had already unilaterally proclaimed that it had no territorial claims in Azerbaijan: Artzakh was a human rights issue.

These new developments, of course, give Armenia and Armenians in Artzakh some breathing time in which they can consolidate at the negotiating table what they have gained on the battleground. The new factor in this turmoil is the realization by the new Baku government that Artzakh has been and will continue to be a tough nut to crack. This can be inferred from its overture to the head of the Artzakh Parliament, Arthur Mekertichian. This is the first instance that the Baku government has consented to talk to Artzakh officials. It had maintained all along that Artzakh was an internal problem and that Armenia had to refrain from meddling in Azerbaijan's internal affairs. Well, that political line seems to have run its course, and recent events have led Baku to the conclusion that the conflict is not just an internal problem but has become an issue of international proportions.

That was the first reasonable reaction from Baku, which has also contacted Armenian officials in Yerevan to negotiate the issue in the context of its new dimension.

Still, the region is very explosive and will remain so for some time to come, given the convergence of many conflicting interests in that area. Armenia has a very long and perilous road to travel until some sense of security and normalcy is restored in its neighborhood.

All recent developments indicate that a breakthrough may be in the offing, albeit for the short term. Armenia is desperate for any respite, and any movement towards a settlement would be welcome. The fact that Cyrus Vance has spent less than one day in Yerevan and more than two days in Azerbaijan indicates that the problems are mostly with Baku, and that Armenia is the willing partner in the dialogue for a peaceful solution.

The days ahead are replete with dangers. It is to be hoped that a settlement is in the cards, bringing peace to the peoples of the region.

March 28, 1992

A Window
of Opportunity

The historic parallels are too painful to forget. Indeed, there are striking similarities between Cilician Armenia in the aftermath of World War I and Artzakh today. In the first instance the Allies armed the Armenian Legion, which marched triumphantly into Cilician territory, a promised land for the Armenians, only to be disarmed and left to the mercy of emerging Kemalist forces. The Armenians were too polite to resist disarmament and too credulous to doubt their Christian allies' ulterior motives. They suffered the bitter consequences: Cilicia was depopulated and left to the Turks, while many Armenians lost their lives in a stampede to follow the retreating French occupation army, which had made a treacherously unannounced decision to leave the region.

With the collapse of the Soviet Union and the withdrawal of the Red Army, Armenians faced a very similar situation in Armenia and particularly in Artzakh. Strategists in Moscow could not care less if the Cilician scenario were repeated, this time in Artzakh; they decided to withdraw the army and leave the Armenians defenseless. But the lessons of history were too fresh and too bitter to forget. Therefore, the Armenians resorted to self-defense, with the full realization that this was the last frontier in Armenian history that they were destined to defend.

Four years of unequal struggle, resulting in many casualties, finally paid off; the conflict was internationalized and the Azeris were convinced that there was no military solution to the issue. Armenian military advances on the battlefield enhanced their political position.

Last week a group of Armenian-Americans were invited to Washington to be briefed on the Artzakh issue by White House policy makers; they left with an encouraging degree of optimism. This writer was privileged to be in that group.

With the demise of the Soviet Union, fifteen republics have emerged, each one charting its own course of development. Armenia was the first republic to uphold the laws of the existing constitution in planning its dissociation from the Union. The referendum, the election of a true democrat who is untainted by any old Soviet ties, as president, a functioning democratic parliament, the success of land reform, and privatization of agricultural land have all helped to project Armenia's image as a true democracy. That was not missed by the West.

The Bush administration has taken note of these developments and has already established very special relations with President Levon Ter Petrossian. Armenia's commitment to the democratic process has been in stark contrast to the autocratic rules emerging in neighboring republics, particularly in Azerbaijan, which is trying to keep Artzakh within its grasp.

Until Secretary of State James Baker's trip to Baku, the US administration did not see a role for itself. But following that visit the US has taken a very active role. Secretary Baker has made a strong statement against the economic blockade imposed by Azerbaijan on Armenia and Artzakh.

On the other hand, Turkey has been assigned a very crucial role in projecting Western power and interests into the emerging Central Asian republics, which are rich in natural resources. In view of this strategic planning, the US administration seems to have convinced Turkey that it is not in her best interest to foment another hot spot on her eastern borders, in addition to the flare-up of the Kurdish insurgency. The Turks seem to have been convinced that they would be better off integrating Armenia into that development plan than antagonizing her. That is why the earlier belligerent statements by President Turgut Özal have been toned down by Prime Minister Süleyman Demirel, whose political fortunes have been enhanced against those of the President. That rules out the possibility of a military strike by Turkey against Armenia.

Resisting the mounting internal pressure, Turkey has also refrained from arming or advising the Azeri army. All statements to this effect were denied by White House officials during the briefing.

The recent peace mission by Iranian Foreign Minister Ali Akbar Velayati was successful in brokering a cease-fire in Artzakh. That success has enhanced Iran's influence in the region and had an adverse impact on Turkey's position. Turkey has been pressured by the US to play a more even-handed and constructive role in order to neutralize Iran's influence, which the US has come to watch with apprehension. No Iranian influence is welcome to the US administration.

The White House did not make any secret of the fact that President Bush views Armenia as a democratic role model for the newly-independent nations emerging from the former Soviet system; therefore it has a vested interest in Armenia's survival and development.

After much hesitation and mixed signals, Russia is now demonstrating a renewed interest in Armenia's strategic position. With superpower interests converging on Armenia, the Artzakh conflict has been pushed to center-stage. The first phase of the peace process is the tripartite negotiations involving Armenia, Azerbaijan, and Artzakh. The Baku government had resisted all attempts to give a voice to the Artzakh representatives. The first breakthrough came when Azerbaijan conceded to Armenia's demand that Artzakh be included as a partner in the negotiations. Cyrus Vance's fact-finding mission provided the basis for these negotiations. The next step moves to Minsk, where negotiations will take place under the auspices of the Conference on Security and Cooperation in Europe (CSCE), with the active participation of three major players, among others: namely, the US, Russia, and Turkey.

We are told that while the Armenians hold an enhanced strategic position on the battleground and the conflict is sensitizing the international community and threatening many interests, this is a once-in-a-lifetime opportunity to sign a peace treaty, get the painful struggle over with, and put the country on the path to economic recovery.

The Minsk meeting provides a rare "window of opportunity" for war-weary Armenians to consolidate a political settlement which has already been legitimized on the battleground.

April 2, 1992

The Spectre of War over Armenia

After a few hopeful developments in Karabagh, the specter of an all-out war between Armenia and Azerbaijan looms once again over the region. The flurry of diplomatic maneuvers aimed at bringing the parties to the negotiating table has been bogged down because of Azeri intransigence; no date has yet been set for the peace conference, which was scheduled to take place in Minsk under the auspices of the Conference on Security and Cooperation in Europe.

Meanwhile, the cease-fire brokered by Iran is repeatedly being violated, with more dangerous ramifications to the entire region. In addition to the continued bombardment of civilian targets in Karabagh's capital city, Stepanakert, the violence has escalated right into Armenian territory, in a very obvious attempt to draw Armenia into an all-out war with Azerbaijan. Indeed, last week witnessed the shelling of Khentzoresk and Nerkin Khentzoresk, villages inhabited mainly by Armenian refugees who were driven out of Hadrut, Guedashen, and Martunashen in Artzakh by the Azeris two years ago. But the most ominous escalation of the conflict emerged on the Armenia-Nakhichevan border, which had been quiet throughout the conflict, thanks to an understanding between Armenia's leaders and Haidar Aliyev, who has been using Nakhichevan as his power base for a potential comeback as the uncontested leader of Azerbaijan. Acting on his own political agenda, he has been waiting in the wings for a possible comeback. He is a well-known Soviet mafia chief, former head of the KGB in Azerbaijan, and a Brezhnev darling, who served on the powerful Politburo of the Communist party in Moscow.

It seems that Aliyev is ready for action, and peace on the Armenia-Nakhichevan border is no longer to his advantage. Indeed, the occupation of the Armenian village of Kerky on the Nakhichevan border introduces a new dimension into the conflict.

After Mutalibov's[1] ouster in early March, there is a realignment

---

1. The leader of Azerbaijan; see the earlier essay in this collection: "Should Fate Strike Once Again" (page 46).

of forces within Azerbaijan itself, as the radical forces in the National Front position themselves for a leadership role following the parliamentary elections scheduled for June 7, 1992. It is characteristic of any weak regime to try to solve its internal problems through foreign exploits. Accordingly, Karabagh and Armenia have become the centerpieces of Azerbaijani internal politics, as each party offers its own version of a military solution to the conflict. Mutalibov is being blamed for his failure to resolve the issue through military force. Turkey's support has encouraged the militant forces in Azerbaijan, who see only one solution: brute force.

Aliyev may precipitate a border war with Armenia in order to derail the election and deny power to the National Front, thus facilitating his own emergence as the true power in Azerbaijan, a man who can lead the country to stability. Developments inside Karabagh (Artzakh) and Armenia have further complicated the conflict for the Armenians and diluted their recent victories on the battlefield. Those impatient to see Shushi, the last Azeri stronghold in Karabagh, recaptured by Armenian forces have to bear in mind that such an action at this moment would play right into the hands of Azeri extremists and would be the straw that breaks the camel's back, precipitating a war.

Arthur Mekertichian's mysterious assassination, which was followed by the trading of charges and counter-charges between Azeris and Armenians and insinuations of a power struggle among Armenians (see Khurshudian's accusations in the Armenian Revolutionary Federation paper, *Yerguir*), seems to have offset recent Armenian advances in Karabagh.

The spectacular fire at a Commonwealth[2] ammunitions depot in Balahovit, Armenia was another unexpected shock for the beleaguered Armenian population, which had to sustain the additional loss of a billion rubles in damage and political fallout which has yet to be assessed. It is widely believed in Armenia that the fire--which fortunately, and perhaps deliberately, claimed no human lives--was staged by the Russian military to justify an eventual withdrawal from Armenia.

Daniel Sneider, in an incisive article in the April 14th issue of *The Christian Science Monitor*, outlines the conflict's grim prospects in the following statement:

The Karabagh war is the most intense inter-ethnic conflict among

---

2. I.e., the confederation of former Soviet Republics
   (the Commonwealth of Independent States.)

the former republics of the Soviet Union. It is a war that many fear could widen to include neighboring states including Turkey or Iran, and could threaten the shaky Commonwealth of Independent States.

Indeed, Iran has been playing a very subtle role and accumulating goodwill and political points in the area, to the displeasure of the United States administration. And contrary to the assurances given to us at a recent White House meeting, Turkey has not been playing a constructive role. It seems that in order to counter the Iranian advances, Turkey has been given some leeway to abandon its mediating role and pursue its ambitions to reach the Central Asian Republics and integrate them into an economic system, in the overall plan of which Armenia would be treated as a partner rather than as a foe. Indeed, Turkey has been giving military assistance to Azerbaijan, training its officers and supplying its Army. And, in a challenge to the United States position, Turkey has suspended all humanitarian aid flights to Armenia, including airlifts carried out by United States military aircraft. Scheduled civilian flights from Syria, which overfly Turkish territory, have also been canceled.

All of these hostile acts are inconsistent with what the West, and particularly the United States, perceive as Turkey's benevolent role.

With Russia's vacillation in its support of Armenia, while the United States is locked into a one-track policy as a virtual hostage to Turkish stewardship in the area, Armenia is left alone against the growing threat of a war which it can neither win nor avoid and which brings back vivid memories of the 1915 genocide.

The conclusion of the *Monitor* article is most telling in this respect:

> *"Despite their military successes, the Armenian strategy in Karabagh has reached a `dead end,'"* argues Namazow *[of the Center for Strategic and International Studies], who advises the Azeri government. "Armenia has a choice--either give concessions on the Karabagh issue and settle the conflict or prepare for a long-term war." "Armenia's geographic isolation makes it vulnerable in a long conflict," he says, "while Azeris have support from their ethnic brothers in neighboring Turkey."*

It is most ironic that the specter of an all-out war and a second genocide should emerge at a time when Armenians around the world prepare to commemorate the 1.5 million victims of the first genocide.

April 25, 1992

Genocide Revisited

The horrors of the genocide continue to torment the collective memory of Armenians. There are still Armenians who think that should the opportunity arise the Turks will repeat their crime against the Armenian nation, because in their perception whenever an armed Turk has come across an unarmed Armenian he has never hesitated to use that arm to destroy or intimidate the Armenian.

Since 1915, Turkey has never admitted responsibility for her horrendous crime and, if anything, many Turkish politicians, journalists, and demagogues have grudgingly regretted not having finished their grisly task during World War I.

There are historic parallels between today's events and the Turkish designs of yesteryear which lead us to believe that genocide is still on Turkey's political agenda. Indeed, following World War I, Enver Pasha dreamed of carving out a Turanian Empire, although his incursions into Central Asia ended in disaster. Nevertheless, at that time Armenia, as the only Christian nation in the area besides Georgia, was considered a spoiler of Turkey's geopolitical plans.

Today descendants of Enver are once again vying for Central Asian republics, and Armenia (although decimated) is once again in their way. This time around Turkey's ultimate goals have been rendered more perilous by her designation as the protector of Western and American interests in the region.

Many people believe that in this day and age another genocide is unthinkable. But evolving political events indicate otherwise. Turkey has occupied 38% of Cypriot territory since 1974. Many nations have paid lip service to the injustice of this case, but no one has made a serious effort to remedy the situation and force out the aggressor.

In more recent times, before the very eyes of the world, a war of "ethnic cleansing"--similar to the Armenian genocide--is being waged by the Serbian Army against the Bosnians. It is very obvious that Europe does not wish to find a Muslim state in her midst following Yugoslavia's disintegration. Once more, on the nightly news, the world watches as terrible events unfold, events which are leading Bosnia to her virtual destruction. Once more, other than some token lip service, no action is being taken to stop the slaughter.

Although the Bosnians are Muslims, their plight is very much like the plight of the Karabagh Armenians, who are fighting for their very survival.

In view of the cynicism of European policies and the insensitivity of the world conscience, no one will stop Turkey if she begins another genocide against the Armenians. In fact, no power in the world has raised its voice against the ferocious slaughter recently perpetrated against Turkey's Kurdish population. Many nations--Turkey included-- have been condoning or justifying the extermination of children, women, and the elderly under the guise of "cleaning up" so-called "Marxist guerrillas." Therefore, no Armenian must be lulled into believing that help may be on the way should Turkey undertake such an aggressive plan, because there is always a convenient political formula to justify inaction. Especially when the justification is already there and the West has subscribed to it: namely, to open up Central Asia to Europe and the West.

The second genocide is already in the making. Turkey cannot afford to use the same ruthless methods of extermination on all fronts; as her army is engaged in the massacre of the Kurds, she has been using a more sophisticated policy of strangulation against Armenia. After all, the Kurds are Turkish citizens and in dealing with Armenia Turkey is facing an independent country. Therefore, she has been applying indirect tactics which will achieve the same results: to depopulate Armenia and facilitate her own march to Central Asia. Turkey has been supporting and arming Azerbaijan, with the intent of suffocating Armenia economically and militarily. She has also been implementing her own blockade by intercepting international flights to Armenia, including US military cargo planes carrying emergency relief supplies to our besieged and beleaguered country. On the other hand, PR firms have been working overtime to portray Turkey as a benevolent state. Turkey has been and continues to be able to deceive the world ever since the 1988 earthquake, when she announced her intention to aid the victims of that earthquake. But not only did she not help, she also found a most profitable opportunity to make money at the expense of the victims. In fact, Turkey allowed her trucking companies to haul much-needed supplies across her border into Armenia, but at an exorbitant price. And those supplies were not even donated by the government of Turkey, but were paid for by the Armenian community in Turkey.

Very recently, Turkey found another opportunity to overcharge Armenia and still pretend to be a benevolent state to the outside world.

After many Byzantine tactics and months of delay, Turkey finally agreed to ship Armenia 100,000 metric tons of wheat, which the European community had promised to replace. After humiliating Armenia's entire population in bread lines, Turkey at last began shipping the wheat across the border, at a very slow pace and at a very high price. The transportation of wheat all the way from Russia to Armenia costs only two dollars per metric ton, payable in devalued rubles; Turkey charged $56 per ton in hard currency. Armenia was forced to deplete her foreign currency reserve to avoid bread riots.

Today Turkey and Azerbaijan continue to implement their joint blockade against Armenia. Azerbaijan has also been successful in pressuring Georgia to enforce the blockade against Armenia. Their intentions are very transparent: to destroy Armenia's economic and political infrastructure, to force the population into starvation, and to squeeze that population out of existence.

Armenia has taken many initiatives, some of them even most degrading, but Turkey has yet to establish the promised diplomatic relations.

The harsh winter and the lack of food, heat, electricity, and medicine have forced President Levon Ter Petrossian to issue an urgent appeal to world leaders to help Armenia avoid a disastrous collapse. Independence has cost Armenia very dearly, but we are on a path of no return.

As thousands in Armenia have been facing starvation, disease, and freezing death, Azerbaijan continues to bombard civilian targets in Karabagh and in Armenia itself, inflicting new casualties. Calls for a peaceful settlement of the Karabagh conflict have been falling on deaf ears.

Recently Ashot Bleyan led a parliamentary delegation on a peace mission to Baku, with a document signed by 55 members of the Armenian parliament. Azerbaijan's response was intensified bombardment of towns and villages in Armenia's south.

Turkey has proven to herself that genocide pays. Therefore, what reason could compel Azerbaijan and Turkey to sit down at a negotiating table and resolve the conflict through peaceful means, especially when they find that no sooner does a tragedy unfold than the world turns the other way? Turkey and Azerbaijan have no incentive to stop the war when they are convinced that starving Armenia out of existence will achieve their political agenda.

For some time now political pundits have been advocating that Karabagh be abandoned to save Armenia. Unfortunately, that does not reflect Turkish logic, just as it did not reflect Nazi logic when Chamberlain sacrificed Czechoslovakia to appease Germany and satisfy her territorial ambitions. The Azerbaijanis have made it crystal clear that they will not stop at the Armenian border when they have succeeded in depopulating Karabagh: they intend to occupy Zangezur and they even claim Lake Sevan as a water resource. Therefore, giving up Karabagh will mean the beginning of the end for Armenia. This is the true geopolitical rationale of the region.

There should be no moral or legal conditions to Armenia's survival. The Armenians gave up their arms before World War I, especially after the 1908 Young Turkish Revolution, and again in Cilicia in 1920, in order to appear civilized. They turned out to be civilized and dead. Our centuries-old history with the Turks has taught us to appear less civilized but remain alive, as there is no substitute for life.

Karabagh is the last frontier of Armenian history. Armenians wish to live in peace with their neighbors, but they cannot trust their survival to the tender mercies of the Turks and Azeris without reliable and ironclad international guarantees, especially when Azerbaijan's interior minister makes no secret of his intention to wipe Armenia out of existence through the use of nuclear force.

Armenia faces a gloomy, even hopeless situation and there is no viable recourse to guarantee her survival.

The earthquake in Armenia and the war in Karabagh have put to test the ability of diaspora Armenians to come to the rescue of their homeland.

Except for a few responsive souls, the diaspora as a whole remains insensitive to the pain, suffering, and deprivation in Armenia. It is in complete disarray when it comes to marshalling its resources and consolidating its political clout and potential.

Unfortunately, thus far the Armenian government, which deserves all of our support in this national emergency, has demonstrated its inexperience in receiving and coordinating of the diaspora's resources. It has chosen to ignore existing diaspora structures, opting for individual contacts which may or may not prove beneficial.

On the home front, the government has steered a prudent course of restraint. Thus far it has avoided all Azeri provocations intended to engage Armenia in an all-out war which would serve as Azerbaijan's long-sought cover and pretext to legitimize her territorial ambitions.

But should Armenia maintain her strategy of non-engagement,

the Turks and Azeris will try to bring about the fall of the Armenian government by creating social and economic havoc within the country. The rise to power of the Dashnak party--known and criticized for its belligerence by Turkey--or even Vasken Manoukian's assumption of power, will provide the Turks with a convenient opportunity to incite a border war. Therefore, no matter how inefficient and inexperienced Ter Petrossian's government may be, it will continue to guarantee the pursuit of that prudent policy, denying the Turks what they have been itching for.

Armenia's government certainly realizes the seriousness of the moment, and its Artzakh policy, with all its flaws, has thus far paid off. What is required now is the formation of a National Salvation Coalition in Armenia, bringing together all groups to assume responsibilities and to work in coordination. Similarly, that same spirit and format have to be applied in the diaspora, bringing together all factions and pooling their financial and political resources. The emergency is too serious for any single party to take Armenia's destiny into its own hands. We must learn from history: in 1920, one party grew so presumptuous that it decided to handle Armenia's fate singlehandedly; we all know the disastrous outcome, which resulted in the demise of the First Republic. To ignore that lesson would lead inevitably to the repetition of the same mistake, which may cost us the Second Independent Republic--perhaps for good.

We are at a crossroads, and blaming scapegoats will not dispel the national emergency.

Armenia faces genocide under a new guise. That is the naked truth, and it must shake us into action.

Before a sense of helplessness and desperation prevails, it is high time to realize that we are facing one of the worst emergencies in the history of the Armenian nation.

December 19, 1992

There is No Substitute for Peace

There is no end in sight for the ongoing war between Armenia and Azerbaijan. The world is too preoccupied with the plight of the Bosnians and Somalis to spare time and concern for Armenia and Karabagh, whose disastrous plight is no better than the two countries in civil war. Somehow the world seems to have forgotten Armenia's plight, partly also because of our inaction. Indeed, Armenia and Armenians around the world underestimate the value of aggressive public relations and media campaigns. It is very characteristic of the mentality of Armenia's leadership to overlook the importance of news coverage. A case in point was Robert Mavisakalian's dismissal from his position as vice-president of the Yerevan TV station after being trained for ten weeks at CNN headquarters in Atlanta, Georgia. Yet Mavisakalian was the only reporter who had been dispatching news coverage to CNN *World Report.* It has now been more than a year since his dismissal, and no replacement is yet in sight; therefore, no news coverage presenting the Armenian side of the conflict has appeared on *World Report,* whereas CNN has been allocating generous coverage on the Karabagh issue filed from Ankara. How can we expect the world to sympathize with our cause, let alone support our position, when that position has not been articulated or enunciated to the world properly!

In the meantime the war is raging, with devastating results to all participants. The people of Armenia have been waiting for a ray of hope to break and, in the meantime, have been speculating on a number of options which may resolve the impasse. For the Turks and Azeris, there seems to be only one solution: Armenia's elimination, as a step to fulfilling their imperial ambitions.

On the other hand, Armenians seem to be too creative or imaginative to consider the probability of extermination. But there are too many indications to rule out that possibility: with Turkey's economic and military support of Azerbaijan, Iran's courting of Baku, Britain's vying for Caspian Sea oil, and Russia's selling of arms (unquestionably destined for Azerbaijan) to Turkey, we are not left with too many options or illusions to console ourselves with. Recently there was a sobering commentary in *Platt's Oilgram*, considered by many to be a very respected oil industry publication, which openly discussed Armenia's dismemberment; indeed, the magazine indicated that in their quest to strike oil agreements with the West, Turkey and Azerbaijan have been planning to grab the Meghri region at the southernmost tip of Armenia, which would further isolate it from Iran, the only quasi-friendly nation in the region, but above all would achieve two major goals: to extend Baku's administrative grip over Nakhichevan, and to open up the way for a gas pipeline from Central Asia to Turkey and thence to Europe.

The Nakhichevan Autonomous Republic, historically an Armenian territory but appropriated by Stalin and given to Azerbaijan, has been posing serious problems to leaders in Baku for some time now, ever since the independence movement in the region began: first, because the 300,000 Azeris in that Autonomous Republic have been experiencing the same fate as the 3.5 million citizens of Armenia as a result of the blockade imposed by the Baku government; and second because Nakhichevan's wily leader, Haidar Aliyev, a former Brezhnev darling, has been posing a serious leadership challenge to the populist novices in Baku.

It is becoming very obvious that Azerbaijan and Turkey would have much to gain from Armenia's dismemberment. While the plot is being actively discussed in both capitals, the West has conveniently been ignoring the situation, realizing full well that they will still have on their hands the grateful remnants of the Armenian people, who may survive to receive the relief and charity extended to them after the disaster!

Ashot Bleyan, has suggested that a respected member of the Armenian Parliament make a trip to Baku. This suggestion has been gaining more ground. It looks as if the Bleyan proposal was a trial balloon which is finally sinking in to war-weary Armenians as the only solution left. That proposal calls for cultural autonomy for Karabagh Armenians under Azeri rule. No final details are available yet, but very few Armenians, if any, will trust the Azerbaijani government to guarantee the safety of Karabagh Armenians: that would be tantamount to entrusting a flock of sheep to the care of a wolf.

As the war continues, proposals and theories abound. Recently another proposal has surfaced: that of humanitarian corridors or, to be more exact, humanitarian tunnels. A point in case, a veteran designer-engineer, Diran Maroutian, has come up with a proposal in the official government organ, *Hayastani Hanrapetoutioun*. His idea entails digging a tunnel under the Lachin humanitarian corridor linking Armenia with

Karabagh. He believes that Armenians are capable of digging that three-mile tunnel in two years. Perhaps he is still thinking in terms of the technology of the Soviet era, when such huge projects could be achieved at a relatively low cost and in a shorter period of time. Armenians have yet to undertake such ambitious projects under the new regime, to find out if they still possess that capacity.

Maroutian also proposes Azerbaijan to dig a tunnel in the Meghri region, extending under a fifteen mile stretch of Armenian territory. One could rightfully ask why Azerbaijan would undertake such an expensive project when its leaders believe that they can grab that territory from Armenia at no cost? And why would they allow the Armenians of Karabagh access to Armenia when they are convinced that their war of attrition has been paying off and they can depopulate Karabagh in no time? Maroutian further stretches his imagination by proposing that Armenia may negotiate a similar tunnel with Turkey or Georgia, giving her access to the Black Sea.

The foresight of Turkish diplomacy should never be underestimated because even in the 1930s they were able to convince Iran into a territorial swap in order to gain land access to Nakhichevan, as one of the building blocks of their future pan-Turanian designs.

But if the parties were on friendly terms to be able to sit down at the negotiating table and seek solutions to the conflict, it would be just as easy to negotiate an agreement for above-ground access across each other's territory rather than resorting to costly subterranean tunnel projects. The problem thus far has been to bring the parties to the negotiating table.

During his visit to Turkey, President Levon Ter Petrossian was confronted by a similar question posed by Turkish reporters: they were looking for an answer to the Paul Goble proposal of exchanging territory between Armenia and Azerbaijan. His answer was very remarkable. He noted that all these notions, theories, and proposals were being made on the assumption that the parties would remain perpetual enemies. But, he said, if we turn the tables and think in terms of peace and cooperation, it would be very easy to solve all the problems: the trucks, trains, and pipelines entering Armenia might easily enter Nakhichevan and extend wherever the other parties please.

Come to think of it, there is no alternative to peace.

January 9, 1993

Act before Armenia Becomes History

While Bosnia and Somalia capture the headlines, Armenians are dying in silence and obscurity, and the independent Republic of Armenia is near collapse.

This dire situation was forced on Armenia because of the continuing blockade by Turkey and the raging war between Armenia and neighboring Azerbaijan, which was also instigated and armed by Turkey.

With no food, no gas, no electricity, and no energy in any shape or form, people are starving, newborn babies are frozen to death, the economy is at a standstill, and a very gloomy future looms over Armenia.

The policy planners in Ankara must be watching developments in Armenia with a measure of satisfaction, as the resilience of the population is breaking down and the first signs of political and social unrest have been surfacing; indeed, last week 50,000 Armenians took to the streets and demonstrated, demanding relief from hunger, cold, illness, and rampant unemployment.

All this seems to be the continuation of the Turkish government's genocidal plan to bring Armenia to her knees and destroy her as a nation.

There can be no other interpretation to this tragic situation.

Armenians around the world have been mobilizing their forces and resources to provide relief assistance to their beleaguered homeland. The United States government has launched its "Winter Rescue Operation," assigning three ships to transport food, clothing, and medicine to Armenia. Thus far the US government has assisted Armenia to the tune of 70 million dollars, and relief assistance is still flowing. Armenians are truly grateful for the humanitarian aid their homeland has been receiving; relief operations, however, are not enough to save Armenia from her current predicament, unless they are coupled with political action.

Turkey is considered a "trusted" ally, armed and supported by the US government; a single warning to that ally to lift the blockade would mean more than all the humanitarian aid in the world. Indeed, if Turkey and Azerbaijan were to lift the embargo, humanitarian assistance would not even be necessary; after all, Armenia is not Somalia or a third-world country. Her industrial infrastructure is still intact, giving her the capability to bounce back within the matter of a few short months.

Turkey has promised to open the borders, establish diplomatic relations with Armenia, and proceed with normal neighborly relations. Agreements were signed to provide electricity and to allow the passage of additional power donated by Bulgaria.

All of these pledges, promises, and agreements remain on paper.

On a recent visit to the US, Turkish President Özal made some conciliatory remarks towards Armenia, and Prime Minister Demirel echoed those remarks by announcing in Ankara that Turkey had agreed to allow the French government to trans-ship food and medicine to Armenia over Turkish territory.

But these pronouncements seem only for public consumption in the West. As such, they have been effective: so much so that they succeeded in duping Congressman Joe Kennedy into believing that Turkey was about to make good on her promises. An unwarranted statement to similar effect was also made at the beginning of a CNN report on Armenia. But Armenia's population is still freezing, the store shelves are still empty, and the homes and factories are still dark.

With the demise of the cold war, Turkey has lost her significance as a strategic asset, and her government has to demonstrate through deeds--and not through empty words--that she still deserves to be considered a US ally, sharing the same values and political goals. Starving Armenia to death certainly cannot be considered demonstrable proof.

Last week the Armenian community's lay and religious leaders met in an emergency session in New York, to map out goals and strategies to address Armenia's needs. They determined that political initiatives, acting in parallel with the humanitarian assistance programs, were absolutely necessary to save Armenia from irreversible destruction.

All parties agreed that:

1. Turkey has to lift the economic and political blockade against Armenia;

2. The borders between Armenia and Turkey have to be opened immediately and diplomatic relations established between the two countries, as agreed, without any preconditions;

3. Turkey pledged to stay neutral in the Nagorno-Karabagh conflict and play a constructive role, yet she has been helping Azerbaijan politically and militarily;

4. As an ally of Turkey, the US government bears a major respon-

sibility to exert the necessary pressure on Turkey to lift the embargo and to live up to her pledges, if she seriously believes herself to be a major player in implementing US goals in the area.

Grave concern over the dramatic situation in Armenia has been mounting throughout the Armenian communities in North America--and the world, for that matter--and that concern has surpassed the stage of relief assistance and has been translating into political action. Unless that action moves fast and moves effectively, Armenia may become history.

February 10, 1993

The Georgian Factor in the Caucasian Equation

The second explosion of the gas pipeline across Georgia into Armenia within a matter of two weeks leaves no doubt that either the political situation in Georgia is out of hand or a conspiracy of collusion is surfacing between Azeri saboteurs on Georgian soil and the government of Georgia. Recent developments give increasingly more credence to the latter scenario.

In Caucasian political circles Georgia has been getting off the hook under the pretense that the government is not fully enough in control to maintain a coherent policy. But Shevardnadze's recent tilt towards Azerbaijan, coupled with a few other developments, has been making Armenians painfully aware that their only Christian neighbor in the region is not a benign ally it can depend on.

Georgia's Edvard Shevardnadze recently made a demonstrative official state visit to Baku, extended olive branches to Iran and Turkey, and excluded Armenia from the Georgian goodwill offensive. All Armenia received was a public announcement that Shevardnadze was mediating between his two hostile neighbors, who were locked in an undeclared war. This friendship bridge extending from Tbilisi to Baku and beyond, all the way to Ankara, did not sit well with political observers in Armenia.

Additionally, the Georgians have long been systematically looting all goods destined to Armenia which pass through their territory. At first, Georgian highway robbers had to be bribed to allow safe passage of trucks and passenger cars through their territory. All along the excuse was that the central government could not control the rebel groups; today it is becoming increasingly clear that the Georgian officials are behind those extortionists, as they are behind the Azeri saboteurs living along the gas pipeline.

The conflict in Abkhazia gave another dimension to Georgia's sentiments. Armenians were peaceful and neutral bystanders in that conflict, yet they became scapegoats from both ends; they were murdered and deported by the Georgians as well as by the Abkhazian rebels. Also, Armenian youth on the one hand were drafted by the Abkhazians in the rebel-held territories, and on the other were drafted into the Georgian army, and were thus forced to fight each other: Armenians killing Armenians in a conflict in which they had no reason to be involved.

Three shiploads of US relief assistance are being directed to the Georgian Black Sea port of Batoum, and that will be a test case to gauge Georgian conduct. Armenians have found out the hard way that the Georgians are an underhanded, unfriendly neighbor. It remains to be seen if their less than friendly sentiments will propel the Georgians onto the international scene as outlaws.

All these hostile acts by Georgia have met with a cool and calculated reaction in Yerevan. Even during the struggle to oust former President Gamsakhurdia, Armenia remained clinically objective and aloof from the conflict.

Early last November, when President Ter Petrossian was scrambling to reach Turkish Prime Minister Demirel on the phone to secure the flow of wheat across the border, he confided to this writer that relations with Georgia were very friendly and that he was in daily consultation with Shevardnadze. That statement, of course, reflected the President's prudence more than the unadorned truth, which is far more complicated and unsavory.

Georgia's treatment of Armenia could have been reciprocated in kind, had the Armenian government chosen to play dirty. Indeed, Yerevan had a powerful political card in Javakhk (Akhalkalak), a neighboring Armenian province under Georgian administration. The 300,000 Armenians in that province have been restive for a long time, because official Georgian treatment of Armenians on that territory has been no different from Azeri treatment of Armenians in Nagorno Karabagh. But the Armenian government has been restraining all potential flare-ups in the area, for a number of reasons:

1. A government cannot always play the political cards at its disposition, unless it is strong and stable enough to withstand the reactions;

2. To avoid further complications in an already difficult situation, it was considered a wise course to continue the pretense of neighborly friendship;

3. To avoid jeopardizing 500,000 Armenian lives throughout the Georgian territory as they were endangered in Baku and Sumgait;

4. Armenia cannot afford to open a second border front while the conflict with Azerbaijan is still raging. As an astute historian, President Ter Petrossian is always mindful of the lessons of the past, and

he seems to have determined to avoid the mistakes of the First Republic.[1]

The leaders of the First Republic were so inexperienced that they overreacted to the first provocations, and before they knew it Armenia was at war on three fronts at different times or even at the same time. Their rashness and shortsightedness were partly responsible for the collapse of the First Republic. The situation in the Caucasus region was so complex at the time that political historians are still debating whether the Republic could have been salvaged if its leaders had acted more prudently. That does not change the fact that their inexperience contributed to the demise of the Republic.

Georgian jealousy and hostility are rooted deep in history. Ronald G. Suny develops an interesting theory in his book *The Making of the Georgian Nation.* He says that, besides being a class struggle, the socialist revolution in Georgia had an ethnic dimension. The Georgians revolted against the capitalist class and overthrew it, and in their case that class happened to belong to another ethnic group: to the Armenians. Georgian resentment dates all the way back to those days, then, and it does not seem likely to subside any time soon.

Ter Petrossian is painfully aware of that history and so far he has successfully avoided the political pitfall, which is for real.

No matter how safely Armenia plays its hand, the duplicity of Georgian politics is far from inspiring confidence in Yerevan.

February 20, 1993

---

1. May 28, 1918 to November 29, 1920.

Artzakh Alone with Its Destiny

After the rejection of the Tripartite Agreement by Artzakh Armenians, the five-year old conflict enters a new and dangerous stage. The agreement, which was negotiated by Russia, the US, and Turkey, was readily accepted by Azerbaijan. Armenia accepted it with some reservations and Artzakh rejected it outright, because it did not provide enough guarantees for its security.

No one was surprised by Azerbaijan's gleeful acceptance of the agreement, because the treaty promised to return, on a silver platter, the strategic positions lost to Artzakh Armenians on the battleground. For the Armenian government, it was an agonizing and painful decision to accept the treaty. In its initial form, the treaty called for unconditional withdrawal from the occupied Kelbajar region, to be followed by the declaration of a cease-fire and the arrival of international monitors. Behind-the-scenes maneuvering by the Armenian government was able to alter the sequence of events: in its final form, the treaty stipulated that simultaneous withdrawal by the warring parties be accompanied by the declaration of a cease-fire and the arrival of the first monitors to observe the implementation of the terms of the agreement. In addition to the cease-fire, the sides would agree to the cessation of all hostility, forbidding any troop movements or enhancement of strategic positions.

The Armenian government could not reject the agreement and the Artzakh government could not accept it, not because they work at cross purposes, but because they base their policies on different premises to achieve the very same goals: namely, the security of Artzakh, and its right to self-determination. Armenia could not deviate from her avowed principle of respecting her neighbors' territorial integrity, which, by the same token, inherently guarantees her own territorial integrity, whereas the prerogative for Artzakh Armenians is to safeguard their own security and act in such a way as to strengthen that security, if necessary by preventive strikes, such as those of Israel in destroying Iraq's nuclear capabilities, occupying the Golan Heights, and controlling Southern Lebanon.

After a brief meeting between Yeltsin and Ter Petrossian, Armenia announced her readiness to accept the treaty, whereas Artzakh turned it down on the grounds that it did not go far enough. That rejection placed Artzakh's fate on a very dangerous course. It was a gamble, and only history will tell if it was justified. Given their five years of bitter experiences in the conflict, Artzakh Armenians have every reason to remain suspicious of Azerbaijani intentions, as the latter has breached several agreements and cease-fires, although in the State Department's view both parties remain accused of betraying each other.

Artzakh Armenians believe that the arrival of the first contingent of international observers cannot deter Azerbaijan from creating dramatic fait-accomplis, which may prove to be irreversible without renewed bloodshed. Although the treaty stipulates the resettlement of the Azeri civilian population in the Kelbajar region, accompanied only by a token police force, nothing can deter Azerbaijan from moving into the region with her military force, thereby exposing the security of the Lachin humanitarian corridor, as well as the border population of Artzakh and Armenia, to the tender mercies of Azeri Grad missiles.

After Artzakh's dramatic rejection, how events will develop remains anyone's guess. Among so many uncertainties, two major actions seem plausible: 1. Turkey may rearm and encourage Azerbaijan to recapture Kelbajar by force; or 2. The US may pressure Turkey and Azerbaijan to come up with further guarantees to meet the minimum expectations of Artzakh Armenians. Although the US government claims that its even-handed mediation is motivated by humanitarian concerns, the State Department revealed last week that western oil companies are very anxious to have oil and gas pipelines cross through Armenian territory, thus bypassing the Iranian option. Therefore, a peaceful solution to the conflict also remains in the US interest.

Last week, during a State Department meeting with Undersecretary Strobe Talbot and Ambassador Jack Maresca, this writer posed the following question: "Under what provision of international law can Turkey justify and the US accept the contradictory positions of Turkey in the identical situations of Cyprus and Artzakh? In fact, Turkey invaded Cyprus and occupied 38% of a sovereign country's territory, under the pretense of defending Turkish minority rights there. As a result of that occupation, a self-styled government of Northern Cyprus was created, and Mr. Denkdash became a major player in the Cyprus parleys. On the other hand, Artzakh's status as an Autonomous Region was unilaterally annulled by the Azerbaijani government, denying the right of self-determination to its Armenian population with the support of a Turkish government so eager to defend minorities. What do you make of this contradictory policy?"

The answer to this question was that duplicity is one of the inconsistencies of foreign policy, and that Turkey is guided by her own national interests. But surely if Turkey can act in her national interests, the Artzakh Armenians should be allowed to pursue their own national interests as well. In this latter case, their very lives are on the line.

Of course, we recognize that Turkey has the power to pursue that inconsistent policy, citing her national interests, and that Artzakh lacks the power to defend her own existence. International policy boils down to the law of the jungle, where might is considered right!

Silence has fallen over Artzakh and all parties are on the watch, waiting for the next surprise action. It seems that acceptance of the agreement would have given international legitimacy to the Artzakh government, which has not been recognized by Azerbaijan. But that does not seem sufficient for Artzakh Armenians, and additional incentives are needed to bring them to the negotiating table.

No one has gone through the ordeal that Artzakh Armenians have experienced for the last 70 years and especially during the last five years. It is, therefore, impossible to put oneself in their shoes and even harder to dispense advice to them. It is equally hard to blame the Armenian government for dissenting with Artzakh, because Armenia's task is even more difficult. While supporting Artzakh, the Armenian government also has to think of the survival of its own people. Both parties are between a rock and a hard place. It is to be hoped that there will be an internal understanding of each other's position. Otherwise the prospects for both parties will be ruined.

The people of Artzakh and Armenia are guided by their own experiences and the interplay of local politics, with which they alone are familiar. Both have to take the course which they think wisest at this time, and it is to be hoped that those courses will converge down the line, to the best interests both of Armenia and of Artzakh.

Armenia and Artzakh are indeed alone with their destinies at this difficult juncture of history.

June 5, 1993

Too Soon to Take Comfort

Suddenly the situation in Azerbaijan has turned extremely volatile, resulting in a temporary lull on the battlefield, where Azeris have been fighting Armenians.

Last week news reports emanating from Baku confirmed an army insurrection in Genja (Kantzak), the second-largest city in Azerbaijan, leaving about 60 casualties. The rebels have demanded, and have apparently received, Prime Minister Gasan Gasanov's resignation. This new development further undermines President Elchibey's power base.

Finding the enemy ranks in disarray, many Armenians have resorted to jubilation and optimistic prognostications about an early resolution to the Karabagh conflict. Unfortunately, it is too early to take comfort in the turmoil plaguing Azerbaijan at this time. As a matter of fact, the new developments in Azerbaijan do not auger well for the Armenians. On the contrary, when these events are viewed within the context of regional power politics and the various interests that converge in the area, they indicate that more trouble is in the making. As a result of the Prime Minister's resignation, Haidar Aliyev has become the front runner for the office. His candidacy must be considered a most ominous development for the Armenians.

A former Brezhnev darling, Aliyev has proven himself to be a political animal who can survive under any regime. Through his legendary bribing of Brezhnev, Aliyev was able to rise very quickly in the Soviet power structure, eventually occupying an influential position in the Kremlin's Politburo. It was during that period that Aliyev ordered the creation of a pseudo-historiography to justify the Azeri occupation of Karabagh. He also took advantage of his position to develop roads and communications channels between Azerbaijan proper and Nakhichevan--another piece of historic Armenian territory which was ceded by Stalin to Azerbaijan--even though that enclave does not enjoy a common border with that country. That helped the Baku government to maintain a tighter grip on the isolated enclave.

Since the collapse of the Soviet Union, Aliyev has been waiting in the wings to make a comeback. He was elected President of the

Nakhichevan Autonomous Republic and was at odds with the Baku government, cutting separate deals with Armenia and Turkey at the expense of irritating the leadership in Baku. He still maintains close ties with Moscow and he may be considered the prime candidate who can return Azerbaijan to the Russian fold.

Ever since Georgia and Azerbaijan refused to be part of the CIS,[1] their internal problems have erupted openly and degenerated into civil war. The Southern Ossetians took up arms against Tbilisi, seeking to unite themselves with their brothers in Northern Ossetia, a constituent region of the Russian Federation. The Abkhazians revolted and demanded independence from Georgia, adding to the woes of the Tbilisi government, which is already fighting a civil war against Gamsakhurdia[2] forces from a tenuous position. Edvard Shevardnadze openly blamed Russia for destabilizing his country by arming and encouraging dissident rebel forces against the central government.

On the other hand, Azerbaijan has its hands full with the Karabagh conflict. On top of that, the Russians have been negotiating with the Baku government about the rights of Lezgis and Talishes in Azerbaijan and Daghestanis in their autonomous republic. The recent Armenian advances at Kelbajar can be better assessed within the framework of Russia's Caucasian policies. In fact, Karabagh represents one of the points on which Russia can apply pressure to bring Azerbaijan (and Georgia, for that matter) back into the Russian sphere of influence. The Russians have made no bones about their intentions and interests in the region. They will continue to destabilize those two republics until they are brought to their knees accepting Russian supremacy in the Caucasus.

The reason Armenia has been spared similar problems is that it has opted to become a CIS member and has been coordinating its policies with Russia. But as soon as pro-Russian rulers rise to power in the two neighboring republics, the pendulum may swing in their favor and Russia may return to its earlier policy of duplicity, continuously pitting one neighbor against the other, as Gorbachev did and as the present Moscow leadership is perfectly capable of doing again.

---

1. I.e., the confederation of former Soviet Republics
   (the Commonwealth of Independent States.)
2. Former Georgian President Zviad Gamsakhurdia was deposed by the military
   council in January 1992, but his supporters continued armed resistance against
   the new government.

Especially after the Azerbaijani setbacks, Aliyev certainly offers Moscow the potential to replace Turkey's influence in the region. In fact, after 70 years of oppressive Russian rule, the Azeris embraced Turkey as a cure-all, soon to be disillusioned with Turkey's limitations. That disillusionment may have added fuel to Aliyev's comeback as a pro-Russian leader. In that case, Armenians must be prepared to experience more losses similar to those they suffered in Shahumian, Mardakert, Hadrut, Gedashen, and Martunashen, sometimes at the hands of joint Russian-Azeri forces.

The Karabagh conflict may continue for the foreseeable future and we are far from seeing the light at the end of the tunnel.

And indeed, it is too early to take comfort from recent events in Azerbaijan.

June 16, 1993

Getting the Facts Straight

The news media continue to describe Nagorno Karabagh as an Armenian enclave in Azerbaijani territory. Nagorno Karabagh is historically an Armenian territory and has never been part of Azerbaijan. In 1923 Stalin forcibly formed the Autonomous Region of Karabagh and placed it under Azeri rule. The nations of Eastern Europe were entirely occupied by Stalin, but with the end of the Cold War, those countries were liberated and returned to their rightful owners. Karabagh is the last piece of territory taken away by Stalin which still remains under foreign occupation. The Nagorno Karabagh conflict is not a war between Armenia and Azerbaijan. It is a war of liberation fought by the people of Karabagh against Azeri occupying forces. It is a struggle for self-determination by the people of Karabagh. Azerbaijan has regularly been bombarding border cities and towns inside Armenia in an attempt to provoke an all-out war between the two republics and thereby cover up its war against the people of Karabagh.

Armenia is described in the media as a republic sandwiched between Azeri territories, meaning that it is situated between Azerbaijan proper and the Autonomous Republic of Nakhichevan, which lies beyond Armenia and is completely detached from Azerbaijan. Historically, Nakhichevan was a province of Armenia. In 1920, when Armenia and Azerbaijan became Soviet Republics, the Azeri Communist Party chief, Nariman Narimanov, declared that Nagorno Karabagh and Nakhichevan would belong to Armenia in perpetuity. In 1923, Stalin made an Autonomous Republic out of Nakhichevan and turned its administration over to Azerbaijan, although Azerbaijan and Nakhichevan did not have a common border and had to communicate over Armenian territory. When Nakhichevan was turned over to Azerbaijan, its population was 60% Armenian. Over the years, through a deliberate policy of what we now call "ethnic cleansing," the Armenians have been deported from Nakhichevan and their churches and monuments have been systematically destroyed to wipe out all traces of Armenian life in that land. In 1923 Nagarno Karabagh was also put under Azeri rule, still maintaining nominal autonomy as an *Autonomous Region* with its own legislative body representing the Armenian majority.

July 21, 1993

A Dangerous Precedent

Since the capture of the strategic town of Agdam in Azerbaijan, the Armenians of Nagorno Karabagh have been breathing more easily, while back home tensions have been escalating, not necessarily between the government and the opposition, but because of an invisible hand which threatens the internal political stability of Armenia. Stability remains Armenia's last asset for the building of a secure political future and for the development of the international confidence needed to attract relief assistance and investments. Unlike its immediate neighbors, Armenia has managed to maintain a measure of internal stability through its ethnic concentration and by sheer luck. Once that stability is shaken, the escalation of internal civil strife becomes inevitable.

It is true that the First Republic was destroyed by succumbing to overwhelming external pressures, but it also collapsed because of the impact of forces on its internal socio-political structure. This time around Armenia has been able--thus far--to maintain its stability, almost by an instinctive self-defense mechanism. Any outside power intending to bring Armenia to its knees will have to manipulate its fragmented internal structure; that will certainly unleash a set of unforeseen events which may drive Armenia to its destruction. Azerbaijan and Georgia are vulnerable because of their ethnic make-ups. Any outside power planning to instigate instability in those republics does not have to look too far: ethnic tensions are rife and ready to be fanned.

When Georgia and Azerbaijan refused to join the Commonwealth of Independent States, they underestimated the vulnerability of their fragile ethnic structures, which were skillfully manipulated from outside, triggering civil wars.

To create the same effect in Armenia one would have to resort to a different method--that of aggravating the political polarization--as there are virtually no ethnic tensions inside Armenia. One might also resort to political assassinations. Unfortunately, it is feared that outside manipulation is about to do just that.

Last June Hampartzoum Ghandilian, head of the Railroad Company, was gunned down in Yerevan as he drove to work in the morning. No particular attention was paid, because the victim was one of the big shots under the former regime--a member of the nomen-klatura --therefore it was assumed that his death could have been related to a long-brewing vendetta. Moreover, a new phenomenon has emerged in Armenia, following the collapse of the Soviet system: in the absence of new laws to privatize industry, the former factory managers and directors have taken virtual control of the businesses that they used to run for the government, and today act as the new owners of those businesses. This new system has triggered a turf war among the members of this new class. Therefore, it was assumed by some that Ghandilian's assassination could have been related to that new war.

But the month of July witnessed another assassination, which clearly indicated a pattern of political destabilization. This time the victim was the head of the former KGB, Marius Yuzbashian, as he walked his dog in the park early in the morning of July 21. In the aftermath of this recent assassination, speculations abound and it is of interest to outline some of the most plausible ones here:

1. Some political observers in Armenia believe that the killing was related to a mafia war between former Soviet officials turned mafiosos. Yuzbashian certainly wielded tremendous power under the former regime, and it is not impossible that he may have been associated with one of the groups that derive their wealth from the old system;

2. Other observers have come up with the theory that since Yuzbashian symbolized Moscow's iron fist in Yerevan and was therefore responsible for many deaths, disappearances, and exiles, he may have been killed for revenge, even though, during the declining days of the empire, he was fired by Gorbachev because he proved to be very soft on Karabagh Committee members, who have taken over the government today. Ironically, his services proved valuable to the new Republic as well, since he was asked to serve as an adviser to the former Mayor of Yerevan and was recently on the faculty of the police academy;

3. A third theory speculates that Yuzbashian may have fallen victim to his own revelations. Last year when President Levon Ter Petrossian ordered Hrair Maroukhian's deportation, accusing him of collaborating with the former KGB, Yuzbashian came forward in an interview and provided details of Maroukhian's dealings with that agency. Those revelations were later corroborated by Col. Kaliugin in Moscow, who held a more responsible position in that agency. It was widely believed that Yuzbashian had more documents up his sleeve and that he could make them public at any time. Therefore, he had become

too much of a threat to be left alive. Since historically some of the ARF's[1] objectives have been met through political assassinations, this theory could not be ruled out. The reference here, of course, is not to the elimination of the major architects of the Armenian Genocide, whose assassination was nationally acclaimed and even absolved by a German court; it is rather to political terror employed against Armenian adversaries to advance partisan political interests;

4. Last but not least, one theory maintains that the recent Armenian gains in Nagorno Karabagh have threatened some big-power interests in the region, and that these powers are hitting Armenians back where it hurts most. Indeed, these killings may be intended for the specific purpose of fomenting political instability in Armenia, in order to derail the recent course of events, which has given Armenians the upper hand in the war.

No matter how innocent the authorities may prove to be in this series of events, it is incumbent upon them to stop the chain of political assassinations, because in the end such acts may lead this new republic to its downfall. Those responsible for the crimes should be identified and dealt with, not necessarily to serve justice--to which the victims would be entitled in democratic societies at any rate--but above all to nip in the bud this trend of political destabilization, before it becomes an unconquerable and uncontrollable monster.

It is high time to exercise political prudence and foresight, before it is too late.

August 7, 1993

---

1. Armenian Revolutionary Federation: the Dashnak Party.

A Breakthrough

The war in Nagorno Karabagh passed a new milestone when the Azerbaijani government grudgingly decided to sit down to negotiate with the official representatives of the Armenian enclave, after pretending throughout the war that such an entity did not exist. The breakthrough came following the fall of the strategic Azeri town of Agdam, which had served all along as a launching pad for the Azeri shelling of Nagorno Karabagh.

Many believe--and with good reason--that this may constitute an Aliyev ruse to buy time internationally and to rally political support to the Azeri cause while the Azerbaijani army regroups for fresh attacks on Armenian strongholds and the civilian population of Nagorno Karabagh. That may be true, but the Armenian side must not lose this opportunity to wrest a favorable agreement from their demoralized adversaries while they are in a position of power. After all, we cannot choose our neighbors and we have to settle our differences with them if we are to live in peace. And the ongoing war has proven very costly, both in Nagorno Karabagh and in Armenia proper.

The Azerbaijani government's agreement to negotiate with the Karabagh representatives brings an entirely different dimension to the four-year old conflict. Ever since the beginning of the conflict, the Azeris have maintained that the war is between Azerbaijan and Armenia. This represents an entirely different perspective, since both parties are signatories of the CSCE[1] agreement, which calls on all members to respect the territorial integrity of the other signatories. Azerbaijani insistence on this version of the conflict therefore portrayed Armenia as an aggressor and the usurper of Azeri territory. The Turkish propaganda machine has been expanding this view in the Western news media, so much so that even some countries or their official representatives who are sympathetic to the plight of the Karabagh Armenians continually refer to the conflict as a war between Armenia and Azerbaijan, thereby blocking the solution of the problem for so long.

Following the capture of Agdam, US State Department

---

1. Conference on Security and Cooperation in Europe.

spokesman McCurry came up with a very strong condemnation of the Armenian side, based completely on the Azeri perspective on the conflict. This was followed by an even stronger condemnation by the UN Security Council, calling on the Armenian side to withdraw completely from recently occupied territories, without even bothering to request that those bases no longer be used for the slaughter of the civilian Armenian population. It is ironic that artificial and unfair boundaries drawn by Stalin himself should get so much support from quarters in Washington and New York!

Of course, Armenians may arguably shrug at the consequences of these resolutions and ask that they be shelved in exactly the same files which contain the repeated Security Council resolutions requesting Israel or Turkey to withdraw their armies from the captured territories in southern Lebanon and northern Cyprus respectively. But we are not there yet. We do not command that kind of political clout in the US or worldwide, and we have to take these resolutions very seriously. This one-sided position, however, is a challenge for Armenian-Americans. It is never too late to mobilize our forces in the US, to muster some clout, and sensitize our State Department and somehow impress upon its policy makers that they have taken an outrageous position on the Karabagh conflict.

Every time a US government official refers to Armenia or Nagorno Karabagh we are reminded of how much humanitarian aid has been pouring into that region. Of course we cannot forget or deny that generous assistance, but that humanitarian aid would not have been necessary had the US and/or the UN been able to lift the unlawful blockade of Armenia and Karabagh by Turkey and Azerbaijan, and to stop the indiscriminate killing of the civilian population in the region.

Whatever the outcome, the negotiations between the Azerbaijani government and the Karabagh representatives will introduce a new equation into the conflict, first by getting the Armenian government off the hook and second by directly addressing the party at odds with the Azerbaijani government. Indeed, the Armenians in Nagorno Karabagh took up arms because that was their last and only resort after Azerbaijan unilaterally annulled its status as an autonomous region, a status that was respected, albeit nominally, even during the totalitarian Soviet era. Azerbaijan created an enormous self-determination issue through this arbitrary act of annulment, which unfortunately did not remain on paper but was followed by a policy of deportation. The Azeri depopulation of Armenians from the Nakhichevan Autonomous Republic was still fresh in memories, forewarning Armenians of the outcome of the Azeri position on Karabagh. Therefore, the Armenians in Karabagh decided not to sit idle and allow the Azeris to deport them without resistance.

In their turbulent history, Armenians have been pushed around too much and too far by the Turks and their Azeri cousins. Indeed, they have been pushed to the brink of extinction. Karabagh constitutes the last frontier in Armenian history. Every Armenian realizes that any further push will squeeze Armenia out of existence, and that is why the world Armenian community is so alarmed by the plight of the Karabagh Armenians and so defensive of them.

We do hope that these new negotiations prove fruitful for all parties concerned, because no matter who wins the war, both sides have been suffering miserably.

These negotiations constitute de facto recognition by the Azerbaijani government that their rightful interlocutors are the representatives of the Karabagh Armenians. That in turn brings the conflict to its true perspective: a persecuted minority has resorted to armed resistance out of desperation and its right to self-determination. These negotiations must offer guarantees to the Armenians and convince their tormentors that the slaughter of Armenians by the Turks and Turkic peoples will no longer be so easy as it has been for centuries.

Although the Karabagh Armenians are entering into these negotiations from a position of strength and can trade land for peace, they should not push their luck too far. For it is no secret that the Karabagh Armenians scored their victories through the assistance of internal and external powers, but those powers may have their own agendas which may not benefit Karabagh in the long run. A small nation can achieve political or military success by gearing its cause to the interests of a major power. The challenge for the weaker party to extricate itself from the alliance after its objectives are met, however, may prove more difficult and even seemingly impossible, because Big Brother may have an interest in the continuation of the conflict. It seems that Nagorno Karabagh Armenians are facing that kind of dilemma. It is now time for them to match their political ingenuity with their military prowess, if at this point they are to call it quits and agree to a lasting and guaranteed peace settlement.

At the same time as Aliyev extends an olive branch to the Armenians, he has been actively trying to revive his old contacts in Moscow and making all kinds of conciliatory gestures to the Russians. We cannot even rule out the possibility that Azerbaijan may reapply for membership in the CIS,[2] which would place Azerbaijan on a par with Armenia within the Commonwealth. Then the Russians might take an entirely different stand on the conflict.

This is no time for Karabagh Armenians to be intoxicated by their recent victories, because those successes may soon prove illusory, as the tide of political fortunes in the region may turn against the Armenians. In the light of past history, that dramatic change is a distinct possibility.

It is time for the Armenian side to translate its military gains into an advantageous political settlement and look forward to a period of peaceful coexistence with Azerbaijan, without relaxing its vigilance against a dubious enemy which has proven itself to be very dangerous.

August 14, 1993

---

2. Commonwealth of Independent States.

Peace Now

Armenians around the world have been holding their breaths every time Artzakh scores a victory. But there is no jubilation in Artzakh or in the diaspora. On the contrary, there is apprehension and anticipation of the worst scenarios. There is a certain element of pride in those victories. After losing so many fighters and so much historic Armenian territory, the valiant soldiers of legendary Artzakh are today fighting back and recapturing the towns and villages which laid in ruins at the mercy of the Azeri army only a year ago. Armenians are also proud that the Turks and their Azeri cousins have been taught the lesson that they can no longer continue butchering Armenians with impunity. But the conflict in Artzakh has passed that stage and Artzakh has become a pawn in the power struggle which has gripped the region. It certainly makes strategic and political sense to occupy Azeri towns and cities which were being used to launch devastating Grad missile attacks and the indiscriminate shelling of the civilian populations of Artzakh and Armenia. The capture of those military bases and the surrounding areas has already helped the civilian population breathe more easily for a while, free from the threat and devastation of bombs. The control of those areas will also give the Artzakh government the upper hand, allowing it to establish its legitimacy and to have a bargaining chip at the negotiating table. But there is still cause for concern, for the following reasons:

1. The Armenian forces are spreading themselves too thin to be able to hold on to the captured territories over the long haul;

2. Azerbaijan is a country of seven million, supported and armed by Turkey; as soon as it settles its internal political instability, it may return to the battlefield with a vengeance and cause more devastation than we have witnessed thus far.

The Azerbaijani army is not dead yet, nor is it demoralized to the point of surrendering, as our wishful thinking would have us believe. It is fighting back vigorously. That army has already crushed the Talish independence movement in the Lenkoran region.

On the political front, Aliyev has been aggressively exploring

---

1. Nagorno Karabagh.

ways to win over the Russians. The Russian ambassador in Baku has already signalled that a change in Moscow's policy vis-a-vis the Baku government may already be in the offing. Once the Russians get what they want from the Azeris--namely, oil and obedience--the tables may turn against the Armenians, as happened during the Gorbachev era and even in 1992, during Yeltsin's rule.

In the face of these developments, Armenians will have to move more cautiously, without burning all bridges with Azerbaijan.

The original plan of the Artzakh Armenians was to recapture the territories lost to the Azeris and hold on to them until the Baku government was ready to negotiate a solution satisfactory to the Armenian side. But carrying the war beyond Artzakh's traditional boundaries is fraught with unpredictable dangers. After restoring their control over historic Armenian territories, the Artzakh Armenians have moved beyond their originally stated goals, not necessarily by their own choice. Following the capture of Aghdam, Fizuly and Jebrail have also fallen to the Armenians, displacing around 700,000 refugees and alarming the international community.

There are already two UN Security Council resolutions against the Artzakh Armenians, who are not strong enough to ignore them. Mounting international criticism has to be taken into account, no matter how unfair and one-sided we may think it is.

The occupied territories must not be surrendered unconditionally. They have to be traded against the security of the people of Artzakh and Armenia. But further occupied land may prove too costly to maintain and too embarrassing to surrender.

With every new town captured, it becomes obvious that the Artzakh Armenians are playing into the hands of their Russian overlords, who seem determined to dismember Azerbaijan as a punishment for the latter's refusal to join the CIS.[2]

Of course, any criticism of Armenian victories in Artzakh is tantamount to speaking against apple pie and motherhood. Every Armenian rejoices in the Artzakh victories, which have finally turned the tide in Armenia's favor after a millennium of defeats, massacres, and territorial losses. It is perhaps the first time in a thousand years that Armenians have recaptured lost territories and have kept the enemy on the run. But we have to assess the long-term ramifications of these devel-

---

2. Commonwealth of Independent States.

opments, which may please us in the short term but may spell trouble in the long run.

After the Abkhazian and Ossetian uprisings in neighboring Georgia, Russia may also instigate Javakhk Armenians to rise, if she finds it expedient for her own selfish interests to do so, and confirm the general feeling in the region that the Armenians have become tools in the hands of their Big Brother for settling scores through proxy wars. What the Armenians desperately need at this time is to settle their differences with their neighbors and proceed with their own lives. Armenia and Artzakh cannot live in peace so long as the general area is in turmoil. It would be very shortsighted to believe that the Armenians can enjoy peace and prosperity at the expense of their neighbors, just as the Armenians themselves proved that those other parties could not enjoy peace and comfort so long as they persecuted Armenians in their traditional homeland.

Every Armenian victory is greeted with a sigh of relief around the world, but worry and apprehension accompany that relief. Questions will arise about how far the Armenians will push before they sit down to earnest negotiations. After all, their goal is not the occupation of enemy territory, but peace within secure boundaries.

It is not in the interest of the people of Armenia and Artzakh to continue the conflict for too long. The toll is too heavy. The effects of the continuing brain drain and the increasing level of emigration from Armenia and Artzakh may prove too onerous to allow Armenia to recover from this untimely conflict.

Peace must be the ultimate goal, not territorial expansion. Now that the Armenians are in a strong bargaining position, they have to strike a deal.

Peace now!

September 4, 1993

THE TURKISH BLOCKADE:

Burden or Blessing?

After tremendous efforts by Armenia and the diaspora to force the lifting the Turkish blockade, which has been imposed on Armenia since the beginning of the Karabagh conflict, a dilemma emerges as the light is revealed at the end of the tunnel. President Demirel's repeated announcements, at the Black Sea Economic Summit and during his recent visits to Kars and Germany, that the blockade may soon come to an end raise hopes as well as concerns in Armenia. Hopes because Armenia will be able to breathe more easily and develop normal economic relations with the outside world, and concerns because of the long-term implications that arise from this development.

The Armenian government may feel gratified that, without a major concession of principle in its relations with Turkey, it was able first to open the air corridor and now the land routes through Turkey.

The dichotomy arises when we analyze the impact and long-term ramifications of the blockade. Certainly the blockade came at the worst possible period in Armenia's history, as the population was struggling to adjust to the rigors of a new system while at the same time wagging a war, settling refugees, and recovering from the ravages of a devastating earthquake. Armenia managed, however, to survive and not give in to Turkish-Azeri blackmail to abandon Karabagh. Indeed, Armenia paid a very heavy toll to circumvent the blockade.

It is now evident that the blockade has equally hurt Turkey in many ways. Indeed, the economic and military blockade of Armenia turned out to be a double-edged sword for Turkey, for the following reasons:

a) The blockade became an irritant in Turkish-American relations and allowed the Armenian lobby to score a few political victories in Washington (the Corridor Act and others). Also, long-standing unconditional American aid to Turkey became conditional, signaling the emergence of a new era, in which Turkey is no longer considered by Washington to be the strategic asset that it was during the heyday of the cold war;

b) Much as Armenia suffered from the blockade, that policy also turned out to be a self-inflicted wound to Turkish internal affairs, since it severely hurt the economy, especially in her Eastern provinces. The damage to the economy goes far beyond the drop in living standards of the population in that particular region and has become a strategic concern as well. For a long time now, economic depression has been causing a rise in the urban population of Turkey at the expense of the rural areas; and that trend, besides having social and economic implications, has historical and political consequences: in the short term, it is not in Ankara's interest to have all the Turks move to the West, leaving the eastern rural areas completely to the Kurds, with whom a deadly war has been raging for a long time. On the other hand, no matter how remote the realization of Armenian territorial claims may seem at this time, it is in the best interest of those claims to keep Eastern Turkey depopulated and underdeveloped as long as possible, until such time as Turkey's history may take an ironic turn;

c) The blockade has not only hampered the economy of Kars province, but it has also handicapped Turkey's far-reaching ambitions in Central Asia. Recently the Turkish business tycoon Alathon commented publicly that some Turkish economic projects in Central Asian republics have cost Turkey twice as much because of the need to circumvent Armenia. As Turkey's dreams of integration into the European Economic Union fade, her Central Asian option becomes all the more attractive. And in this case time is not on Turkey's side, as Iran has been actively seeking to project its political and economic influence into the region and very recently Afghanistan has become a factor, with the advent of Taleban in Kabul. In the meantime, Russia has become increasingly nervous and is trying to mend fences in the area to protect its defense parameters in the South;

d) Apart from the Western oil consortium, Turkey stands to benefit most from the flow of Azeri oil. As long as Turkey ties the lifting of the blockade to the resolution of the Karabagh conflict--thereby remaining a hostage to Azeri intransigence--no Azeri oil will flow to the oil refineries at Yumurtalik, on Turkey's Mediterranean coast.

Therefore, if Turkey eases the embargo, it will certainly cause a sigh of relief in Armenia, but only for the short term. For as trade develops between the two countries the economy of the Kars region will receive a boost, encouraging the Turkish population to remain in place and attract others with the newly revived economic opportunities. But above all Turkey will have unhampered access to Central Asia, consolidating its long-standing designs of Pan-Turkism and turning Armenia into a Christian island in the increasingly turbulent ocean of Muslim fundamentalism.

Therefore, just as the blockade proved to be a double-edged sword for Turkey, its lifting will have the same significance for Armenia.

Political observers find an irony in this new prospect and wonder whether the blockade, in its historic dimensions, was not a blessing in disguise.

Clouds over Armenia

Armenians have been rejoicing every time their kin in Nagorno Karabagh score a victory against their Azerbaijani oppressors. But it looks as if any advance made from this point on will prove a Pyhrric Victory, because the neighboring powers, which have an interest in the outcome of the Karabagh conflict, have already become alarmed. Russia is no longer a superpower, but is still a major regional presence. Turkey and Iran have also been major players in the region for the last several hundred years, and they have all influenced the course of Armenian history. Armenia has been a bone of contention between these empires, which have alternately dominated the region. Of the three, Russia has proven itself to be a more tolerant ruler than the others, sometimes for religious but most of the time for political reasons.

As Russia recedes from its position as a world power, its policy becomes more focused on the region, reviving the historic rivalries between the three countries with all the opportunities and dangers inherent in that rivalry, and Armenia is once again in the thick of things.

Never in recorded history was Azerbaijan a sovereign nation until 1918, when the Western powers created an artificial nation in order to tap its oil resources. It looks as if that country is returning to the same role today, with the support of those very same countries, especially Great Britain. Ever since Prime Minister John Major announced his government's determination to guarantee Azerbaijan's territorial integrity (denying self determination to Nagorno Karabagh), Britain has taken the driver's seat in all international resolutions and outcries, defending Azerbaijan's position, human rights issues notwithstanding.

But today the immediate threat comes from Turkey, which mobilizes international public opinion against Armenia every time the Karabagh Armenians score a victory on the battlefield. Mind you, Turkey's threat is directed less at Karabagh than at Armenia herself, because to Turkey's disappointment the 1915 genocide remains unfinished. Prime minister Tansu Çiller and President Suleyman Demirel have repeatedly requested the government in Yerevan to withdraw its forces unconditionally from the occupied Azerbaijani territories. Yeveran points to the Karabagh government. But, matching her words with action, Turkey has already massed her forces on the Armenian border for so-called military exercises. Unprovoked shots have even been fired across the border into Armenia. Turkey's late President Özal had already made it very plain what those exercises meant when he rhetorically questioned: "What if a few bombs were dropped on the Armenian side of the border during those exercises?" It is, therefore, very obvious that those exercises are intended to provoke a conflict. The Turkish threat is real, and the latest threats have become more specific, as Turkey has announced that should Armenian forces enter the territory of the Autonomous Republic of Nakhichevan, they would face Turkish soldiers there. Turkey has not yet relinquished her imperial designs and dreams, and she will always find Armenia in her path to the realization of those dreams. But this time around there are two more contenders in the way, namely Iran and Russia.

Iran has a very critical role to play in this odd triangular tug-of-war, because Iran herself has not been in conflict with Armenia, at least since the Russo-Persian war early in the last century. Armenia has been benefiting from Iran's de facto neutrality during the Turkish blockade. But Iran is also in a very peculiar and sensitive position; furthermore, it is to her advantage to see Azerbaijan weakened or even dismembered, but she cannot ignore her own Azeri population, which expects Teheran to take an active role in defending their brothers across the border. She is compelled to outperform Turkey in her role as the defender of the Azeris, because the rivalry between the two countries for the domination of the region has taken a sharper turn. This is why the government in Teheran has been so vocal during the past several weeks, echoing Ankara's threats. It has also been reported that Iranian tanks have crossed the border into Azerbaijani territory. Moreover, Iran is concerned about the influx of Azeri refugees as the conflict draws closer to her borders; and despite all the precautions taken by the Karabagh self-defense forces, some refugees have indeed crossed the border, justifying Iran's legitimate concerns. Iran already has her hands full with the Iran-Iraq war and the Afghanistan conflict.

In this entire scenario, Russia's role is crucial for both Armenia and Nagorno Karabagh, which have been taking bold and risky steps in line with Russian policy in the area. And although Russia has been joining the rest of the UN Security Council members in condemning the occupation of Azeri territory, it is no secret to anyone that the capture of strategic Azeri towns and cities could never have been achieved without Russian acquiescence and, yes, without Russian military help. But the question is how far Russia is willing to pursue a consistent policy. What happens to Nagorno Karabagh and to Armenia after Moscow achieves its military, political, or economic objectives in the region? Aliyev is already in Moscow, courting Yeltsin and expressing a desire to join the CIS. Is Russia going to abandon Armenia and Armenians, or will she be willing to pay the price of gratitude for their allegiance? It would indeed be very tragic should Russia ignore the Armenians once the Azeris are back in her fold.

As the clouds gather over Armenia and Nagorno Karabagh, at least there is one bright point: Aliyev's willingness, for the first time, to negotiate directly with the government in Stepanakert. And for this purpose Aliyev's deputy, Jelilov, has flown to Moscow with him to meet with Karabagh's foreign minister, Arkady Ghougassian.

Prime Minister Tansu Çiller's visit to Moscow indicates that Turkey is striving to influence the outcome of those negotiations. This will add a political dimension to the military pressure which Turkey has been exerting on Armenia's borders.

Çiller's visit may have two additional reasons: to send a message to the Armenian side that demoralized Azerbaijan is not alone at the negotiating table; and to stop or moderate Aliyev's tilt towards Russia.

Although the situation in the region is very tense, especially on Armenia's borders, the Russians seem determined to call the bluff of all Turkish threats and defend Armenia in any eventual major conflagration. Russia has countered Turkish troop concentrations with its own concentrations in Armenia. She has also warned Turkey that Moscow will live up to its treaty obligations and defend Armenia's borders. But that offers no comfort to Armenians, given the bloody past of Armenian-Turkish relations. Should Russia turn her attention to an emerging internal problem, the Turks might seize the opportunity to complete their old design of overrunning Armenia.

Armenia had to sidestep the issue of genocide for very obvious political reasons, even at the risk of touching raw nerves in the Armenian diaspora, which has made the genocide the centerpiece of Armenian politics. The charter which declares Armenia's independence does not give the genocide issue the full weight it deserves because Armenia is in no position (and will not be for the foreseeable future) to provoke a confrontation with Turkey. That does not in any way deny the right of diaspora Armenians to pursue the issue, especially in these critical times, when the Turks may use any opportunity to wipe Armenia out of existence. The genocide is an incontrovertible priority, and diaspora Armenians have to watch the political situation vigilantly and alert international public opinion to the potential threat of a new Turkish genocide caused by the blockade of Armenia.

That economic and military blockade has already been bleeding Armenia dangerously. It is reported that close to one million Armenians have left their homeland during the last four years because of unbearable living conditions there. Many have left for good. Others have been waiting for an improvement in the economic situation before returning to their homes. Should the crisis drag out, as it seems it will, the temporary absence of many refugees might become permanent, with devastating consequences for Armenia. The Turks are counting on the Armenians' lack of resilience. Should Armenia collapse economically, the Turks would not even need to invade that small republic, since she might already be doomed.

We cannot, then, sit back and relax and take pride in what our brothers and sisters have been achieving in Nagorno Karabagh, because the Turkish threat is too real and too imminent for Armenians to ignore. Turkey has determined to destroy Armenia, either peacefully or through armed intervention.

It is high time, at the dawn of the 21st century, for diaspora Armenians to act now to stop a second genocide.

September 18, 1993

Armenia's Independence Day

Two years ago on September 23 I was in the Parliament Building in Armenia, witnessing the historic declaration of Armenian independence. There is a profusion of independence dates and some confusion about them. Many make their choice according to their taste and political orientation. Did Armenia attain independence on May 28, 1918, November 29, 1920, or September 23, 1991? The answer depends on whom you have been talking to. But in this day and age, when all Armenians are free to express their opinions without instigating a fight, it is time to determine objectively the place of those momentous dates in Armenian history.

Indeed, May 28, 1918 marked the restoration of Armenian statehood after almost six centuries of foreign domination. The last Cilician kingdom fell to the Mameluks of Egypt in AD 1375, and since that date Armenia's historic territory and the Armenians themselves had been ruled by a variety of kings and despots. Therefore, May 28 is most significant, because it marks a historic milestone in Armenia's destiny.

Armenia regained statehood as a result of the collapse of the Russian empire, although most of historic Armenia remained under Turkish rule. Independence came to Armenia when it was least expected. Russia's withdrawal from World War I led to the creation of the Transcaucasian confederation known as the Seym, which was to serve as a buffer state between Russia and Turkey, long-time enemies. No sooner had it been formed than Turkey began undermining that confederation, in an attempt to eliminate the last obstacles on its way into Central Asia, where Enver Pasha was already making incursions. Armenia, Georgia, and Azerbaijan, the constituent republics of that confederation, were virtually forced to declare their independence, thereby becoming easy preys to Turkish machinations. Armenia was the last republic to declare independence and did so reluctantly. That, of course, does not minimize in any way the significance of that historic date; nor does the fact that the independence attained at that time was disappointingly short-lived.

The newly independent republic fell to the Soviets on November 29, 1920. Armenia's Sovietization was nothing to celebrate, especially in light of the ruthless rule that inevitably followed. But in viewing events in their historic perspective we do not have the right to allow our biases to color our objective judgment. In fact, on the day Armenia was declared a Soviet republic it had already lost its chances of independent survival, because Turkish General Kazim Karabekir was already in Gumri (Alexandrapol), and had forced the leaders of the republic to sign the most humiliating Treaty of Alexandrapol, which reduced Armenia to a Turkish vassal state. The handwriting was on the wall and the Turks, who had planned and executed the extermination of the Western Armenians, were not about to tolerate the survival of the Eastern Armenians. Armenia's Sovietization, then, sealed its destiny and at least assured its physical survival.

The collapse of the Soviet empire in 1990 paved the way for the emergence of the present Republic of Armenia. Armenia had no choice but to declare independence, because the Union was about to be dissolved and all the constituent republics had to determine their own destinies. Credit, of course, must be given to the Karabagh Committee, which spearheaded Armenia to its independence.

Given the sequence of these historic events, questions naturally arise about when to celebrate Armenian independence. Some still insist on May 28, others nostalgically remember November 29, and the majority are poised to celebrate independence on September 23, the most recent date of Armenian independence. There is confusion even in Armenia itself. Indeed, this year May 28 was celebrated with great fanfare, whereas no similar enthusiasm has been shown thus far for the date that the present government itself declared independence. Most certainly everything will fall into place as the confusion clears up and historic facts replace demagoguery and emotions. When the dust settles it will not be hard to evaluate these dates in Armenian history. But in the meantime the confusion will continue.

The leaders of the present Republic were so unprepared for independence that they were unable to create their own flag, a new coat of arms, and a new national anthem. In particular the coat of arms, which fails to reflect the modern spirit of liberated Armenia, was adopted in a dubious, underhanded manner, as a measure of shortsighted political expediency. The present government emulated the first Republic in every respect. It is hardly surprising that they have not yet gotten around to fixing a date for celebrating Armenian independence.

May 28 will remain in our history as the date of the restoration of Armenian statehood. There should not be any controversy about that.

Some people would like to confuse the issue by insisting that the ARF[1] was instrumental in keeping May 28 alive, and that other groups have reluctantly been forced to accept its historic significance. That story has another side to it, however; indeed, the groups which opposed ARF politics and tactics always made a distinction between their opposition to those policies and the significance of May 28, which at times was abused for narrow partisan purposes. The same holds true for the Tricolor flag. And if any insult is directed to that flag, it should certainly be condemned as a misguided attack on a sacred symbol.

November 29 can assuredly not be celebrated as a day of independence, but what ensued after that date has to be objectively recorded and historically evaluated. Armenia's Sovietization saved her from complete annihilation. The Turks were already prepared to strike the final and decisive blow when the government in Yerevan changed hands with the full cooperation of the ARF leaders, who were able to read the handwriting on the wall. This, of course, does not justify the atrocities and injustices which were later perpetrated in the name of socialism and other noble ideals.

In addition, it is a fact that the language and culture were preserved and academic and economic infrastructures were built during the Soviet years. Indeed, after the collapse of the Soviet empire, Armenia emerged as a technologically advanced country and not as a third-world country, and had it not been for the war with Azerbaijan, Armenia would long since have become a self-sustaining independent state. Armenia's Sovietization also marked the beginning of its pro-Russian policy in modern times, which even today has proven prudent.

The republic which continued as a constituent political unit within the Soviet framework can therefore be considered the continuation of the First Republic and could rightfully be called the Second Republic.

Some people may argue that Soviet Armenia cannot possibly be construed as an independent republic, and cannot therefore be known as the Second Republic. But they should be reminded that France, which is considered the cradle of modern European democracies, is currently living under the Fifth Republic, founded by General de Gaulle, and that this enumeration, of course, takes account of the Vichy Republic under Marshal Pétain, who went down in French history as a traitor.

---

1. Armenian Revolutionary Federation.

Independence, which came to Armenia on September 23, 1991 following the referendum held two days earlier, marked the beginning of the Third Republic. And, as is the tradition with most countries, September 21 can rightfully be claimed as the legitimate independence day. Of course, counter arguments may also be brought, since France is presently under the Fifth Republic, founded in 1958, but the official French celebration of independence falls on Bastille Day, July 14, which commemorates the beginning of the French Revolution in 1789, three years before the establishment of the First Republic. That is a valid argument too, in favor of a May 28 celebration. But it is up to the Parliament of Armenia to make a final determination and celebrate one nationally agreed date as independence day. That date, of course, cannot be November 29. And should May 28 be adopted as the national day of independence, September 21 will lose its historic significance. Therefore, after rendering unto Caesar that belongs to Caesar, a trend must be established to celebrate Armenia's independence on September 21, and to observe May 28 as the date when Armenian statehood was restored.

September 29, 1993

Armenia in the Wake of the Moscow Crisis

As the battle lines are drawn in Moscow streets, with unpredictable consequences, our instinctive concerns are directed to Armenia. How will this crisis impact on Armenia? How is it going to influence the outcome of the Nagorno Karabagh conflict? What will be the long-term fallout in Armenia? These are legitimate questions that every Armenian will ask at these trying moments, perhaps with no satisfactory answers at this time. Developments in Moscow and in Russia as a whole are extremely dangerous, and the situation is too volatile for anyone to predict a tangible outcome with any measure of accuracy.

Armenia's destiny is closely tied to that of Russia, and the recent crisis in Russia does not augur well for Armenia. The repercussions of the current developments on Armenia are too serious to discount. First, authorities in Armenia may be tempted to emulate Yeltsin's treatment of the parliament, perhaps in a clumsier manner, although the Parliament of Armenia does not pose similar challenges to the executive branch. If anything, the leadership of parliament at this time is docile and the opposition is too tame, given the very delicate situation in Armenia.

But the danger does not lie so much in the impact that the crisis may have on Armenia internally, as in the impact it may have on Armenia's relations with its neighbors, and in particular with Azerbaijan.

A number of factors saved Azerbaijan from disintegration when it was on the brink of complete collapse. First, Haidar Aliyev's rise to power brought Azerbaijan back into the family of CIS countries, assuring it parity with Armenia in relation to Moscow. Aliyev's recent election further legitimizes his position in the eyes of the Western powers. Second, Aliyev corrected his country's pro-Turkish tilt by returning it to Russia's fold. And the Turks exercised the wisdom of King Solomon in allowing Azerbaijan to maintain its territorial integrity, albeit grudgingly, in the hope of bringing that oil-rich country back under Turkish control at a more opportune time. And third, the cease-fire declaration between Azerbaijan and Nagorno Karabagh gave much-needed respite to the demoralized Azeri forces, allowing them to regroup for fresh battles or to return to a position of strength in dealing with Armenia and

Nagorno Karabagh. The Armenians of Nagorno Karabagh had scored several impressive victories which had brought the Azeris to their knees and had impressed on the leaders in Baku that it was futile to hope for a military solution to the conflict. Also, the Azerbaijani leaders had come to the realization that they could no longer pursue an ostrich policy, pretending that the elected officials in Nagorno Karabagh did not exist. Finally, they had resigned themselves to that fact that they needed to negotiate with the authorities in Stepanakert. Even Aliyev himself was forced to call the Armenian enclave by its legal name, the Republic of Nagorno Karabagh.

Despite all these positive developments, Armenians followed the unfolding events with serious apprehension. This writer earlier expressed concern that even given the positive turn of events, should any crisis emerge in Moscow and Yeltsin's attention be diverted from the Caucasus for a brief period, political developments might take a sour turn for Armenia. It seems that we are now faced with that unpleasant possibility.

This is not the first time that Armenians have encountered such dramatic downturns in their fortunes. During World War I, even after experiencing the genocide, Armenians managed to muster enough strength to enlist five thousand volunteers to fight along with the Allies to achieve their dream of home rule in Cilicia and independence in Armenia proper. And yet, even after the signing of the Treaty of Sèvres in 1920, allied animosity and back-stabbing gave the Turks a free hand to become the real victors in a war which they had lost. Unfortunately, this precedent is too vivid in our minds for us to take any comfort in the recent turn of events in Moscow.

The cease-fire declared between Azerbaijan and Nagorno Karabagh was to last until October 6. No one will be surprised if that cease-fire is broken by the Azeris to test the political waters. Also, the Minsk group[1] was to convene in early November to finalize agreements reached at informal meetings in Europe. Those negotiations have not produced any tangible results. The Azeris have been dragging their feet, certainly waiting for the outcome of the Moscow conflict. Azeri troop movements have also been observed on the Karabagh borders.

---

1. A peace conference on the Nagorno Karabagh conflict, scheduled to take place in Minsk under the auspices of the Conference on Security and Cooperation in Europe (CSCE). See the earlier essay in this section, "The Specter of War over Armenia" (page 67).

Now that the Yeltsin government is fighting for its life, Armenia and Nagorno Karabagh can have only a low priority on Moscow's political agenda.

Armenians have done well both politically and militarily. Let us hope that history does not return upon us with a vengeance. We are living in most sensitive times, and any possibility may be in the cards.

The leaders in Yerevan and Stepanakert have to move with extreme caution, as they have been doing recently, to avert a catastrophe. Otherwise, events in Moscow may indeed prove critical for Armenia.

October 9, 1993

Armenia's Foreign and Domestic Policies

With the collapse of the Soviet system, the old cadres disappeared overnight, and new ones were nowhere to be found. That is why a young and inexperienced president had to grope his way when making appointments, many of which were simply not justified, to say the least. But President Ter Petrossian learned statecraft on the job in phenomenally record time, and steered the nation safely through most dangerous times and circumstances. Today Armenia enjoys relative peace and stability, in a region plagued with turmoil. That miracle has been brought about partly by the Armenian people's sense of history and destiny, but mostly by the policies developed and implemented by the leadership in two short years. One can only shudder at the thought of Armenia's prospects to be entangled in the civil strife which grips the area and especially her immediate neighbors, Georgia and Azerbaijan.

Early in the game Armenia's leadership realized that courting Turkey or the West could not lead the country anywhere and that Russia had determined to maintain its geopolitical and economic interests in the region, Czarist, Soviet, or Republican labels notwithstanding. Only after they had courted disaster did it dawn on the shaky leaders of Georgia and Azerbaijan where their vital interests lay.

It is a well-known axiom that any given country's foreign policy is an extension of its domestic policy. Armenia was able to maintain its functioning parliamentary system, albeit at a primitive level. It was the first former Soviet republic successfully to implement the privatization of farmland and embark on plans to privatize industry.

In July, 1992, when one-third of the territory of Nagorno Karabagh was lost to the Azeris, some opposition groups called for Ter Petrossian's resignation, arguing that any president who tolerated the loss of Armenian territories did not have the moral right to continue ruling. When the tide turned against the Azeris and the Karabagh self-defense forces extended their control beyond the traditional borders of the enclave, those opposition quarters did not reverse their position. If anything, they maintained complete silence.

Ter Petrossian's foreign policy has been especially vindicated on two counts, which had raised controversy in Armenia and the diaspora:

1. Armenia's conciliatory stand vis-a-vis its arch-enemy, Turkey. Armenia's leadership took pains to resist all temptations to lay claims or accusations against Turkey at a time when nothing could be achieved. Ter Petrossian knows better than any other Armenian that Turkey is guilty of the crime of genocide and that it has been occupying 90% of historic Armenian territory. But one has to be at the helm of a government, with the destiny of millions of lives in one's hand, to realize that claims cannot be raised when Armenia is at her weakest and when Turkey still enjoys the status of a regional superpower. Successful statesmanship would dictate biting the bullet, while fighting for the lifting of the blockade in order to be able to feed the people, and hoping only for survival;

2. Opposition groups demanded immediate recognition of Karabagh's independence. That, in the minds of the Armenian foreign policy planners, was a futile point to press, since it could only prove to be counterproductive, provoking Azerbaijan into an all-out war against Armenia and inviting the international community to condemn Armenia for officially threatening Azerbaijan's territorial integrity, contrary to its commitment to the CSCE charter.

Armenia's support of Nagorno Karabagh helped the latter to regain its lost territories and even to push further, to control additional Azeri territories, in effect forcing Azerbaijan to come to terms with reality in the embattled enclave. It was indeed a long and arduous road, which eventually paid off. Today Azerbaijan is resigned to the fact that it has to negotiate with Stepanakert as a legitimate party to the conflict, which may, of course, eventually lead to full recognition of Nagorno Karabagh's independence.

Armenia's domestic policy evolved through a bumpy course. It had its highs and lows. The country owes its territorial integrity to its internal stability. But that stability may have resulted from a number of factors: (a) the political maturity of Armenia's population; (b) the telling and bitter lessons learned through its historic experience, which dictates extreme sobriety in dangerous times; (c) a general apathy towards politics, as people spend most of their time in bread lines to feed their families; and (d) the checks and balances (although as yet imperfect) exerted by the opposition forces in parliament.

On the other hand, the mentality carried over from the Soviet era has been wreacking havoc, as the scarcity of food and fuel drives people to perpetuate the corrupt life style, through bribes, lawlessness, assassinations, and blackmail. Although the country is in dire need of foreign investments, it has not yet developed laws to protect foreign capital. Almost all joint ventures have turned sour. Diaspora Armenians who (motivated by patriotism or profit) have tried to start businesses or engage in joint ventures have soon found out that they are being ripped off. But the saddest realization comes when they learn that their corrupt partners enjoy protection from higher echelons in the government. People driven by greed are able to see only their own short-term interests, which can only jeopardize the country's future. They are Armenia's worst enemies and have already damaged society's moral fabric, perhaps irreparably. Another factor is the attitude of the ruling class to the opposition. The tolerance level of that ruling class is dangerously low. Once again, Soviet tradition is very much alive there: the Soviet regime used to retaliate against the slightest criticism with enmity. There is still too much of that. Even responsible people make irresponsible pronouncements; they deplore the multi-party system, or naively call for a docile opposition policy, completely ignoring the dynamics of social and political forces in a healthy democracy.

It is to be hoped that when normalcy is restored in the economic and social spheres, people will become less greedy and will think twice before committing extra-legal acts. In addition, the promulgation of new laws will regulate the market economy and protect foreign investments, paving the way for Armenia to integrate successfully into the economy of the industrialized world.

Today we have reason for cautious optimism. The sorry situation in Georgia and Azerbaijan is at least a source of consolation for Armenia, if nothing more. After being forced to integrate Georgia into the CIS, Shevardnadze has appealed to Russia, Armenia, and Azerbaijan to help him repel Gamsakhurdia's rebel forces, which control the Black Sea ports. Armenia's winter supplies have been trapped in those ports, waiting to be shipped to Yerevan. This gives Armenia an incentive and the best opportunity to move in and take control of the supply lines until stability and normal transportation are restored in Georgia.

Once normal life resumes in the streets and the workplace, things may improve dramatically and pull the country out of its current predicament. After all, who are we to teach patriotism to leaders who go through the thick and thin of Armenia's turbulent life day in and day out?

October 30, 1993

AFGHAN ZEALOTS FACING KARABAGH FORCES:

Not So Scary a Prospect As It May Seem

As the UN Security Council issues its fourth resolution calling for the return of territories captured by Karabagh defense forces, and as religious leaders from the Caucasian republics gather in Moscow to declare that the Karabagh conflict is not a religious war, an ironic twist has been introduced into the conflict by the participation of the Afghan Mujahedin on the Azeri side. President Haidar Aliyev's public invitation and documents captured by the Armenian forces leave no doubt that at least 1500 Mujahedin soldiers have been fighting alongside demoralized Azeri forces against the Armenians of Karabagh. This new turn of events may eventually prove not to be so disastrous as it seems. It may even turn out to be a blessing in disguise. Afghan leader Gulbuddin Hekmatyar's forces, armed, trained, and financed by fundamentalist Iran, do indeed pose a serious threat, not only to Armenia but to Russia and the West as well. With the collapse of Communism, Islamic fundamentalism has emerged as a major danger to Western interests from Indonesia to Algeria. Last year, when the Algerian armed forces averted a landslide election victory by Muslim fundamentalists, the West heaved a collective sigh of relief, accompanied by some lip service to democratic principles.

The arrival of the Afghan volunteers will affect the equation in the Karabagh conflict:

1. Armenian and Afghan forces have met on the battlefield in the past, as Armenians fought in the Soviet Army in Afghanistan. Although seasoned and tough fighters, the Afghan volunteers have already proven themselves no match for the superior Armenian forces, who are well trained in the use of sophisticated modern weapons systems and driven by anger at a thousand years of oppressive Turkish and Azeri rule;

2. The same Afghan forces have been fighting in neighboring Tajikistan, where they are challenging Russia's political and

strategic ambitions in that region. The arrival of the Afghan volunteers in Azerbaijan signals the opening of yet another front against Russian interests. Russia, then, has as much at stake with the advent of fundamentalism to her soft southern underbelly, as the Armenians, if not more. Hence, there is reason to believe that Russia will do everything within her capacity to nip this new hotbed of religious fanaticism in the bud;

3. The Iranian and Sudanese theocracies have already caused enough concern and aggravation that the West and particularly the US cannot stay indifferent or neutral in the face of this new development, especially in view of the fact that Iranian fanaticism may be extended into Turkey, potentially linking up with a fundamentalist Azerbaijan.

The US has already put herself in an awkward position by voting in the UN Security Council for the preservation of Karabagh's borders, which were drawn by none other than the despot Stalin himself.

Thus, it becomes amply clear and convincing that all the powers concerned with the proliferation of fundamentalism have a common goal: that is, containing the danger everywhere in the world, including Karabagh.

Despite the contentions of the religious leaders gathered in Moscow, the Karabagh conflict has become tainted with religious overtones. Unfortunately, the introduction of the Afghan zealots into the conflict will seriously prolong a bloody war.

Last week this writer witnessed a measure of cautious optimism in Armenia regarding the outcome of the Karabagh war. The Azeris have begun to pay the Armenians back what they have been looting from Karabagh for the past 70 years. Indeed, the fleeing Azeri forces and civilian population have been abandoning tremendous amounts of food, vehicles, and war materials, which will enable the Armenians to defend their positions for at least another ten years.

This writer has also shared the concern of some members of the Armenian parliament, however, that Armenia and Karabagh are caught up in the chess game of a regional power struggle which they are unable to control, and that even if some semblance of peace returns to the area they will be viewed in the region as surrogates for big-power interests, very much as Israel has been viewed for the past 50 years. President Levon Ter Petrossian and Karabagh leader Robert Kocharian have been walking a tightrope, in a balancing act which aligns them with Russian interests while reducing the threat of long-term animosity with their neighbors.

The old Communist fox, Aliyev himself, seems to have gone off the rails: the participation of Afghan forces in the conflict is a desperate act. He has once again reneged on his commitments to Moscow and begun courting Turkey and Iran. The exasperated Russian rulers seem determined to punish Aliyev through the Karabagh Armenians. Recent flare-ups in the conflict are indications of Russian impatience. It seems that the storm is gathering, and no one in the region will be surprised should Aliyev be replaced in yet another power shuffle.

Karabagh and Armenia are not able to determine the outcome of the conflict in which they are caught, yet they must suffer its bitter consequences.

November 27, 1993

The Gathering of the Storm

It was all too obvious from the very beginning that the emerging great Russian Federation could determine the fate of its former republics at will, citing Russian national interests, and the world community would just look the other way. It happened in Tajikistan and it even happened in Azerbaijan, where Moscow tightened its grip on former allies, in the latter case with the help of the Armenians.

At this point it seems that the tide is turning, at least in the Caucasus region, and the Armenians will be on the receiving end of this Russian policy, through no fault of their own: Russian objectives in Azerbaijan have now been met and the Karabagh army, which the Russians built and used as their political tool, has already outlived its usefulness for them.

For Armenians, some soul searching about what went wrong with Armenia's Karabagh policy is well warranted at this point. The truth of the matter is that Karabagh and Armenia played it very safe and went into Azerbaijan at Russia's urging and goading. Now that Moscow's political and strategic goals have been fulfilled, the Armenians will be discarded like an old rag, until they can be called again to be of use in the pursuit of yet another Russian venture.

Unfortunately, the signs of a switch in Russian policy which will translate into a change in the plight of Armenia and Karabagh are too many to ignore.

The recent blistering verbal attack on the Armenians by Russian Foreign Minister Andrei Kozyrov is only the beginning, setting the stage for more criticism and for an eventual toughening of policy. Kozyrov seized on the opportunity of the attack on the convoy of Kazimirov, the Russian mediator in the Karabagh conflict. He demanded a public apology from the Armenians for the attack, for which no one has yet claimed responsibility. The Armenian government has dispatched a panel of experts to the scene of the attack--which, incidentally, claimed no casualties--and has promised to extend a public apology, as requested, should the panel determine any blame on the Armenian side.

A change in the Karabagh situation is all too imminent, and the reasons are many:

1. The Armenians in Karabagh have demonstrably taken the upper hand in the conflict, and should the disintegration of Azerbaijan continue at the present rate, Russia's role as a referee in the region would be diminished dramatically. Therefore, in the estimation of Moscow's policy planners, the other side must be equally weakened to warrant a strong Russian presence in the area;

2. Acting on their own, the Karabagh Armenian forces pushed the war front farther than the Russians had tolerated, at the expense of frustrating their overlords. Therefore, Moscow believes that it is now time to downsize the Karabagh forces;

3. Russia had been disillusioned by Aliyev's ascendance to power, as the latter did not fulfill his pledges: he had promised to cancel all oil agreements with the West and re-negotiate them in the light of Russian economic interests. But recently Azerbaijan announced that agreements had been signed to exploit Caspian Sea oil jointly with Russia. In return it is believed that Russia has agreed to political concessions, probably at Armenia's expense;

4. It was most revealing when Russia's ambassador to Baku, Mr. Shonia, announced that Russia's only ally in the Caucasus has been, and will remain, Azerbaijan;

5. In addition to these political maneuvers, the scene at the battlefront has been changing rapidly and an unholy alliance among many competing forces in the region is shaping up. The presence of 1500 Afghan Mujahedin was already a well-publicized fact. Now Ukraine has supplied Azerbaijan with 75 tanks, which have been heading towards the city of Genja, the next flash point in the conflict. Over 200 Turkish officers have been sighted, along with several hundred Russian "volunteers," who definitely could not show up in Azerbaijan without Moscow's acquiescence or even official sanction. It is not unlikely that the Abkhazian scenario may be replayed in Karabagh: in that case Russia helped the negligible Abkhazian forces to rout the Georgians and then threw in their lot with Tbilisi when the latter decided to join the Commonwealth.

The battle lines in and around Karabagh have been drawn, and something sinister is in the offing. Informed sources in Yerevan believe that an invasion of Armenian territory is planned in order to draw

Armenia directly into the conflict, a plan which Azerbaijan has thus far failed to achieve alone.

The Armenians are faced with a superhuman challenge, and have no choice but to muster their courage, wisdom, and military prowess to beat the odds and prove that they are the only force in the region that must be reckoned with, Azerbaijani oil notwithstanding. The alternative is an unthinkable catastrophe.

December 4, 1993

The Stalemate

Once again the Karabagh Armenian forces have warded off an Azerbaijani offensive, which was launched in the middle of winter against the strong objections of the Turkish officers who were advising the Azerbaijani army. This time the freezing cold, which hampers the movements of both troops, helped the Armenian forces, which were on the defensive. President Haidar Aliyev desperately needed a battlefield victory to solidify his political bargaining position and to justify Turkish military involvement in the conflict. Despite early jubilation in the Azerbaijani and Turkish news media, heralding victory, the Azeri forces were desperately trapped in the Omar Pass, which they had hoped would lead them to the recapture of the Kelbadjar valley. Five hundred of them perished and another three hundred fled to the snow-capped mountains, to face the prospect of freezing to death. For the Azerbaijani side, human life has no value; they can sacrifice their own and they can sacrifice their enemies'. Armenian losses were relatively small, but not negligible. The Armenians can ill afford to lose men in this unequal war.

Aliyev has been stalling on his pledge to Moscow to allow Russian troops on Azeri territory, and his untimely offensive, designed to score victories against the Armenians in order to put himself into a position of power from which he could negotiate more independently with the Russians, proved unsuccessful. He has also been postponing the signing of oil contracts with Western and Turkish companies, waiting for a time when he can negotiate with the West free of Russian encroachment.

In view of the heavy human toll taken by the last offensive, Russia intervened and for all practical purposes has enforced a cease-fire. Baku is adamantly refusing to sign a cease-fire, insisting on her earlier terms: i.e., the return of captured Azeri territory, the disarming of the Karabagh army (who are "Armenian terrorists" in Aliyev parlance), and insistence on dealing only with Yerevan. The Azerbaijani government demands that the destiny of the Karabagh Armenians be left to its tender mercies, on the vague promise to "treat Armenians as rightful Azerbaijani citizens." A people that has been on the receiving end of the 1915 genocide and the Baku and Sumgait pogroms understands full well the meaning of those vague promises. The Armenians in Karabagh are between a rock and a hard place--they have two choices: either to give up their arms and allow themselves to be slaughtered like sheep, or to fight to the bitter end, even if the outcome would be the same. It seems they have opted for the latter alternative.

Azerbaijan has internationalized the conflict by soliciting help from an odd assortment of interests: Afghan religious zealots have joined Ukrainian Christians, Turkish advisers, and US, British, and Russian mercenaries to fight the Armenians with Chinese rockets, modern Soviet tanks, and an array of armaments. On the other hand, the Russians have reduced their arms shipments to the Armenian side to a trickle, in an effort to entice Aliyev back into their fold. Yet the latter has been stubbornly trying to breathe life into his predecessor's failed pro-Turkish policy by visiting Ankara and by appealing for more Turkish help.

Turkey has its hands full: Iran has been pumping money into the country to promote militant Islamic radicalism, which may win in the upcoming March elections. Despite huge human losses, the Kurdish independence movement has been raging fiercely in southeastern Turkey. Ankara stands to lose face in the Muslim world should it fail to live up to the pledge made during the recent Çiller-Bhutto visit to that part of the world that Turkey would help Bosnian Muslims. Latent tension is also building up on the Syrian border as a result of an ongoing feud with Turkey over Euphrates River water resources.

Turkey's actions are limited by all the above restrictions, and Ankara cannot bully any nation behind the borders of the former Soviet Union, since Moscow has made it abundantly clear that it considers those borders to be its own international boundaries.

Yet Turkey maintains the illegal blockade against Armenia, as a continuation of its genocidal policy. Many Turks have openly lamented the fact that they did not finish the Armenians off earlier in this century, when they planned and executed the genocide. Talaat[1] was a shrewd politician, as he foresaw the danger to his pan-Turkic designs: he told US Ambassador Henry Morgenthau that the government had determined to complete its grisly task because, he argued, "even if we spare the children, they will grow up and plan their revenge." Thus, Armenian survival, albeit on only a minute portion of its historic territory, is already partial revenge.

In retrospect, the Turks also resent having spared their Kurdish minority at that time: today the Kurds have multiplied to 16 million in

---

1. Talaat Pasha: Turkish Minister of the Interior during the Young Turks regime.

Turkey alone, and are seeking independence. The Turks can read history well, and they know that in any territorial dispute, 90% of the argument is with the inhabitants of the land.

Back in Karabagh, a stalemate of forces has been created, since neither side will negotiate under humiliating conditions. This stalemate may continue indefinitely, unless Russia stations its forces between the warring factions and imposes its version of peace, which may not please either party.

One important fact must be kept in mind: time and numbers do not favor the Armenian side.

March 5, 1994

Is Peace at Hand?

After so many cease-fire violations in the Karabagh conflict over the past several years, very few people on either side of the fence believe that this time around the cease-fire agreement will be sincere and durable. But the July 27 agreement, which was brokered in Moscow by Russia, has generated a measure of optimism, with some compromises on the horizon. After one million displaced refugees, 15,000 dead, and so much misery on both sides, the warring parties seem to have realized that there can be no military solution to the Karabagh conflict and that acceptable compromises have to be worked out if the people of the region are to have any respite from destruction, violence, and misery.

Unlike the stipulations of past cease-fire agreements, this time the parties have pledged to refrain from violations, which gives the negotiations a chance. Also, the status of the cease-fire has been upgraded to that of an armistice, which has a more permanent nature.

Many factors have contributed to the present atmosphere of optimism. Some of these can be traced to the policies of the parties involved, others may surface later. To place the conflict in the right perspective one must recognize that, like many other flash-points in the world, the Karabagh conflict is a proxy war between Russia and Turkey and, by extension, between Russia and the West.

Azerbaijan's old fox, Haidar Aliyev, who climbed up through the hierarchy more easily during the Soviet period, went through a tough time recently when he tried out his old tricks on Moscow, Ankara, and Teheran, tailoring his policies to make them sound more palatable in each capital. Instead of developing confidence, the Azeri president succeeded only in making all three capitals more suspicious about his real motives.

On the other hand, Moscow has been able to convince Azerbaijan, through both subtle and not-so-subtle means, that without a Russian military presence in the conflict area there can be no durable peace in Azerbaijan. It suffices to study the Georgian precedent, when the fiercely independent-minded Georgians had to acquiesce to Russian military presence after Abkhazia broke loose from Georgia and the rulers in Tbilisi found themselves unable to govern Southern Ossetia. And it seems that American collusion has also played a role, as indicated in a *Christian Science Monitor* editorial on August 5: "The Haiti vote was secured by giving Moscow a 'peace-keeping' mandate in Georgia."

Every Azeri president who has pledged to regain captured territory through force has failed miserably, and every flare-up in the conflict
has incurred additional territorial losses for Azerbaijan. Had there been
another round of fighting, the strategic cities of Ganja in the north and
Yevlakh further west would have become new casualties, splitting
Azerbaijan in two and encouraging two other restive minorities to rise up
demanding autonomy, namely the Lezgis and the Talishes. That dreadful
prospect must have frightened the Baku rulers into accepting concessions.

As the Azeris were coming to their senses, other international
factors impacted favorably on the peace process.

Deteriorating relations between Russia and Turkey are at their
lowest ebb. President Demirel's provocative statements in Kiev and in
Crimea, whipping up Ukraine's antagonism against Russia, and Chief of
Staff General Cures' remarks in Baku touched a few raw nerves in
Moscow. At the present time Turkey and Russia are at loggerheads, with
confrontational postures on Bosnia, the Black Sea, and on Armenia's
borders. Turkey's hands are too full at this time for it to be able to prod
Baku into a full-scale war over Karabagh. Turkey is in the process of waging a war of extermination against its 16-million strong Kurdish population, its economy is in shambles, rising Islamic militancy has been
threatening internal stability, and its relations with Washington have
soured after the US decided to cut its foreign aid by 25% pending
progress in the stalled Cyprus negotiations and improvements in
Turkey's abominable human rights record.

The Turkish leaders are highly experienced and shrewd statesmen, and they realize that they can ill afford to add a new burden to their
present predicament.

Turkey was behind Azerbaijan's intransigence in refusing to
come to the negotiating table before a complete Armenian withdrawal
from the captured territories. That, of course, was an inadmissible condition, because after the return of the captured territories the Baku leaders would have had no inducement to talk seriously about peace. It seems
at this point that they have already dropped that pre-condition, which
will pave the way for earnest talks.

The Azeris have always portrayed the conflict as a war between
Armenia and Azerbaijan, refusing to recognize Karabagh as a legitimate
party to the negotiations. Yet this time around the cease-fire has been
signed by the defense ministers of Azerbaijan and Armenia, along with
the commander of the self-defense forces of Karabagh, which amounts

to de facto recognition of the Karabagh government.

The entire month of August will be devoted to technical discussions about a military disengagement and the simultaneous formation of peace-keeping forces for deployment in the conflict zone. Despite their earlier resistance, the Azeris seem to have agreed to a major Russian role in that peace-keeping force. Otherwise, it would have been impossible to imagine any progress in the peace talks.

There is further a realization by both major powers--the US and Russia--that in a rising ocean of Islamic fundamentalist militancy, Armenia can play a balancing role and can serve as a reliable ally should that fundamentalism become a real threat to any of the major powers.

The negotiations may drag on, and in the meantime political fortunes may change directions. But at least for now the prospects that the Karabagh Armenians may attain a measure of autonomy, which will allow them to live in peace, seem promising.

Every cease-fire agreement in the past has been fraught with many dangers of a new flare-up. Azerbaijan has once more been using the respite to replenish its arsenals with Turkish weapons. Turkish advisers and mercenaries are arriving in Azerbaijan in alarming numbers. They certainly have not been invited for any peaceful intention. On the other hand, nobody believes that the Armenians are sitting idly by and watching these alarming developments without concern.

The peace process has many dangerous roads to travel, but the factors contributing to a peaceful settlement seem to have increased, inspiring some cautious optimism among political observers.

Should peace be achieved in Karabagh, the Armenians would be vindicated and President Ter Petrossian's prudent policy would pay off.

Let us hope for peace.

August 13, 1994

The Karabagh Issue Must Be Addressed by the Powers

The following letter was sent to The Wall Street Journal *in response to an editorial, "War and Peace and Russia," published in the Journal on November 30, 1994.*

December 2, 1994

Editor,
The Wall Street Journal,
200 Liberty Street,
New York, N.Y. 10281.

Dear sir:

Your November 30 editorial, "War and Peace and Russia," was a welcome departure from the international conspiracy of silence over the burning issue of the Nagorno Karabagh conflict, now in the sixth year of its bloody course. The Karabagh conflict, which has the potential of becoming a far broader conflagration than the war in Bosnia, has been overshadowed by the latter for too long.

Now that the handwriting is on the wall for Bosnia, it was a wise move by *The Wall Street Journal* to place the Karabagh issue on the front burner, to explore more positive options, based on the lessons of the war in Bosnia.

But we need a clearer perspective on the situation in the Caucasus: we must identify the premises of the conflict properly if we wish to avoid another catastrophe.

1. You have defined the conflict as "this awful war between Armenia and Azerbaijan," whereas all UN Security Council resolutions identify the parties to the conflict as Nagorno Karabagh and Azerbaijan. Armenia is mentioned only in reference to using her good offices to reach a negotiated settlement.

2. You define Nagorno Karabagh as "an Armenian enclave inside Azerbaijan." That definition needs to be expanded if one is fully to grasp the historic context of the conflict; in fact, Nagorno Karabagh has been part and parcel of Armenia. In 1923 Stalin decided to put the territory under Azerbaijani jurisdiction, in order to curry favor with Turkey. A sliver of territory was also given to Azerbaijan outright, in order to cut the enclave completely off from Armenia. A similar fate befell Eastern Europe, which also came under Stalin's hegemony in the aftermath of World War II. With the demise of the Cold War, all the walls have been falling down. The border between East and West Germany was wiped out overnight. Since all of Stalin's diabolic maps are being redrawn, why would anyone, especially in the West, defend his borders in the Caucasus? Why should Stalin's gift to Azerbaijan continue to be honored by the West?

The last figment of legitimacy for Azeri claims on Nagorno Karabagh was that provided by the Soviet constitution, which is now extinct. Indeed, UN Secretary General Boutros-Ghali himself provided an argument against keeping Nagorno Karabagh within Azerbaijan when he recently stated in Baku that in reference to territorial integrity the UN understands the borders which a country possessed when it joined the world body: when Azerbaijan joined the UN the status of Karabagh was being hotly contested and indeed the war was in progress. For all practical purposes, Baku had already lost its grip on the Armenian enclave, which has since declared its independence;

3. It is true, as you have pointed out, that the Conference on Security and Cooperation in Europe (CSCE) has played a positive role in moving the parties towards a cease-fire, which is still holding, albeit precariously. It is also true that "the plan would deploy 1,400 troops and 1,400 personnel at an estimated cost of $42 million per six months. *Turkey has pledged to supply up to one-third of the forces on the ground.*"

To consider Turkey's pledge as a positive factor, however, throws the entire concept of peace out of balance, because Turkey has been and continues to be part of the problem: therefore, she cannot become part of the solution. Ankara has been arming Azerbaijan and training its troops to continue the war. By imposing a military and economic blockade around Armenia and Karabagh, Turkey has virtually declared war against them. Many in the region view the Turkish blockade as the continuation of the genocide which Turkey launched against the Armenians in 1915. Turkey even denied trans-shipment of US humanitarian aid to Armenia following the devastating earthquake which ruined one-third of Armenia's territory and claimed 25,000 casualties. The Turkish army is viewed in the area as an instrument of extermination even at this very moment, when it is engaged in a war against Turkey's Kurdish population. If Turkey is to provide cease-fire troops, the same opportunity must be given to Armenia.

It seems that some thinkers in the West continue to harbor lingering cold-war illusions about Turkey's alliance with the West. Turkey is looking out only for her own selfish interests, as can be seen today in Turkey's attempts to break or circumvent UN sanctions against Iraq.

The West would better serve its own interests by pledging US, British, or French troops, which are a far better match for Russian troops; they would symbolize a Western presence in the region and would be welcomed by all parties to the conflict.

Projecting Turkish forces into the Caucasus will not serve Western interests and will only jeopardize the prospects of a lasting peace.

Sincerely,
Edmond Y. Azadian

December 10, 1994

Destination Deir Zor

Every human being is curious about how and when his/her appointment with death will come, but is happy that the ultimate truth will never be revealed until it happens and at that time it no longer matters to know!

Similarly, we Armenians are curious about how and where the mass slaughter of our nation took place, but we constantly postpone the date of actually mustering the courage to make the trip and experience first hand the locale and the environment where millions of Armenians met their deaths.

How many times had I planned a trip to Rakka, Deir Zor, Hassakeh, and all the death camps where my mother had walked and miraculously survived to tell me all the gory details of her death march, which, in my childish imagination, had become a legend because I could not countenance that men could be so inhuman to their fellow men!

My heart was pounding in my chest as I relived stories of the horrors which my mother experienced along with her entire nation. I looked from the window of my racing bus, and I felt terribly uncomfortable in that air-conditioned atmosphere as I remembered my twelve-year old mother walking over these burning sands, while the Turkish gendarme goaded her and the caravan to march towards their final destination.

It was an unforgiving August day and the sun violently burned the white sands of the desert. It seemed as though the sun also burned the blue sky, which had turned pale on the horizon where it met the desert.

Every once in a while we passed by slopes and hills where the open mouths of caves gaped at the sky. It seemed like a movie sequence to me, but it was the real thing: these were the caves where hundreds of emaciated women, children, and old people were huddled and burnt to ashes. I even felt guilty for being alive in this God-forsaken desert where so many innocent people had perished.

Our destination was Deir Zor; a name that had always fascinated me. It may sound crazy, but all along I had imagined that Deir Zor was a ghost town; that once you stepped into that city you would witness skeletons dancing. But to my surprise, a completely different scenario unfolded as we entered the city: Deir Zor is a bustling rural town; the region is Syria's bread basket. Deir Zor is crowded with black-robed people struggling their way through the narrow streets, trying to avoid farm equipment or donkeys laden with sacks of grain. It is devoid of memory; people live there, thrive, earn their livings, oblivious to the fact that a human tragedy took place in that city, and that the wells are still full of human remains from the people thrown there to drown.

As we entered the city we crossed the calm waters of the Euphrates River, where children were swimming, heedless of the pollution hazards. I was surprised to see the waters so serene and blue, when throughout Armenian history and poetry the Euphrates has been portrayed as a raging river sweeping corpses along in its blood-red stream.

The townspeople were kind and friendly; they all know about the Armenian tragedy. Anyone in the street can direct you to the chapel that has been erected as a monument to the martyrs. I was told that one can still find Armenian survivors who have been assimilated into the local population.

As we approached the chapel, we passed through run-down streets. The somberness of a death camp or a memorial is not to be found here. The people continue to crowd the streets, tending to their own daily chores. I wondered how the neighborhood of Auschwitz looks today. One is offended at such insensitivity to the place which proved to be the last station on earth for so many Armenians.

A huge iron gate opens onto that nameless street in Deir Zor. Marble walls bear inscriptions and carvings symbolizing our nation's martyrdom. Once inside, one is awe-stricken. As you hear your own footsteps on the marble, you feel them ascending towards the spirits of all the martyrs who seem to hover somewhere above.

To the left is a chapel built in the beautiful tradition of Armenian architecture. Stairs in the middle of the chapel lead to the inner sanctum below, where bones found in the desert are collected with loving care and displayed.

It is in this destination that an Armenian faces the ultimate truth about the genocide. No emotions, no philosophizing, no sermons, no acrimonious debates. You are there, alone with the bones and spirits of the martyrs. A skull stares at you with blind wisdom. No words are necessary. He or she knows what happened, you know what happened, but you do not want to spoil the dignity of the moment by thinking about a world which denies the truth, which wishes to forget a tragedy of atrocious proportions. No, there is no time to spoil the sanctity of spiritual communication with the souls of the martyrs.

Suddenly I find myself lighting a candle, and the flickering light of that candle seems more eloquent in the silence than a thousand words and a million debates.

As I leave the sanctuary I look once again at the skull. It seems almost to be smiling, perhaps out of a sense of gratification that the martyrs here have not been forgotten.

It seems that extreme emotions desensitize human beings. Once outside the chapel, I touch myself and once again feel my flesh. I feel that my soul has returned to my physical self after making a celestial journey.

x x x x x x

We are told that sixty miles north of Deir Zor, highway builders have discovered another mass grave. A hill of skeletons covered with earth. We hire a cab, a 1952-model Mercedes, and race towards Markadeh, where the bones were recently discovered.

As we arrive there, we are disappointed to find that the bones have been bulldozed to make room for a chapel at the foot of the hill. The construction workers inform us that the bones have been taken away. They point to a nearby hill, where they say you may still find some bone fragments.

After ten minutes out of the car you are already burning hopelessly. The scorching sun penetrates your bone marrow. It is so hot. I start thinking once again about the caravans which passed by here. Those helpless bodies were exposed to this sun not only for ten minutes, but for days and months on end.

Suddenly a young man from our group spots a skull. We rush over to him. The bones are ivory white. We look into the face and determine that it must have belonged to a young girl. The cheek bones have graceful lines.

I wish that the anthropologist Dr. Jougharian were alive and could reconstruct the face for us, as he once did the face of the poet Bedros Tourian, so that we could figure out exactly what this young girl looked like.

As I stare at the skull, the sun makes me extremely uncomfortable. Every cell in my body craves for a cool place, and suddenly I find my mind hovering over the mountains in Shushi, in Karabagh, which I had visited exactly one year ago. There, the balmy mountain breeze and the stars celebrated the restoration of Armenian dignity, for Shushi became the symbol of Armenian victory, the turning point in Armenian history. After a thousand years, Armenians recaptured a portion of their historic territory in Shushi.

The Battle of Shushi has the same significance for Armenians as the Battle of Tours has for Europeans. In 732 the Frankish ruler Charles Martel, the first king to bring most of what is now France under his control, turned back the tide of Arab conquest, which was pushing northward from Spain into the heart of Europe, in a celebrated battle at Tours, near Poitiers. Similarly, Shushi turned back the Turkish-Azeri onslaught, which was aimed at the extermination of Armenians and the obliteration of Armenia.

As I looked at the skull I began to wonder if this young girl knew that her death, and that of many others, had been vindicated at Shushi.

Will she ever know?

October 28, 1995

THE MURDEROUS DUPLICITY CONTINUES:

Reflections on the 80th Anniversary of the Armenian Genocide

After the lapse of eight decades, a call for revenge against the genocide of the Armenian people would sound belated and rather uncivilized. But a call for caution is both timely and necessary, even after such a long period, because the potential for a new genocide is inherent in Armenia's geopolitical position and the long-term national and political ambitions of her neighbors.

The genocide was planned and executed during the Ottoman period by the Young Turks. That premise provides a cop-out for apologists and even to some Turks, who continually argue that the wholesale murder of Armenians was committed under the old regime, which was overthrown and repudiated by the Kemalist government, whose founder, Atatürk (literally, Father of the Turks), put a totally different perspective on the Turkish self-image.

Some dramatic changes in Turkey's social and political structure were indeed brought about by Mustafa Kemal,[1] but that does not absolve Turkey of the crime perpetrated under the old regime, because modern Turkey inherited the territory and the wealth of historic Armenia and has never condemned her former leaders for the crime they committed against Armenians. On the contrary, unlike modern Germany, she has denied it and is currently in the process of rewriting history to defend herself against potential demands of restitution.

By virtue of inheriting the legacy of the Ottoman Empire, modern Turkey is accountable for all its deeds, including its usurpation of

---

1. Mustafa Kemal Atatürk (1881-1938) led the Turkish nationalist movement. He was a general in WW I, and was President of Turkey 1923-38.

Armenian national territories.

Even after the lapse of eight decades, the geopolitics of the region remains basically the same: the Turks still maintain their pan-Turanian designs, which Ittihadist[2] leader Enver Pasha tried to revive and which modern Turkey has recently (after the collapse of the Soviet Empire) attempted to realize, under the guise of extending "democracy" to Central Asian Turkic nations. During all of these periods Armenia has remained an obstacle in the way of the Turkish drive to the East. As long as Turkey does not abandon her great design of uniting all Turkic nations under one banner, the annihilation of Armenia remains a possibility at any given time that conditions allow.

Documents recently discovered by Professor Vahakn Dadrian, the foremost scholar in the field of the genocide, reveal that Republican Turkey was no different than her predecessor, Ottoman Turkey, when it came to wiping Armenia off the map, and used the very same rationale.

On the eve of Armenia's Sovietization,[3] the Kemalist government invaded Armenia and imposed on her beleaguered government the demeaning terms of the Treaty of Alexandrapol, forestalling any hope of resuscitating the Treaty of Sèvres, which had been signed on August 10, 1920. The Turkish expeditionary force, under General Kazim Karabekir, had exactly the same purpose as the Ottoman government--to eliminate Armenia--and intended to use identical methods: that is, to try to soothe world public opinion on one hand while performing the grisly task of genocide on the other.

Professor Dadrian quotes a telegram dispatched in November, 1920 by Kemal's foreign minister, Ahmet Muhtar, to General Karabekir, commander-in-chief of the Eastern Front army: "Buried in a 1200-page tome," says Prof. Dadrian,

> the document consists of a cipher telegram dated November 8, 1920.... On November 6, prior to the receipt of the cipher, Karabekir had transmitted his own set of armistice terms to the Armenians. But Ankara's instructions obliged him to withdraw these terms, which the Armenians had accepted the previous day, substituting new terms that were deliberately harsh in order to preclude their acceptance. Following the anticipated rejection of these new terms by the Armenians on November 10,

2. The Union and Progress Party.
3. Armenia was proclaimed a Soviet Republic in 1920.

Karabekir resumed his military campaign with a drive to Yerevan, the capital of Armenia.[4]

The political purpose of these negotiations was not to achieve a successful outcome; rather, they were designed for other ends, further revealed in another cipher telegram which Professor Dadrian has uncovered, drawing his own conclusions:

First, the ground was prepared for justifying the crime through the following assertions: by virtue of the provisions of the Treaty of Sèvres, Armenia will be able to cut Turkey off from the East; together with Greece she will impede Turkey's general growth; furthermore, being situated in the midst of a great Islamic periphery, she will never voluntarily relinquish her assigned role as a despotic gendarme, and will never try to integrate her destiny with the general conditions of Turkey and Islam.

After the enumeration of these rationales, the following decision was transmitted: "Consequently, it is indispensable that Armenia be eliminated, politically and physically."[5]

Note, this is not Ottoman Turkey which is deciding to annihilate Armenia; it is the very same Kemalist Republican Turkey in whose name modern Turks claim to have achieved democracy and to deserve membership in and integration into the community of civilized European nations!

Unfortunately, the very same conditions still exist in the neighborhood in which Armenia is located. That is why the late Turkish President Turgut Özal threatened to drop "a few bombs on the other side of the border," because "the Armenians have not learned the lessons of 1915" (a tacit admission of the genocide by none other than Turkey's President).

Professor Dadrian's further quotations and analyses reveal that there are striking similarities between Turkish actions, goals, and methods in 1920 and those of 1995. Indeed, the scholar continues by stating:

To enhance the level of plausibility, Turkish Foreign Minister Muhtar repeated the method of two-track orders practiced by Talat[6] during the World War I implementation of the genocide.

---

4. Vahakn N. Dadrian, "Genocide as a Problem of National and International Law: the World War I Armenian Case and Its Contemporary Legal Ramifications," *Yale Journal of International Law*, 14.2 (1989).

5. *Ibid.*

6. Talat Pasha, the Minister of Interior at the time when the Young Turks were in power.

He sent the same commander of the Kemalist forces parallel cipher telegrams on the same day. One contained completely opposite instructions, which were meant to be made public and relayed to the tottering Armenian government as Ankara's official terms for an armistice. The use of subterfuges highlights another cardinal feature of the genocidal legacy under review here. Under the pretext of protecting the rights of the Azerbaijanis, who are related to the Turks by ethnic and religious ties, the General was advised to "militarily occupy the entire territory of Armenia," temporarily arrange the frontiers of Armenia in such a way that "under the pretext of protecting the rights of Muslim minorities there is ground for constant intervention," and disarm the Armenians, at the same time arming the Turks of the area, little by little, with the goals of linking up East and West in the area and molding Azerbaijan into an independent Turkish government through the creation of a national force structure.[7]

At that juncture, fortunately, the 11th Red Army marched into Armenia and Turkish designs suffered a delay of 70 years.

These extensive quotations from Dadrian's study and the Foreign Minister's telegram sound exactly like a scenario of modern Turkish political behavior in the region. Indeed, in 1974 Turkey occupied 38% of the territory of an independent neighbor, namely the Republic of Cyprus, under the pretext of "defending" the Turkish minority on the island. Twenty-one years after their brutal aggression on that island, the Turkish army of occupation is still there, formulating even harsher demands and threatening to annex Northern Cyprus to Turkey, despite the fact that the Turks tried to justify their presence on the island by claiming that they were there to prevent the annexation of the island by Greece.

Turkish duplicity is a specially apparent on the European front, where Turkey swears to respect democracy and human rights, hoping to meet European conditions for admission into the family of civilized European nations, while on the other hand using torture as political means and slaughtering Kurds in the name of curbing terrorism.

Turkish plans are even more dreadful in the Caucasus region: once again "under the pretext of protecting the rights of Azerbaijanis," the Turks have imposed a blockade against Armenia, in an attempt to sti-

---

7. Dadrian, *op. cit.*

fle that landlocked nation into annihilation. Ironically, the Turks would prefer to see the conflict prolonged in order that they might achieve the plans laid down by the Kemalists in 1920: namely, to cause a brain drain in Armenia, cripple its economy, encourage voluntary emigration, reduce the country to the third-world status of dependent countries, and impose their own will on that beleaguered nation.

Unfortunately, some Western powers are behind Turkish plans to move East, trampling Armenia on the way, because, as the Kemalist foreign minister put it, Armenia "will never try to integrate her destiny with the general conditions of Turkey and Islam." Armenia will never integrate into those general conditions and may have to pay dearly for that in the foreseeable future.

Recently a British newspaper was calling for "forceful negotiations" to carve away a chunk of Armenian territory and create a free passage for the realization of the Turanian grand design. The very same proposal was being advanced as a trial balloon by a former State Department expert, Paul Goble. It is no surprise that Bülent Ecevit, the former socialist Premier of Turkey who engineered the Turkish occupation of Cyprus, was advancing a similar solution, i.e., a land swap between Armenia and Azerbaijan. His proposal was that Karabagh be exchanged for Zangezur: one piece of Armenian territory for another piece of Armenian territory! Not to mention the fact that Karabagh has attained its independence and Azerbaijan is in no position to barter it for another piece of Armenian territory. The position of the region of Meghri, which has been the focus of attention for all potential land grabbers, has actually been enhanced by the capture of additional Azeri territory in the South, all the way to the Iranian border, by Nagorno Karabagh forces.[8]

The truth of the matter is that all Turks, be they Ottoman, Ittihadist, Republican, or Socialist, have the same goals: to occupy Armenian territory, to depopulate it, and to exterminate its inhabitants. Unfortunately, Armenia cannot choose its neighbors and, given who those neighbors are, it will constantly face the same threat from Turkey. But the genocide and seventy years of Soviet rule have taught our homeland many lessons which will help it to survive. While seeking neigh-

---

8. Meghri is on the southern tip of Armenia, sandwiched between Azeri territory from the East (Nakhichevan) and from the West. The land on the West, adjacent to Meghri was captured by Karabagh Armenian forces, creating a buffer zone between the borders of Azerbaijan and Armenia.

borly relations with Turkey and Azerbaijan, Armenia has been preparing itself for the worst. Today, while Armenia emerges as the strongest nation in the Caucasus, Turkey is in decline, plagued by war, terrorism, internal unrest, and economic chaos. That does not in any way mean that Armenia is yet a match for Turkey. Far from it.

Despite the mobilization of most of her forces to combat Kurdish insurgency, Turkey knows that she is waging a losing battle. Sooner or later Ankara will be forced to come to terms with Kurdish demands for autonomy. If history is any indication, we might remember Nixon's bombing of Hanoi and escalation of the war into the territory of North Vietnam just before beginning the Paris peace talks. Similarly, Israel intensified its war against the Palestinians before shaking hands with Arafat on the White House lawn. Consequently, the incursion of 35,000 Turkish forces into Iraqi territory, without achieving the intended results, may only lead to conciliatory moves.

As long as Turkey has her hands full Armenians may breathe more easily, but they can never be lulled into complacency, as the Turks will never give up their imperial dreams. Turkey refuses to lift the blockade to establish diplomatic relations with Armenia and engage in commerce and cultural exchanges because she can never tolerate a strong and stable Armenia. Our relations with Turkey must be based on that assumption, if we are never to endure another genocide.

President Ter Petrossian has always been quiet and conciliatory on the issue of Nagorno Karabagh. He has even stated publicly that the Armenians in Karabagh may trade territory for security, but he has never made bellicose statements. Once he felt secure and strong, however, he dared to state that Armenia will never allow another genocide in Karabagh. And he meant it.

Today, as Armenia is embroiled in the complex political games of the region, every Armenian believes that we must be prepared to prevent a repetition of the genocide. We must never again be caught unprepared. NEVER AGAIN!

December 4, 1995

The Controversy over the Presidential Elections in Nagorno Karabagh

It seems that the violence which erupted following the presidential election in Armenia will continue for some time to cast a shadow over the present government's conduct in its international diplomacy abroad. It was the clear intention of the forces with vested interests, like Turkey and her allies, to portray Armenia as the weaker party in foreign policy negotiations and thereby impose unacceptable terms on her. Unfortunately, the opposition fell into their trap, playing into the hands of outside powers by drawing the controversy to the verge of violent confrontation.

One obvious indication of this new development is the pressure currently being exerted by the international community on Nagorno Karabagh to cancel its own presidential elections, set for November 24, because Armenia (and consequently Karabagh) is perceived as the weaker party at this December's upcoming CSCE Minsk Group conference in Lisbon.

Many of the foreign ministries of CSCE member countries have been critical of Nagorno Karabagh for proceeding with plans for the presidential election. Particularly disturbing is the position of Russia--which has traditionally sided with Armenia--because, the conflict is as much a Russian problem as an Armenian one. Washington has always been too eager to downplay the right to self-determination in favor of the principal of territorial integrity, which happens to favor Azerbaijan.

Iran, which is not a member of the Minsk group but is vitally interested in the solution (or rather in the continuation) of the conflict, has also announced that the election is "unacceptable."

The countries which are critical of the election speculate that it will bias the negotiations in Lisbon and further complicate the outcome of those negotiations. But Nagorno Karabagh held its first presidential election two years ago, as stipulated by its constitution, and the election in no way biased or complicated the negotiations, which are deadlocked at this time.

There are a number of compelling reasons for the election to take place on the scheduled date:

a) The Karabagh government has not deliberately and only recently chosen the date in order to cause problems: the date was set two years ago, when the first election took place. The newly-adopted constitution called for the election of the president by Parliament for an initial term of two years; at the end of that two-year term, the president was to be elected by the general electorate, for a term of four years;

b) The Russian Foreign Ministry argues that since the Azeri population has fled Karabagh, they will be denied the vote in the upcoming election. That is very tenuous reasoning, because no such arguments were raised, either by Russia or by any other government, when Azerbaijan held its own parliamentary and presidential elections, in which a half-million Armenians expelled from Azerbaijan were denied their right to vote. There is also a distinction to be made among Azeri refugees, who are not all from the original territory of Nagorno Karabagh, which had a population of 175,000 before the war, (a number which today stands at 150,000). The rest of the refugees have been displaced from towns and cities within Azerbaijan and outside of the Nagorno Karabagh territory as a result of war: they are not entitled to participate in this vote anyway;

c) Even if Nagorno Karabagh had remained an autonomous region under Azerbaijan's jurisdiction, it would have held elections in any case.   Postponing the election will enhance Azerbaijan's position during the upcoming negotiations.

d) The demands that the CSCE countries intend to impose on the people of Nagorno Karabagh are contradictory: on the one hand, the CSCE makes it a condition that they will deal only with the elected representatives of the enclave, and on the other hand, in one breath they deny that enclave the right to hold the elections which will produce those elected representatives! President Robert Kocharian's term expires in December, 1996. In order for him (or any representative, for that matter) to be able to negotiate on behalf of the people he claims to represent, he needs to renew his mandate at the conclusion of that term;

e) The Turkish government, which has been pursuing the cancellation of the election, should be the last one to complain about that election. Turkey invaded the sovereign island of Cyprus in August, 1974, and ever since then it has maintained the self-declared government of Northern Cyprus, which has been holding elections under the shadow of the 30,000-strong Turkish expeditionary force while negotiations have been continuing on and off, for the last 22 years; and the end of those negotiations is not yet in sight. It is ironic for Turkey to occupy 38% of a country's territory under the pretext of protecting the Turkish minority's right to self-determination while denying other people the very same right to self-determination. Incidentally, the Turkish minority happens to represent only 18% of Cyprus' total population. If Turkey can tolerate and even encourage elections in Northern Cyprus, it should also understand and tolerate elections in Nagorno Karabagh, based on their very own logic.

Karabagh seems determined to proceed with the election as scheduled. "We are concerned that everyone should know that the elections in Karabagh will be open and fair" Nagorno Karabagh President Robert Kocharian declared recently, adding that international observers have been invited to participate. As for the existence of opposition candidates and their platforms, Kocharian explained that all of the candidates have a common approach to the fundamental issues, including the future of Karabagh. "The candidates are not fighting over different platforms," he said, "but over how best to implement the same program."

The three candidates running for the office of president are NKR[1] member of parliament Boris Arushanian; chairman of the NKR Communist Party, Hrant Melkumian; and, of course, the incumbent president, Robert Kocharian. By all indications Kocharian seems to be a sure bet, as he enjoys solid support at home and popularity abroad. During his first term he has demonstrated wisdom, prudence, and courage, thereby generating overwhelming confidence and respect at home.

His travels and negotiations abroad have exposed him to the world political scene. During his visit to the US last year he impressed his interlocutors as a consummate statesman. In his public appearances and rebuttals he was sharp and very succinct. In his private discussions with legislators he was able to articulate the Karabagh conflict brilliant-

---

1. Nagorno Karabagh Republic.

ly and convince them of the legitimacy of his cause. For diaspora Armenians he symbolizes the legendary Karabagh heroes David Beg and Mekhitar Sparabet, who fought valiantly to preserve the freedom of the Armenian people in Karabagh. Kocharian has been able to give a modern aspect to his legendary legacy by building an efficient army, which has been able to defeat overwhelming Azeri forces.

A case in point which demonstrates Kocharian's ability to articulate Karabagh's position was his October 28 interview on Yerevan TV, in which he was able to outline his government's stand on the current negotiations over the Karabagh conflict through brief sound bites and rational arguments.

Indeed, in response to the statement by Aliyev's adviser Gulizadeh that Azerbaijan is ready to grant the highest level of autonomy to Nagorno Karabagh, Kocharian stated that today Azerbaijan has nothing to offer to Karabagh: "We have already obtained our freedom and independence, and we are not in the mood even to consider autonomy. Azerbaijan is offering Karabagh something which it does not possess itself, and is seeking in return to wrest from us something real which Karabagh already possesses. The party which has lost a war has more problems to solve than the party which has won that war. Therefore, it is incumbent upon the losing side to take the first step."

Few Armenians realize the extent of the pressure on the governments of Karabagh and Armenia to cancel or postpone the presidential election on the eve of the Lisbon Conference.

But the Karabagh representatives at the negotiations need a popular mandate in order to have a strong hand in the upcoming Lisbon Conference, and that strength can only be obtained through the democratic election which Karabagh will soon hold.

Diaspora Armenians cannot remain indifferent at this critical juncture in Karabagh's history. Some diaspora Armenians fought in the battlefields of Karabagh and sacrificed their lives. Short of that supreme sacrifice, we may raise our voices through our elected legislators in order to sensitize our State Department to our concerns and to the democratic principles upon which the United States was founded.

Karabagh needs a popularly mandated president if the elected officials of Karabagh are to play a significant role at the conference. Therefore, the show must go on and the election must be held on schedule, unhampered.

A Time for Healing

A somber mood is still reigning in Armenia as a result of the events which took place on September 25, when the Parliament was stormed by the opposition leaders and the Speaker, Babken Ararktzian, and his deputy, Ara Sahagian, were beaten so badly that they had to be rushed to the hospital.

The ensuing barrage of propaganda and accusations by the opposition, both in Armenia and abroad, has inferred that the violence was instigated and begun by government forces. Many ambassadors, parliamentarians, senators, and diplomats, who have received additional information from some interested quarters, are already accusing the government of resorting to violence.

But what if we turned the tables around and asked how any other government would have reacted if its parliament had been attacked and its elected officials wounded? What would the US government do, for instance, if Congress were attacked, public property destroyed, and legislators wounded, if not restore public order, by a show of force if necessary? That is exactly what the Armenian government did.

The daily newspaper *Aravod*[1] has commented in an editorial that the opposition was hoping and praying that some shooting would take place and result in casualties, in order to create martyrs and incite the mob against the authorities, "who are massacring their own people."

Fortunately for all parties concerned, the turmoil did not reach that stage.

Foreign observers had raised questions about voting irregularities which have no bearing on the outcome of the election. The central election committee has not contested their allegations. It looks as though the last word will come from the Constitutional Court.

But even when irregularities and fraud were admitted, the place to redress them was not the street, nor was the method mob violence.

Unfolding events have revealed that there were several layers of varying responsibility and influence underlying the violence, which reached the point of the lynch-mob. Right in the middle of the turmoil,

---

1. *Morning.*

one of the most vocal leaders of the opposition, Baruyr Hayrikian, protested that Vazken Manoukian had gone far beyond what the leadership had agreed and planned. In turn, Vazken Manoukian extended an olive branch to the government, indirectly admitting that things had gotten out of hand. What remains is for him to reveal all his funding resources, as Ter Petrossian did; otherwise his campaign will remain tainted with rumors that it was heavily financed by the ARF.[2]

Whose interests, then, did this situation serve?

We should be mindful that Armenia is in a state of no-war-no-peace with neighboring Azerbaijan over the issue of Nagorno Karabagh, and has been trying to reach a negotiated settlement from a position of strength. There are regional and international powers who wish to see Armenia weakened in this stand-off. That wish is very obvious in the coverage and commentaries of the news media, which seem to have discovered a golden opportunity to denigrate Armenia, while those media kept silent when more momentous events were taking place in and around Armenia. *The New York Times* has taken the lead, along with *The Washington Post*, which has never missed an opportunity to smear Armenia. Even *The Christian Science Monitor*, which has always demonstrated more objectivity in the past, has come up with a most alarming headline: "Armenia's Fallen Hero Tries to Recover in Second Term." The European and particularly the French press, which monitor the situation in the region more closely, have also come up with negative comments.

As if this international conspiracy were not enough, the ARF and the ANC[3] have been engaged in a very violent and vitriolic campaign, not only in their own media, but also by feeding legislators and the foreign press with grossly exaggerated ammunition. This is enough to demonstrate that the ARF had a stake in pushing the tension beyond its limits and have an interest in its perpetuation.

It is true that the ARF has a legitimate axe to grind with President Ter Petrossian, as does the ADL.[4] But this is no time for settling scores, when the destiny of a people and its homeland are at stake. This negative campaign can only weaken Armenia's resolve in its ongoing struggle in Karabagh. It may also result in a suspension of aid and loans from governments and international agencies, much needed to

---

2. Armenian Revolutionary Federation.
3. Armenian National Committee.
4. Armenian Democratic Liberal Party.

feed the people and to develop a viable economy. Already sources close to the State Department have confided that had the chronology been different and the election held before the $95 million grant had been earmarked by the US Congress, the fate of that grant would most likely have been jeopardized. We have to be mindful that Armenia will be needing the same or a larger grant next year as well, and the continuing campaign will not be conducive to that kind of generosity from the US Congress. In an attempt to punish Levon Ter Petrossian, an entire people is being chastised. This is throwing out the baby with the bath water. The continuation of this campaign will only be self-serving.

Many diplomatic observers in Yerevan believe that this is no time for change. The initiatives taken by the present administration have to run their full course.

Armenia should be allowed to go through a healing process in order to be able to pursue her own national agenda. Already voices of moderation are being heard. Rafik Hovhannessian, a writer in the Yerevan daily *Azg*, has proposed a formula which may pave the way to national reconciliation (ironically that article has been reprinted by *Horizon*, the ARF weekly in Montreal, alongside many vitriolic articles). Mr. Hovhannessian states that Levon + Vazken = stability and progress; Levon - Vazken (i.e., Levon without the support of Vazken) = instability and regress.

The President has already made a conciliatory speech on TV, on September 30, in which he acknowledged the legitimate dissatisfaction of our one million citizens who live below the poverty line. He has also admitted that corruption has been plaguing certain levels of the government. He has gone even further, stating that the government is not bent on beginning a witch hunt. People of good will have to seize the opportunity and begin the peace process if foreign influences are to be forestalled from making inroads into Armenia's political infrastructure. National interests have to take precedence over partisan considerations and political expediency.

This we can do, both in Armenia and abroad, if we recognize the seriousness of this historic moment.

November 4, 1996

Part Two

ARMENIA AND THE WORLD

"Favors"
We Can Live Without

The emigration of Armenians from Soviet Armenia has become a hot issue in superpower relations. Officials at our State Department, which was so reluctant to acknowledge the extermination of 1.5 million Armenians in their ancestral homeland, all of a sudden demonstrate an inordinate compassion and have become champions of human rights by encouraging Armenians to leave their homeland.

In the aftermath of World War I, when Western Armenia was completely depopulated, General Kiazim Karabekir's forces moved against the last stronghold of the Armenians, in an attempt to wipe Armenia off the map. Fortunately, historic events did not evolve the way the Turks had planned, and the survivors of the genocide were spared that last devastating blow. With all its shortcomings, Soviet Armenia became the focal point of the entire Armenian nation. Armenians mustered their remaining strength to reverse the trend of history and gradually replenish Armenia's population. The 20s and 30s saw the first influx of immigrants to Armenia. Almost 200,000 repatriated to Soviet Armenia during the three years following World War II. Many among them realized in advance the personal sacrifices they would undertake in Armenia, but they were also convinced that their immigration would make a historic statement. Armenia had survived many foreign dominations, and the current state of affairs could not last forever.

In 1920 the population of Armenia consisted of 700,000 starving peasants and refugees. Today 3.5 million Armenians live in our homeland, despite losses suffered during World War II and the atrocities and exiles of the Stalin era.

We must look beyond today's political realities to see the need to perpetuate Armenia in history. One does not have to be a sympathizer of the Soviet system to see the danger of depopulating Armenia. The Armenian people's will to survive may not jibe well with the political expediencies of today's superpowers. Encouraging Armenians to abandon their homeland may score insignificant and temporary political victories against the Soviet system, but in the long run will constitute a serious blow to Armenia's very existence. Politicians eager to score those victories may not see or may not care about the consequences of such short-sighted policies, but Armenians must care, and must rise above the intrigues of international diplomacy for the sake of perpetuating Armenia and the Armenian people.

Kathleen Teltch reported in the January 11 issue of *The New York Times* that "Whereas 1,000 Armenians were expected in 1988, Church World Service, which provides care for most of them, reports that 1,000 are showing up monthly at the American Embassy in Moscow and telling officials, 'there are thousands more behind us.'" She further quoted Carl D. Zuckerman, executive vice-president of the International Jewish Migration Agency, as saying, "It is ironical and kind of dumb that the United States had an enormous foreign policy victory in getting the Soviet Union to allow Armenians and Jews out...."

One immediately asks, "a victory against whom?" A propaganda victory against the Soviet Union, perhaps, but also a far-reaching "victory" against Armenian history.

No Armenian has sought or needs such a "victory," which adds up to bleeding Armenia to death by undoing what Armenians have built over the past 70 years. No one can dispute the right of an individual to live a more affluent life in a freer society, yet what seems to be the natural right to choose for an individual may be tantamount to collective suicide for a nation. We should have learned the lessons of history better.

We should also draw a very clear distinction between the Jewish and Armenian cases when emigration from the Soviet Union is an issue. We appreciate the implementation of the Helsinki Accord, which is intended to help people resettle in their ancestral homelands and reunite with their families. The Helsinki Accord does not, however, stipulate the eradication of indigenous peoples from their homelands by breaking up their families, which is the case with Armenians and Armenia. One should not play with the destiny of a tormented people by acting on a lopsided view of humanitarian ideals or by engaging in politics based on wrong assumptions.

We have a challenge facing us: the challenge of educating our State Department officials as well as our congressmen and senators who believe they are doing us a favor by depopulating Armenia.

If the State Department is truly anxious to show humanitarian support to the Armenians, it would do better to drop its objection to the Genocide Resolution.

Whatever the case, we can live without the "favors" presently being forced upon the Armenians.

February 6, 1988

The Kurdish Issue
Blew Up in Demirel's Face

A year after the Gulf War, which enhanced Turkey's political stature in the Middle East, Prime Minister Süleyman Demirel's coalition government faces the perennial Kurdish problem, which refuses to wane away despite ruthless military repression and the hot pursuit of Kurds into Iraqi territory by the Turkish military.

President Turgut Özal shares Gorbachev's fate in one respect: he enjoys much more popularity abroad than at home. Thanks to his smile, political skills and, at times, his patronizing advice to world leaders such as President Bush, he has been able to humanize to a degree Turkey's image in the West. Turkey has always been on the hit list of human rights advocates in the West for her record of political repression, torture, and the outright extermination of minorities.

Because of their proximity to the West, several major Turkish cities such as Istanbul and Izmir have acquired a Western facade, and Turkey has been able to put that facade to good use in the past as well as today, in an attempt to mask internal political realities. In the Ottoman years, that political gambit won over even Armenian leaders in Istanbul, to the extent that they disassociated themselves from the suffering masses in the interior provinces. Even today, many European leaders and journalists tend to base their judgments of Turkey on conditions in those admittedly more sophisticated western cities, but in fact conditions there are in stark contrast to those in the interior provinces.

No one knows exactly how many Kurds live in Turkey, but estimates run anywhere from 9 to 16 million, and sometimes even higher.

After having been used against the Armenians during the 1915 genocide, the Kurds became second- or third-class citizens in Republican Turkey and, since the days of Atatürk, the official Turkish line has been to deny that there even are Kurds in Turkey, and any assertive move to define the Kurdish national identity has invited harsh reprisals from the authorities.

The use of the Kurdish language was forbidden, and even singing a Kurdish song would cost the offender many years in jail. At best, Kurds were known as "Mountain Turks!"

But the world has been changing, and in order to convince the West that Turkey truly deserves to be considered a European country, Özal had to make a turnaround, admitting the existence of the Kurds and, at least on paper, allowing the use of the Kurdish language, as parallel measures to a campaign to stop the use of torture in prisons as a means of obtaining confessions. But Özal's party lost the recent parliamentary election and Demirel's True Path Party formed a coalition government with Erdal Inönü's Social Democratic Populist Party in late October 1991.

Demirel has been on the Turkish political scene for many years--even serving as prime minister on several occasions--but he has never given a hoot about Kurdish national aspirations. This time around he recognized the realistic nature of Özal's policy towards the Kurdish problem, especially in the face of rising Kurdish militancy: the militant Kurdish group called the Kurdish Workers' Party had been staging more and more violent raids against Turkish military and civilian targets. The election of Kurdish representatives or sympathizers to Parliament also played an important role in Demirel's conversion, so much so that he made it one of his political priorities to appease the Kurdish provinces. And indeed, early last December Demirel took a tour of the restive Kurdish regions of Diarbakir and Siirt, accompanied by Deputy Prime Minister Erdal Inönü. He promised the cheering crowds in that region a "new dawn in Turkey." He even claimed to be against torture, trying to gloss over the fact that many Kurdish nationalists continued to be subjected to medieval tortures on Turkey's death rows.

Simultaneously, the new education minister, Köksal Toptan, pledged to revise textbooks and "recognize the realities."

But it seems that all these promises and appeasement measures were too little and too late: despite all these cosmetic pronouncements or because of them, the Kurdish nationalist drive blew up in Demirel's face. In fact, the explosion occurred December 25, in the very heart of Istanbul. Until that date, the Kurdish militants had confined their operations to rural areas, but now the violence suddenly shifted to the metropolitan stage in a bid to dramatize the Kurdish plight before a larger audience. The Kurdish Workers' Party hit the Çetinkaya store in the Bakirköy area of Istanbul. Eleven shoppers died and 18 were wounded. The target was not chosen at random; the store belonged to Fehmi Çetinkaya, the brother of Governor Nejat Çetinkaya, who is responsible for the implementation of the harsh rule of martial law in the Kurdish region. Before staging their violent attack, the Kurdish militants shouted such slogans as "Kurdistan will be fascism's graveyard," and "The Mara, Lice, and Kule massacres will be avenged." The Turkish military had organized the wholesale slaughter of Kurds in recent months in those cities.

Demirel's cautious moves towards recognition of Kurdish rights came to an abrupt halt when Parliament met in a stormy session the very next day and the members of the True Path party shouted down the Kurdish apologists. Later, at the funeral of the victims of this latest violence, Chief-of-Staff General Dogan Güven vowed revenge against the Kurds. The right-wing religious fanatic, Necmettin Erbakan, did not miss the opportunity to snipe at the Armenians during that stormy parliamentary session. He claimed that many of the "terrorists" slain by the Turkish military were Armenians because they were discovered to be uncircumcised!

The Kurds had coordinated their bloody attack with simultaneous demonstrations throughout Europe, hitting hard where it hurt most. Indeed, since his election, President Özal had carefully cultivated an image of a Turkey that had finally achieved internal peace, but this well-orchestrated Kurdish explosion was a devastating blow to that image.

Demirel's government faces two real alternatives today: either to continue the appeasement policy by trying to improve the economic and political plight of the Kurds and integrating them into Turkish society, or to proceed on the traditional path of trying to contain violence with military terror. Demirel himself knows full well that violence breeds more violence, until chaos is created and inevitably the generals step in to rule the country by military decree for another decade.

The first scenario seems more likely for a seasoned statesman like Demirel, because the latter would not be admissible, even by Turkey's closest allies, in this era of a new world order.

January 25, 1992

Betting on the Wrong Horse

Recently the US news media came out with severe criticism of the Reagan-Bush Administration's foreign-policy blunders. "The Soviet Union wasn't the only superpower that bet on the wrong horse in Afghanistan. The US did too, and that may prove embarrassing to Washington in the months ahead," writes Robert S. Greensberger in *The Wall Street Journal* (May 11, 1992), and he expands on this assessment in the following paragraphs:

Gulbuddim Hekmatyar, a hard-line Islamic fundamentalist guerrilla leader who built his significant fighting force in large part with US equipment and acquiescence, has emerged as a major obstacle to patching up war-torn Afghanistan. He's bent on seizing control of the fractious nation.

US policy was to assist the Afghanistan resistance to get rid of the Soviet-installed regime, presumably allowing a more democratic government to take hold. But it turns out that miscalculations by the Washington strategists have paved the way either for more bloodshed or for the installation of a more fundamentalist regime in Kabul, promising worse calamities to the Afghani people than they suffered under the previous Communist regime. An extremist regime would also generate instability in the area. Therefore, Greensberger concludes, "If Mr. Hekmatyar succeeds in disrupting the peacemaking efforts [...] the administration would bear the blame."

As the dust settles in the Middle East and on the Southern flank of the Soviet Union, it becomes more and more apparent that miscalculation was not only confined to Afghanistan, but followed a pattern which betrays an ignorance of the area and an unwarranted over-confidence on the part of the Washington planners in mapping out their strategy. Another case in point, which has made William Safire of *The New York Times* spit fire, is Iraq. In a recent essay (May 18, 1992), Safire blames President Bush for his pre-Gulf policy: "Americans know now," he says, "that the war in the Persian Gulf was brought about by a colossal foreign policy blunder: George Bush's decision, after the Iran-Iraq war ended, to entrust the regional security to Saddam Hussein."

As though these foreign policy blunders were not enough, the Administration is betting on yet another wrong horse in the region:

Turkey. With the collapse of the Soviet Union, the Central Asian Turkic republics seem to be up for grabs. Although the only competitors for control of the area seem to be Iran and Turkey, Pakistan cannot be discounted from that equation either.

The US government has been encouraging Turkey to take over the leadership to bring the newly-independent Soviet Muslim republics under its sway. This policy was stated very bluntly at a recent White House briefing to Armenian representatives; but knowing Armenian sensitivities to the issue and trying to soften the blow, it was added that the Republic of Armenia has also been figured into development plans and that the US Administration has been successful in convincing Turkey to integrate Armenia into the economic and communications systems, as a partner rather than an antagonist.

Given their historic experience, Armenians have reason to harbor reservations about Turkey, and the White House seems to appreciate that fact. But those reservations notwithstanding, the Bush Administration is determined to go ahead with the Turkish option. The assumption is that Turkey has long-standing ties with Central Asia and that the Turks understand those republics better than anyone else.

But piecing facts together, it is not difficult to prove that the Administration is on the verge of sponsoring yet another foreign-policy blunder, very much in line with those in Afghanistan and Iraq. Apart from Armenian fears of pan-Turanism, Turkey seems to be very far from the position which Washington policy-makers wishfully attribute to that country. Our worst fears materialized recently when Turkey threw away its mediator's mantle and assisted Azerbaijan in its bloody war to exterminate the Armenians in Artzakh.

From the standpoint of US foreign policy, it does not make sense to extend Turkish hegemony over the area, because Turkey may have its own hidden agenda, which may not necessarily include US interests. Nor does Turkey have the knowledge and the local reputation to pass itself off as a model of Muslim secular government.

In a most cynical article in *The New York Times*, the syndicated columnist Leslie Gelb articulates US policy in the following manner (May 22, 1992):

> To Administration officials, Iranian fundamentalism represents the immediate threat to Western interests in Central Asia. They hope to build up Turkey, a Muslim but secular nation, as the alternative. And they do not want Armenian military successes against Turkic people to put Ankara in a position where it must

either stand aside and look impotent or intervene with force. Mr. Gelb also confesses that "while US diplomacy has been evenhanded, Administration feelings are increasingly anti-Armenian."

There are certain intrinsic fallacies in the US assumptions:

1. Turkey cannot serve as a secular model in a Muslim region which enjoys even stronger secular traditions. Turkey has nothing more attractive to offer than what those nations have already achieved and continue to experience;

2. If it comes to a showdown, the US has to project its military might into the area to do the job, as happened in Iraq, where the UN provided the fig leaf. Therefore, it makes better sense for the US to take the lead and promote its own interests at the outset, rather than rely on surrogates of questionable allegiance;

3. No matter how much wishful thinking is invested by the Washington policy makers, Turkey cannot project a benevolent image or a democratic model while it is in the process of waging a vicious war of extermination against a third of its population. Indeed, no one can yet assess the outcome of the insurrection of the Kurds (a distinct ethnic group with devout Muslim traditions) against Turkish military suppression. Foreign policy cannot be formulated on false assumptions or wishful thinking;

4. Contrary to Administration assertions, the Turkish government does not have a firm handle on Central Asia, nor enough knowledge and experience to chart a coherent policy. Indeed, upon returning to Ankara from a Central Asian tour, Turkish Prime Minister Süleyman Demirel confessed in a public speech on May 5: "I realized that we know nothing about these [Central Asian] republics, and my mind is full of confusion on the issue at this time";

5. The Administration's fear of Iran is no longer justified, as that country has recently tilted towards the West, after President Rafsanjani consolidated his position at home. Despite its past extremism, Iran proved to be an honest broker between Armenia and Azerbaijan, without projecting its fundamentalist policies. On the other hand, the Administration has already set a precedent of conducting business with regimes that are not very palatable to Washington. A case in point may be Angola, where Chevron was drilling oil wells while Washington tried to topple the Marxist government in Luanda by supplying arms and training to Savimbi's opposition guerrilla forces.

The Armenian leaders in Yerevan are painfully aware that a war with Azerbaijan is not in the best interest of their country, yet a conflict is being concocted on the Nakhichevan border to precipitate such a war and to cut a passage through Zangezur linking Turkey to Central Asia.

It is of major importance to keep in mind that President Levon Ter Petrossian's recent spectacular visits to three Muslim countries--Iran, Syria, and Egypt--demonstrate fully that Armenia does not harbor any hostile intentions towards Muslim nations. Our problem is only with Turkey, which has a long-standing objective of destroying Armenia. Armenia has also signed a defense pact with four of the Central Asian Muslim republics, to the displeasure of Turkey and Azerbaijan. Therefore, our task is to try to dissociate the Turkish leadership role in Central Asia from US policy interests. Not only do they not converge, but they actually diverge.

Fortunately, Armenia and Armenians are not the only ones critical of the unrealistic US policy towards Turkey. The US congressmen and senators who have visited the area on fact-finding missions also realize that Turkey is not the country to entrust with the promotion of US interests in the region.

Indeed, after a fact-finding mission in the Central Asian republics, Arizona Senator Dennis DeConcini voiced his criticism of the Administration's decision to meet the threats of Islamic militancy through a policy of encouraging Turkey as a model for Central Asia. Administration officials say they have agreed on a joint technical pact with Turkey, which is Islamic but secular, to "foster democratic and market reforms, and orient their trade and other ties Westward." "Turkey has immense problems, including in human rights" said Senator DeConcini in an interview given to *New York Times* staff writer Barbara Crosette (May 31, 1992).

Other experts in the area tend to concur with the senator's assessment. Barnett Rubin, Director of the Center for the Study of Central Asia at Columbia University, said: "The main obstacle to intelligent policy-making in Central Asia is the repetition of the cold-war pattern of looking for a threat and for a partner against that threat--and then finding that the partner has a regional agenda that isn't yours." In this case, it is the spread of Turkish influence across the region and the accompanying revival of long-dormant pan-Turkic aspirations which have nothing in common with US interests.

"At the moment, the new threat perception is some kind of Iranian fundamentalism, and our partner is so-called secular Turkey," Mr. Rubin added; "I think that the Central Asian nations are not going to be the passive recipients of somebody else's models."

Edward Allworth, also of the Columbia Center, said that making Turkey the model was "a simple-minded solution to a very complex problem."

All these statements by politicians and experts prove one point: that all the pieces are falling into place. It is wiser for the US Administration to distance itself from Turkey, in order to open up a broader vision over this relatively unknown area, enabling itself to develop a more objective and realistic policy.

Not only is it in Armenia's interest to see US policy dissociated from the Turkish factor, but it is also in the best interest of US foreign policy. The mistakes in Afghanistan and Iraq must serve the Washington planners as useful guides, cautioning them against repeating the same mistakes and encouraging them to break away from the pattern of cold-war thinking.

Armenians have an interest in helping to de-Turkify US policy in Central Asia. Political wisdom also dictates that sane policy. An election year is the most opportune psychological period to press that point across, which, in this case, happens to correspond to a sound US foreign policy objective.

The Cold War is over, and there is no room left for cold-war strategic thinking and planning.

June 20, 1992

THE SOLARZ PHENOMENON:

An Opportunity for Political Empowerment

Reading through the Turkish press, one concludes that the Armenian-American political lobby is an all-powerful monster; in fact, the Turks tend to exaggerate Armenian political clout in Washington, in order that they might blame Armenian influence for some of their political setbacks with the US Administration and Congress. Yet we well know that, if anything, the Armenian lobby is in its infancy. That does not, of course, rule out the possibility of potential growth into a force to be reckoned with.

The Armenians in the US definitely possess political, financial, media, and other resources, which lay helter-skelter across the country; they need to be harnessed, coordinated, and directed towards specific targets. And that of course requires political maturity and unity of purpose. As Armenian-American involvement in the democratic process develops, more and more of those resources will be brought into play to serve our political goals.

Today Armenians in the United States are faced with a unique opportunity for political empowerment. That opportunity is provided by none other than a determined opponent of Armenian interests: Congressman Stephen Solarz of Brooklyn, New York. Because of a recent redistribution of his district, the Congressman has decided to run for re-election in the newly-reapportioned 12th Congressional District, which is inhabited by a Hispanic majority. The Hispanic community is up in arms, because they believe they are entitled to elect and be represented in Washington by a Hispanic voice. As Lindsay Gruson wrote in the July 9 issue of *The New York Times*, "Some Hispanic leaders and opponents immediately denounced the decision by Solarz, who has accumulated one of the largest campaign war chests in the country, as an attempt by a carpet-bagger to buy a seat that should go to a Hispanic person." The news media and political pundits have been debating the claim that a candidate's ethnic background should not be an issue, especially in light of other districts in the country where white majorities have elected black or Hispanic representatives.

But Mr. Solarz' questionable track record is gradually emerging in the media, a record which obviously works to his detriment and which opponents have been putting to good use. Indeed, Congressman Solarz has been one of the worst offenders in the Congressional bad-check-writing scandal, so much so that news has surfaced of a State Department advisory to all US embassies not to honor his checks during his foreign trips.

Whereas the Congressman tries to present his involvement in foreign policy issues as his forte, that involvement is being treated as a liability in the economically-disenfranchised district, where issues closer to home enjoy precedence. Mr. Solarz has been on many overseas trips, ignoring major domestic issues in his former district. Some journalists have also investigated his financial dealings, which they believe may damage his credibility and integrity.

Armenians in the New York area are determined to add yet another dimension to the Congressman's woes. In fact, he has been a very vocal spokesman for Turkish apologists on the issue of the Armenian genocide. Initially he supported the Armenian position on the genocide, until the Turks offered him lucrative junkets and generous campaign contributions. He underwent a change of heart at that point in his career, and decided to sell his conscience and vote to the highest bidder. His records indicate heavy Turkish financing of his past election campaigns. In recent years he has also received medals and commendations from various Turkish societies, so much so that he has claimed to be proud to be known as "the Congressman from Istanbul." Hispanic voters in the 12th Congressional District wish that Solarz would move his campaign out of their district--perhaps as far as Istanbul....

His denial of the Armenian genocide first pits Solarz against his own record and secondly singles him out from other representatives of Jewish background. Because of the parallel historic experiences suffered by both groups, the majority of Congressmen and Senators of Jewish background have been very supportive of issues concerning the Armenian genocide, with Senator Carl Levin of Michigan leading the pack.

It is ironic that Mr. Solarz has put himself in an awkward position by defending the Jewish holocaust and denying the Armenian genocide--a double standard does not bode well for a politician and may blow up in his face! Through his duplicity, the Congressman discriminates against not only the living, but also the dead. In his estimation, the victims of the holocaust deserve justice and respect, whereas the victims of the Armenian genocide deserve neither.

A group of New York Armenians, headed by a seasoned public official, Sam Azadian, have taken up the challenge of defeating Solarz. Retired Army Colonel George Juskalian has echoed that initiative by firing a single salvo from Washington, in a letter to the press (*The Armenian Mirror Spectator*, July 25). Sam Azadian and his supporters must not be left to shoulder the awesome responsibility of defeating Mr. Solarz by themselves. We need to network across the country, pooling our resources and sending a powerful message to Brooklyn. It has been done by other ethnic groups, who have successfully defeated candidates who hurt their causes, even in remote areas where those groups have lacked voting power. In fact, they have met their objectives by supporting the enemy of their enemy.

At this point, the Hispanic community in the 12th District is facing the intruder with four different contenders of its own. We urge them to get their act together and face Solarz with one strong candidate. That candidate must also enjoy Armenian support.

Solarz' undignified advocacy has insulted not only New York Armenians, but the entire Armenian community, across the political spectrum. He has insulted the dead and the living.

Mr. Solarz has afforded us a rare opportunity for political empowerment. We have to rise to the challenge. Not only will the experience teach a lesson to Solarz, it will also teach one to us: that we can do it!

We must breathe life into the monster the Turks fear most, and we must send a message to Brooklyn, a message which will also reverberate in Washington and in Istanbul.[1]

August 1 , 1992

---

1. *The combined efforts of Armenians and the voters of the 12th district paid off: Solarz was defeated in the election.*

A Time for Creative Political Thinking

With Ross Perot's entrance (or rather, re-entrance) into the Presidential race, this election year has turned all too colorful and interesting. Although, even after the first presidential debate, in which Perot fared significantly well, very few people, if any, consider him to be a serious challenger to the candidates of the traditional parties, nevertheless Perot may yet become a spoiler, depending on the course and the outcome of the elections.

The presidential campaign got off to a lethargic start this year, with general apathy towards both candidates. Enter Perot, and the race turned more interesting, obliging the other candidates to sharpen their images and focus more on real issues.

The most important problem, of course, is the state of the US economy. Mr. Bush contends that the slow-down is the result of a global trend rather than of any misguided policy at the White House. Mr. Clinton, of course, blames the President for the "trickle-down" economy and promises to do better.

How do we vote as US citizens and how do we vote as Armenian Americans?

Many factors affect our decisions. If we have stocks or real estate to sell, we definitely lean towards Mr. Bush, hoping that he will be able to cut the capital gains tax and thus help our pocketbooks. If we support gay rights, we should stay away from the President (and certainly from Mr. Perot). If we favor universal health care, our candidate is Mr. Clinton, and if we uphold family values, our choice is Mr. Bush. If we are "pro-lifers" or "pro-choicers," we will vote in a certain way.

Many people still refuse to accept the notion of economic determinism--that the economy tends to move in cyclical patterns--and some candidates get lucky by riding the tide, as Mr. Reagan did.

The economy, ecology, crime, and social issues all impact on our daily lives and help determine our choice. But some special-interest groups, and certainly some ethnic groups, are single-issue voters. For example, many Jews vote for candidates who never question Israel's policies. Under pressure from certain rightist groups and opponents of foreign aid, President Bush dilly-dallied on the issue of a 10-billion dollar loan guarantee to Israel, although he later timed his approval of the loan to help his re-election bid. Some Jews will vote for Mr. Bush in appreciation of his positive decision, but many more will cast protest votes because he delayed that decision too long and turned it into an election issue.

On the other hand, Arab-Americans may support Bush's candidacy because he finally revived the peace process in the Middle East.

Many ethnic groups will base their decision about whom to vote for on the treatment their ancestral homelands have received from the present administration, or on the treatment they anticipate from whatever US Government may be elected.

Therefore, as Armenian Americans, are we exercising our franchise well if we vote for the candidate who proves to be most receptive to Armenian issues?

Economic and social issues are determining factors. But Armenian issues have become a more important and, with some Armenian voters, even the overriding factor in making a voting decision this year. We cannot ignore the grass-roots movements all over the country, which indicate a marked improvement in political awareness and which, although admittedly uncoordinated, are certainly growing in scope.

Before we cast our votes we must ask certain questions and demand answers from both camps.

The Bush administration came to the Presidency with the promise of a "kinder and gentler" America. As Armenians, we expected to be the beneficiaries of that "kindness," which, unfortunately, was late in coming. In the wake of a devastating earthquake in Armenia, the richest country on earth came far behind Italy, Germany, and many other countries who rushed to help the victims.

In terms of policy, the Bush administration continued its predecessor's position of fighting the Genocide Resolution.[1] The White House did not even pretend to pursue an even-handed policy. On the contrary, it actively campaigned against the Resolution and the memory of the genocide victims. Its crucial support was handed to the Turks as a favor, on a silver platter.

Armenia faces its fifth cold winter under the Azerbaijani block-

---

1. *The Genocide Resolution has been introduced on the agenda of the Congress many times and unfortunately the votes have fallen short for adoption.*

ade, but we have yet to see any power, let alone a superpower, assert itself
to persuade the reckless Azeri government to lift the embargo and allow
food and supplies to reach the victims of the earthquake and the refugees
from Baku and other parts of Azerbaijan.

At first our hopes were raised by sweet talk from the White
House, where Armenian leaders were invited twice to share and discuss
their concerns.[2] But gradually the Administration's consistent policy vis-
a-vis the Karabagh conflict made it abundantly clear that those invita-
tions were nothing more than election-year gimmicks. The Secretary of
State was sent to the region to convince Azerbaijan to ease the blockade
or face the consequences. We were led to believe that the US would
withhold diplomatic recognition of Azerbaijan until the latter improved
its inhuman conduct. But no sooner had Mr. Baker's plane touched
down in Baku than the US recognized Azerbaijan's left-over government
from the Communist era.

Later, courageous Congressmen and Senators passed the
Freedom Support Act Amendment (907), forbidding the US government to extend direct economic aid to the Azerbaijani government pending the lifting of the blockade. But recent months have demonstrated
that the pro-Azeri tilt of the present administration's policy continued,
as the White House tried to change the language of the Act in order to
mollify or neutralize its effect completely. Fortunately, the Armenian
community was alarmed, and friendly Representatives and Senators
helped defuse this most recent threat initiated by the White House.

More dangerously, it is the proclaimed policy of the present
administration to rely on a Turkish proxy to penetrate the Central Asian
republics of the former Soviet Union, contrary to the warnings of many
knowledgeable statesmen and newsmen. It seems to be a foregone conclusion at the highest level of this administration that Turkey remains the
only country in the region that can be trusted with tending to US interests in Central Asia. Part of that commitment seems to stem from a sense
of obligation to repair any harm to US-Turkish relations which may have
resulted from ignoring the Turkish Government's pleas to abandon the
Kurds in Iraq and consequently deny the Kurds the right to any semblance of self-rule.

In this context it becomes all too obvious that the Paul Goble

---

2. *See the two essays earlier in this section, "A Window of Opportunity" (page 64), and*
   "Betting on the Wrong Horse" (page 157).

plan of swapping land between Armenia and Azerbaijan remains the centerpiece of US policy in the Caucasus, contrary to adamant official denials. The Goble theory maintains that, yes indeed, Nagorno Karabagh belongs to Armenia and must be ceded to that republic and, in return, Armenia must reciprocate that Azerbaijani concession by ceding a chunk of its own territory in the Meghri region, which links Armenia to her only friendly neighbor, Iran. Indeed, the only barrier to Turkish expansion into Central Asia remains the Armenian province of Zangezur, which separates Nakhichevan from Azerbaijan proper. It seems inconceivable that pan-Turkish ambitions can be achieved, with Washington's blessing, without carving a passage through Armenia. On the other hand, it might prove suicidal for Armenia to give up that vital portion of its southern tip, which would further isolate her in the region and make her dependent on Turkish mercy for survival!

This is what four years of the Bush administration has brought to Armenia and Armenians will receive more of the same if George Bush is re-elected.

On the other hand, as yet we have no clear indication of what direction a Clinton administration policy might take, because, as the saying goes, "the proof of the pudding is in the eating." The Clinton campaign has come up with a general but favorable statement on Armenian issues; but the prospect that the pro-Turkish Solarz[3] might be designated Clinton's Secretary of State or even US envoy to the United Nations does not augur well. If we can prevent the nomination of Solarz to any important position before a final decision is made, and help to maintain a Clinton administration policy that is generally consistent with the spirit of the positive campaign statement, we may end up with a more hopeful prospect in this election year.

In fact, no individual or group in the Armenian community has successfully taken either of the two major contenders to task in an attempt to wrench firm commitments from them. We basically remain a fragmented community, in which each faction is trying to score partisan points rather than achieving any substantive political gains.

It is indeed difficult to isolate certain basic issues from the plethora of overwhelming concerns and consider them as determining factors in voting during the upcoming election.

Yes indeed, we have to consider our pocket books, the health,

---

3. *See the previous essay in this section, "The Solarz Phenomenon" (page 162).*

education, and welfare of our children, the environment, and the sustenance of this country's social fabric, along with all the other problems. But it is also time to focus on Armenia's future and the values which have come to determine our own very being. After all, appropriate stands on Armenian issues may not be prejudicial to the resolution of our other concerns. In fact, they may even complement and reinforce them.

Therefore, it is high time to give up on old dogmas and antiquated blind allegiances, and it is also time for fresh and creative political thinking.

October 24, 1992

Is Secretary of State Christopher Conducting an Even-Handed Policy in Karabagh?

The following letter was addressed to US Secretary of State Warren Christopher on April 12, 1993:

The Honorable Warren Christopher,
Secretary of State,
US Government,
Washington, DC

Dear Mr. Christopher:

Armenians in Armenia and in the United States are very grateful for the generous relief assistance that the US Government has been providing for the past two years. As you may well know, Armenia is a highly industrialized and technologically advanced small country, driven back to the Stone Age by the continued blockade which the neighboring Republic of Azerbaijan has been imposing ever since a devastating earthquake hit Armenia's northern region in December of 1988, rendering 500,000 citizens of that tiny republic homeless.

For the past two years the ravages of the economic blockade have been compounded by the indiscriminate shelling of border towns and villages in Armenia and in Nagorno Karabagh.

The historic memory of the Armenian people is filled with horrible events, from the 1915 genocide at the hands of the Ottoman Turks which resulted in 1.5 million martyrs, through the 1920 Baku massacre which took a toll of 30,000 Armenian lives, to the Sumgait and Baku pogroms of 1988 and 1990 respectively. Therefore, when the foreign and interior ministers of Azerbaijan publicly announce that the conflict over Nagorno Karabagh can be settled only on the battlefield, Armenians can draw no other conclusion than that their existence is in danger, very much in the historic pattern.

Despite all of Azerbaijan's attempts to draw Armenia into an all-out war through border provocations, the Republic of Armenia has been restraining itself in order to allow the world to focus on the real issue, which is the struggle of the Armenian people of Nagorno Karabagh for self-determination. That territory was forcibly taken away from Armenians and put under Azeri rule by Stalin. For the past 70 years Nagorno Karabagh has had at least nominal status as an autonomous region. The ultra-nationalist government of Azerbaijan unilaterally annulled that status, contrary to the will of the inhabitants of the region. Azerbaijan's declared determination to wipe out the Armenians of Nagorno Karabagh left the latter no alternative but to defend themselves, which they have been doing under the most primitive conditions.

The even-handed policy of the US Government has been a welcome approach to the resolution of the conflict. However, your recent condemnation of "ethnic Armenian forces," in which you characterized the self-defense struggle as an "offensive" drive, can no longer be deemed the even-handed assessment of an honest broker. Had the United States condemned past atrocities and unjustified encroachments on Armenian territory (when the city of Ardzvashen was seized by Azerbaijan, no protest or condemnation was issued by our State Department), you could claim today that your policy remains even-handed.

Armenians also question why the State Department has kept silence for the past four years, when emergency relief trains intended for the earthquake survivors were being destroyed on Azerbaijani territory and when a continued blockade threatened the extinction of 3.5 million people in Armenia. Are those offenses of lesser consequence than the self-defense measures taken by guerrilla forces in Nagorno Karabagh to prevent an all-out assault by Azerbaijan?

In view of your overwhelming support for Bosnia-Herzegovina, we also have some reason to ask why the US has failed to provide the same level of support to Armenia and Nagorno Karabagh, which are in no better shape than Bosnia.

The Armenian government and the elected representatives of the people of Nagorno Karabagh have repeatedly appealed for a peaceful resolution of the conflict, but the response has always come from the barrels of guns. The Armenians continue to search for avenues for a peaceful settlement, and they realize that they cannot choose their neighbors. Only peace will guarantee normal civilized relations among the nations in the region.

We hope that you continue your even-handed policy by urging all sides to exercise restraint.

Sincerely,
Edmond Y. Azadian

April 17, 1993

Et Tu, Ukraine?

Last year my visit to President Ter Petrossian's office was interrupted by an urgent phone call, after which the President returned to his desk and, with a sigh of relief, exclaimed: "One more serious problem solved!" That statement encouraged me to ask what the problem was. "That was Leonid Kravchuk.[1] Ukraine has decided to withdraw its forces from our borders with Turkey. I convinced him to postpone the implementation of that decision for two more months, until we are ready to deploy our own forces," answered the President.

I began wondering why Ukraine, a so-called Christian nation, would leave Armenia defenseless to face her historic enemy. After all, Armenia and Ukraine had enjoyed long and historic relations, always on friendly terms.

At that time I did not make too much of the incident. But as subsequent events evolved it became all too apparent that Ukraine has steadfastly stood behind Azerbaijan in the Nagorno-Karabagh conflict all along. As if it were not enough for Ukraine to express her hostility against Armenia by setting up a joint gas company with Azerbaijan and building a pipeline which extends from Iran to Ukraine, bypassing Armenia, the authorities in Kiev began supplying Azerbaijan with armaments, contrary to UN Security Council resolutions which forbid third parties to supply arms to parties in conflict. On September 8, 1993, it was reported from Stepanakert that Ukraine had shipped 40 tanks to Azerbaijan. Later that number was raised to 59. Those tanks were airlifted from Ukrainian territory to Azerbaijan, three tanks at a time. Ukraine had also supplied Azerbaijan with Mig-21 attack planes, as revealed by the captured Ukrainian pilot of one of the two planes downed in Karabagh last September.

All of the above reports were denied by the Kiev authorities, who said that Ukrainian assistance was limited to the repair of Azeri tanks in Ukrainian facilities. Of course no one is in a position to verify this limited extent of Ukrainian assistance, which, even if true, still constitutes a hostile act against Armenia.

---

1. *First President of Ukraine after its independence from the former Soviet Union in 1991.*

Last week Radio Liberty in Europe announced the shipment of an additional 75 Ukrainian tanks to Azerbaijan.

Despite its official neutrality, Ukraine has been siding with Azerbaijan, not because of any unfriendly act on the part of Armenia, but because of Armenia's guilt by association. Armenia is perceived by Ukraine as a Russian ally and therefore an adversary of Ukraine. In fact, a fierce rivalry is brewing between Ukraine and Russia. That rivalry was first centered around control of the former Soviet Black Sea fleet, an issue which has finally been resolved, leaving the status of the Crimea and the plight of Ukraine's nuclear arsenal as the last remaining bones of contention between the two most powerful republics. From time to time, Ukraine has been flexing its nuclear muscle, delaying the relocation and/or dismantling of its nuclear weapons. Those maneuvers have been reaping handsome dividends from both Russia and the West.

As long as Russia stands firmly behind Armenia, the damage caused by the Ukrainian tilt can be contained. But Russian support is not the most reliable factor in the entire conflict. Just before the Russian elections, when Moscow needed an excuse to vent its nationalistic fervor, Foreign Minister Andrei Kozyrov blew the Kazimirov incident[2] out of proportion, demanding a public apology from Armenia. Although Yerevan authorities consider that incident behind them, relations between Moscow and Yerevan do not seem to be back on track. We have yet to see the impact of the recent Russian elections on Moscow's relations with "near abroad," as the former Soviet republics are called.

On top of Russia's undependable, inconsistent, and self-centered policy vis-a-vis Yerevan, Ukrainian antagonism further isolates Armenia.

While Georgia is effectively reinforcing and indirectly supporting the Turkish-Azeri blockade of Armenia, it is most discomforting to find Ukraine further aggravating that isolation.

Awareness of all these problems in itself certainly does not lead to their solution. The Government of Armenia already has its hands full with the development and implementation of a prudent foreign policy,

---

2. *See the essay "The Gathering of the Storm" (page 121), earlier in this collection: "Kozyrov seized on the opportunity of the attack on the convoy of Kazimirov, the Russian mediator in the Karabagh conflict. He demanded a public apology from the Armenians for the attack, for which no one has yet claimed responsibility." According to that essay, "the attack ... claimed no casualties."*

while trying to befriend all of Armenia's neighbors and antagonize none.

Armenians in the US can play a positive role in this situation. With the demise of the Soviet Union, Ukrainians in the US have been reactivated and have been supporting their homeland in a meaningful way. The Ukrainian lobby in Washington is alive and well. They have also been developing relations with their homeland and are impacting on their country's march towards democracy. We may approach those groups, their leaders, churches, and clergy, and sensitize them to the cleavage, which is widening with each passing day. We have to convey the message that improving relations with Armenians can benefit both countries and enhance our political partnership in the US. A more stable Armenia can be a better trading partner than Azerbaijan, which is in perpetual turmoil and instability.

Politicizing the Armenian communities in the US and engaging them in the democratic process will render the community a force to be reckoned with. We have been moving in that direction, but the faster we move the healthier the results will be.

Having said all this, we realize that our options are limited. We will find it hard to internalize the crude facts of facing Ukraine as an adversary, and will keep wondering and asking, like a latter-day Julius Caesar, "Et tu, Ukraine?"

December 18, 1993

Azerbaijan's Fragile Ethno-Political Mosaic

Azerbaijan is an artificial country, created only after 1918 as a result of the settlement of geo-political issues in the Caucasus following the Russian Revolution. Lenin considered the present-day Azeris to be Caucasian Tartars. Ethnic consciousness developed among the Azeris during the 70 years of Soviet rule, yet Azerbaijan was never able to become a cohesive nation, since Stalin had bundled up a host of independence-minded ethnic groups within its geographic boundaries.

Just as Nagorno Karabagh Armenians never accepted Azeri rule and used every opportunity to rid themselves of that oppressive domination, so did other ethnic minorities living within the boundaries of what had become Azerbaijan: namely Lezquis, Avars, Talishes, and Georgians. Azerbaijan not only needs to define its borders with its neighbors--Russia, Iran, Georgia, and Armenia--it also needs to settle its internal borders, because, if Karabagh becomes a flash-point, other minority resentment, which continues to simmer, is waiting for a spark to ignite it.

Armenians are sometimes led to believe that tiny Nagorno Karabagh, with its population of 150,000, is standing up to 7.5 million Azeris. In reality, Azerbaijan's population is not comprised of a monolithic ethnic group. If anything, the large size of the population has inversely affected the solidarity of its constituent minorities. Had Armenia been a strong country, she could have used that diversity to her advantage. But it is Russia, which still remains the regional superpower, that has been manipulating Azerbaijan's ethnic makeup for her own political ends, just as she implemented the same policy in Georgia to achieve her objectives.

Russia is determined to maintain her military presence in the Caucasus. The sooner the nations in the region understand this Russian resolve, the better for them. There also seems to be a tacit collusion between the superpowers to allow Russia to implement that policy, public rhetoric notwithstanding, as was amply demonstrated recently when an equation was drawn between the struggle in Nagorno Karabagh and, of all things, the invasion of Haiti! Armenians learned their bitter lesson in 1992, when Russian forces helped the Azeri forces (Omons) occupy one-third of Karabagh territory after Armenia's brief (albeit fruitless) flirtation with Turkey.

To break Shevardnadze's opposition to the Russian military presence in Georgia, Russia instigated Southern Ossetia to rise against Georgian rule in a quest to unite with Northern Ossetia, which is within the borders of Russia. But the Georgians suffered the most spectacular debacle later, at the hands of the Abkhazians, who, ironically, account for only 18% of Abkhazia's entire population, the majority of which is comprised of Georgians and Armenians. Today, after the Tblisi government gave in to Russian demands for a military presence in Georgia, Russia is mediating a settlement between Georgia and Abkhazia.

Since Armenia is more homogeneous ethnically, that divide-and-rule policy can hardly succeed there, although last year some Armenian demonstrators in Gumri, in the north, called for severing their relations with Yerevan and joining Russia!

Azerbaijan's ethnic makeup is ripe for a break-up under any application of outside political or military pressure, although that circumstance is seldom reported in the press. Professor Rosa Kaprielian, a staff member of *Azg*,[1] the most authoritative daily in Yerevan, recently published an article providing a few interesting facts and statistics about Azerbaijan's ethnic composition.

In addition to controlling Azerbaijan's oil resources, Russia is also vying for a military presence in that former Soviet Republic, with a specific interest in its borders with Iran and Turkey.

President Haidar Aliyev of Azerbaijan has been testing Russia's resolve on both issues--oil and border control--ever since he came to power through a military coup. So far Russia has been countering Aliyev's moves by manipulating the Karabagh conflict. But when Aliyev tried to work out a treaty with Iran on customs agreements and border traffic, an irate Moscow sent Walter Shenia, its ambassador in Baku, to Lenkoran, which is located on the Iranian border in the south, as a reminder to Baku that the powder keg in that region may blow up at any time. Indeed, on August 12, 1993 the Talish leader, Alekram Gumedov, had declared the region "the Independent Talish Republic of Mughhan." He was soon arrested and jailed, but the Talish minority has been restive ever since, awaiting an opportunity to free its leader from jail and rid itself of Baku's grip.

---

1. *Nation.*

The region along Azerbaijan's border with Russia in the north is populated by Avars and Lezquis, respectively 500,000 and 800,000 strong. Their kin across the border live in Daghestan, under Russian rule. They also have been agitating for independence, and the situation can conflagrate at any time, at Russia's whim.

Tucked between Georgia and Russia lies the province of Zakatala, which historically belonged to Georgia, and the majority of its population is comprised of Avars. The Georgians have never given up their desire to re-attach that historic piece of territory to their homeland. But every time the issue is raised by the authorities in Tbilisi, the Baku government counters that claim by agitating the Azeri minority in Georgia, forcing the Georgians to back down. Azerbaijan has also been using the Azeri minority in the Marneouli region of Georgia to sabotage gas pipelines that cross that area before entering Armenian territory, thereby making Georgia an unwilling partner or ally in the blockade of Armenia.

As we can see, Azerbaijan is fragmented and vulnerable to outside pressures. But the temptations of foreign oil deals are too great for her leaders to resist. Should Aliyev continue testing Moscow's patience by refusing Russian control of its borders and denying Russia the lion's share of oil resources, it is not impossible that Russia could use Azerbaijan's inherent weaknesses to break that republic up into several autonomous political units, whereby a new ball game might emerge in which all the liberated minorities might negotiate a loose federation with Baku. At that point they would share equal power with the Azeris. The Russian media have suggested many times that a federal system for Azerbaijan would be a way of satisfying all the restive minority groups in that country. It would also serve as a face-saving formula for the Baku leaders and would allow the Armenians in Karabagh to control their own destiny.

Unfortunately, the last round in the Karabagh conflict has yet to come.

November 5, 1994

Turkey under Siege

Despite Prime Minister Tansu Çiller's smiles at the Mediterranean and North African economic summit in Casablanca and during her visit to the Gaza Strip, where she purported to be playing a mediating role in the peace process, Turkey is a house on fire, plagued by many internal and external problems. Some of the external problems are extensions of the internal ones and vice versa.

Relations between the US and Turkey have been deteriorating and the two countries are perhaps on a collision course. Throughout the Cold War period, Turkey was spoiled by generous US assistance. With the collapse of the Soviet Union and the end of the Cold War, Turkey lost its significance as a strategic asset, a few lingering arguments in favor of its regional value notwithstanding. It became very obvious that Turkey was becoming more of a liability than an asset, particularly in regional conflicts. During and after the Gulf War, Turkey demanded billions of dollars from the US for her symbolic participation in the conflict. Ever since, Turkey has been spearheading the lobbying campaign at the UN and around the world to undermine UN resolutions on sanctions against Iraq. She has blackmailed the US into operating the pipeline from Iraq to the Mediterranean coast under the pretext of flushing the pipeline to prevent corrosion. Turkey has been openly violating the embargo against Iraq by sending 700 truck-loads of goods daily across her border with Iraq.

Another sticking point which has been straining relations between Turkey and the US is the raging war in Eastern Turkey against 16 million Kurds, all of whom have been labeled "terrorists" and sympathizers of the PKK (Kurdistan Workers' Party), whose 6000-8000 guerrillas have tied up the huge Turkish army with their hit-and-run tactics. Official figures have placed the number of victims at 13,000 since 1984, but in reality the casualties must run much higher. Indeed, who is there to do the counting? Foreign journalists and observers are banned from the region, where 1500 villages were recently torched and 1.5 million Kurds uprooted.

This war has been going on since the days of Atatürk, the founder of the modern Turkish Republic, and so far has claimed 1.5 million Kurdish lives. At the threshold of the 21st Century, a genocide of monumental proportions is being perpetrated, while the major powers look the other way.

The Turkish leaders have been using the same methods which their Ottoman ancestors used against the Armenian population early in the century, thumbing their nose at the world and giving the same argument: that the government is uprooting the majority of the Kurds for their own protection.

Of course, the world has forgotten the farce of the Turkish trials of the Kurdish Members of Parliament, after they had been stripped of their immunity.

In view of the absence of objective witnesses, the Turkish authorities have been fabricating every conceivable form of lies to justify their brutal actions. They have even alleged that the PKK guerrillas burned the Kurdish villages themselves, wearing Turkish military uniforms. Even Prime Minister Tansu Çiller has been participating in the fabrication of those lies, announcing that the culprits are Armenians who have been crossing the border in helicopters and helping the Kurds!

In this well-planned atmosphere of hysteria, carefully orchestrated in the press by the government, it is no wonder that Armenians in Istanbul have been receiving threatening letters from Turkish extremists.

Finally, the US government, under intense pressure from human rights groups, has acted with what can be construed as a slap on Turkey's wrist.

The US action consists of blocking the shipment of crucial military equipment to the Turkish armed forces, claiming that this equipment is being used in the military actions against Kurdish separatists in southeastern Turkey. The Defense Department has also objected to the delivery of missile-launching systems for Sikorsky and Black Hawk helicopters, with which the US recently supplied Turkey.

Additionally, the US government took minor but very significant legislative action by freezing 10 percent of Turkey's $364.5 million military aid package pending a human rights report. Some people might think that these actions are too little and too late, compared to the European outrage over the Turkish atrocities against the Kurds, but they are important even in their symbolism. Credit is due to human rights activist Kathryn Porter and her husband, Congressman Porter, who sensitized the US Congress and US public opinion in order to force such an action.

On the other hand, while Turkey is desperately trying to join the European Union, the European Parliament has suspended all contact with Turkey's parliament in protest against the trials of the pro-Kurdish political leaders. More than 336 cases of abuse by Turkish authorities are pending before the European Commission on Human Rights. Turkey's own independent monitor, the Human Rights Association, has compiled accusations of torture, electric shock, beatings, and ice-water showers during the maximum 15-day detention period allowed under Turkish law if no charges are laid. More than 600 people are detained each month. In recent years, more than 1200 murders have been carried out by Turkish security forces. The Turkish government has cynically allowed the publication of Kurdish or pro-Kurdish newspapers, only to eliminate their editors one by one at the hands of death squads.

It is ironic that Turkey has become more vocal in denying the right of self-determination to Karabagh Armenians and has laid a blockade against Armenia and Karabagh in an attempt to force the Armenians to relinquish their historic territories, while she still occupies 38% of Cypriot territory, under the pretext of protecting the Turkish minority there.

Last year, when I pointed out these contradictory Turkish policies to our State Department officials, I was told that that was one of the anomalies of international relations.

To offset its plaguing problems, the Turkish government undertook certain initiatives, with negligible results:

1. Following the Casablanca meeting, Mrs. Çiller visited Israel and the Gaza Strip and offered her country's support to the peace process. But apparently there were no takers. In the past, when Israel and her Arab neighbors were not on speaking terms, Turkey could have played--and indeed did play--a role as the only Muslim country with diplomatic ties to Israel. But today, when the Arabs are negotiating with their Israeli counterparts face to face, Turkey's offer and pretensions are superfluous;

2. The Turkish government opened the Atatürk dam on the Euphrates River with great fanfare and offered to sell some of her water resources to Israel and Saudi Arabia. The dam and the reservoir were built at the expense of Syria and Iraq. As soon as Syria signs a peace treaty with Israel, her attention will be turned back to Turkey, who, in addition to stealing Syria's share of the water resources, sits on a chunk of Syrian territory: in 1939 the Allies ceded the Syrian region of Hatay (Alexandretta) to Turkey as a bribe to discourage her from riding with emerging Nazi power in Germany. In time, water may become a hotter issue of dispute in the Middle East than oil;

3. Turkey invited the former Soviet Central Asian republics to Ankara in an attempt to achieve her pan-Turanian designs by wooing those republics away from Russia. Although the meeting officially deplored Russian political influence over those countries, Turkish officials went to great lengths to deny that the meeting was in fact directed against Russia. According to political observers, Turkey came away from that meeting empty-handed, having in the meantime caused severe irritation to Moscow. The conference could not even come up with a common stand on the Karabagh issue.

Turkey is in deep trouble. All of these political factors have had negative impacts on her economy, which is in shambles. Turkey is in no position to serve as a role model of democracy for the Central Asian republics, nor can it serve as a beacon of free-market economy for those emerging nations.

In view of Turkey's woes, Armenians may draw a few wrong conclusions. That would be a most dangerous approach, because nations in despair become more dangerous. They may attempt any risk in the region. As the Armenian saying goes, "The dying bear fights more fiercely in its waning hours."

November 19, 1994

CASPIAN SEA OIL:

A Blessing or a Blasphemy?

Armenians have been fighting for self-determination and historic rights on their own territory in Nagorno Karabagh, but the world does not give a damn about such noble stands. Armenians have came to realize, at a bitter cost, that there are factors over and above their right to live and to live free. One of those over-riding factors is the economic interests of neighboring countries or remote major powers who maintain an interest in the area. At stake today are the huge reserves of Caspian Sea oil, which Azerbaijan wishes to exploit for her own political ends in the short term and for her economic empowerment in the long term. After sealing the deal of the century with seven Western countries, Azerbaijan has positioned herself to reap the rewards of her natural resources. Turkey has been rallying the Western powers behind Azerbaijan in order to encourage the latter to stand up against Russian interests and pretensions in the region.

Thus, the UN and the world powers have drawn an equation between Azeri oil and the Armenian blood shed to achieve sovereignty in Nagorno Karabagh.

With the demise of the Cold War, Turkey lost her strategic significance in the region, but the leaders in Ankara see a residual conflict between the interests of Russia and those of the Western powers, and are trying to cash in on that, still maintaining the pretensions of a strategic asset for the West. The Turkish leaders have been crying wolf to the West, regarding Russian interests and actions in the Caucasus and Central Asia with little success, because the West still views those regions as legitimate zones of Russian influence, based on Moscow's security concerns. Unless the West intends to rekindle the Cold War or pursue a hot war with Russia, Turkey's warnings will fall on deaf ears. In the meantime, however, Turkey has been doing some poking of her own at Russia's soft underbelly, in the hope that the West may take a more resolute posture down the road.

Last October Turkey convened a meeting of the leaders of Azerbaijan, Turkmenistan, Kyrgyzstan, Uzbekistan, and Kazakhstan in

Ankara with a view to reviving the Pan-Turanian designs she inherited from the Ottoman era, and President Demirel of Turkey announced provocatively that since these were all independent states they did not need to get anybody else's permission to meet together.

Turkey has extended $800 million in assistance to Azerbaijan and has been training the latter's army in order to counter Russian meddling in the area and to boost Azerbaijan's intransigence in the Karabagh conflict.

For its part, Russia has made it clear that unless the former Soviet Republics respect her interests on her borders and "near abroad," there will be no peace in the region.

A major bone of contention is the exploitation of Caspian Sea oil. Although Russia's Lukoil has been awarded 10% of the deal, Moscow is raising legal hurdles, questioning Azerbaijan's right to exploit the oil deposits unilaterally now that the Caspian Sea has become an international body of water in which Iran, Russia, Kazakhstan, and Uzbekistan all have interests as well as Azerbaijan.

The second hurdle is the mode of delivery of that oil. Turkey and Azerbaijan have agreed to pump the oil to the Mediterranean seaport of Ceyhan and ship it by tankers to the West. At present Azeri oil can only be delivered through the Russian Black Sea port of Novorossiysk, which will further deteriorate the already congested shipping lanes at the Straits of Bosporus. To discourage Russia's insistence on that route, Turkish authorities staged a collision between a Greek tanker loaded with Russian oil and a freighter. The ensuing fire was dramatic enough to justify Turkish calls for more restrictions on Bosporus shipping traffic. Russia found the restrictions contrary to the Montreux Treaty on freedom of shipping through the Dardanelles, and countered Turkey's proposal with a new route through Bulgaria and Greece.

The most natural and economic route is to run a pipeline through Armenia. That is why Ankara and Baku, with some inspirational help from Paul Goble at the US State Department, have been trying, through alternately peaceful and warlike means, to slice a piece of territory off the southern tip of Armenia, which would allow them to achieve their designs without owing anything to the government in Yerevan. The capture by Karabagh of additional territory to her south has made that goal doubly impossible, as it expanded that sliver of Armenian controlled territory westward.

Of course, the Baku pipeline can be diverted through Iranian territory (which would meet with US opposition), or through Georgia:

the most unstable country in the region. Ignoring the impracticality of this latter option, President Demirel announced in Tbilisi on November 15, at the conclusion of his state visit to Georgia, that he would be very happy to see the pipeline go through Georgian territory. That announcement was probably intended only to annoy the leaders in Yerevan.

Armenia remains the only logical route. It seems that the West has been considering a combination of the Novorossiysk and the Armenian routes, for a number of reasons: 1. to cater to Russian interests (they also believe that since Armenia is Russia's most trusted ally, Moscow might buy the plan); 2. given the region's history of oil embargoes and the volatile nature of its politics and international relations, the West is carefully avoiding making itself the hostage of a single country for the reliable flow of oil; 3. the use of two pipelines would help reduce the congestion at the Bosporus Straits.

Meanwhile, it has been confirmed by private sources that the leaders in Baku and Ankara are not opposed so adamantly to the route through Armenian territory as their public postures might suggest.

The sooner the Karabagh conflict is settled, the better for the entire region. With the construction of a pipeline through Armenia, our energy-starved homeland would have access to an abundant source of oil, in addition to the fees she would receive from the oil consortium. And such a plan would prove a bonanza for Azerbaijan and Turkey, at the two ends of the pipeline.

Once these countries are locked into an economic relationship, any future blockade would be counter-productive.

If only the first logical step were taken, the remaining pieces would fall into place and the prospect of peace and prosperity would emerge.

As long as Turkey remains strong, the leaders in Ankara will continue encouraging Baku in its intransigence. And indeed Aliyev announced once again during his last visit to Turkey that no negotiation is possible until Karabagh withdraws its forces from all captured territories, including the Lachin humanitarian corridor and Shushi. That, of course, would mean suicide for the Armenian side, and will never happen. Aliyev knows that better than anyone.

With Turkey's internal convulsions (with the Kurds) and external confrontations (with the Greeks), Ankara may yet realize that it cannot afford to confront all of its neighbors, and may suggest a more conciliatory policy to Aliyev.

When all parties realize the economic bounty which might result from the present oil deal, perhaps they will see the light at the end of the tunnel and compromise.

Depending on the political course followed by the parties involved, Caspian Sea oil may prove either a blessing or a blasphemy.

December 3, 1994

All Thawing on the Western Front

After Girard Libaridian's[1] recent political swoop into Turkey, a few tangible prospects for a thaw in Armeno-Turkish relations have emerged. For the past two years Turkey has been whipping up mass hysteria against Armenia. Anything that went wrong in Turkey was blamed on the Armenians. And, contrary to some wishful thinking in the West, there is nothing approaching freedom of the press in Turkey, except perhaps for pornography. Turkish editors and columnists are masters at manufacturing outlandish lies or enhancing those provided by government agencies. To raise the ante, even Prime Minister Çiller at one point contributed to this mass hysteria, when she accused Armenians of allegedly crossing the border in helicopters and fighting alongside Kurdish guerrillas.

This campaign, of course, had two main purposes: (a) to justify to the international community the blockade imposed against Armenia; and (b) to distort the facts of the Kurdish fight for autonomy or independence, making the Turkish public believe that were it not for Armenian instigation, the Kurds would quietly submit to the genocidal policy that has been directed against them since the days of Atatürk.

Well today the atmosphere has calmed down, and the very same publications that were pointing fingers of accusation at Armenia are now calling for the normalization of relations between the two countries and are listing the benefits which both countries would reap if such a rapprochement could be achieved.

Of course, these changes were not achieved solely through President Ter Petrossian's and Girard Libaridian's diplomatic skills--which should not be underestimated--but are also the results of certain new factors in the political climate of the area. Armenia's president took advantage of those favorable developments.

Armenia's stability and economic reforms, which qualified her

---

1. *Senior political advisor to President Ter Petrossian.*

to receive international loans, certainly played a part, so much so that strategic planners in Moscow could bank on them and were able to conclude a treaty of military alliance for the next 25 years. A similar treaty with Georgia has been facing enormous hurdles.

This consolidation of Russia's strategic vanguard frustrates the Western appetite for the oil of Azerbaijan and Central Asia, which may become hostage to Moscow's will, should it fully consolidate its grip on the Caucasus and the areas beyond.

This prospect convinced the US to adopt a more pragmatic and determined approach towards its relations with Turkey and refrain from basing its policy on Turkish assumptions. When Deputy Secretary of State Richard Holbrook visited Turkey last month it seems that message was conveyed to Ankara.

The U.S. openly supported the Turks in certain policy areas which are crucial for Turkey and wrested some concessions on issues where Turkey has less to lose by conciliatory moves.

1. Turkey hoped to save its sagging economy by joining the European Customs Union. Washington supported Turkey, although itself not a member of the European Union.

2. The US continued to maintain its hands-off policy on the Turkish occupation of Northern Cyprus, which will mark its 21st anniversary next August. And negotiations towards the resolution of that complicated issue seem to lead nowhere.

3. Despite Turkey's abominable human rights record, Washington seems to have given her the green light to continue the murderous war against her 16 million Kurds, under the guise of eradicating terrorism. That war is costing the Turkish economy and US taxpayers $7 billion annually. It is a full-scale war and, that after the blatant murder of thousands of innocent civilians and the torching of hundreds of villages, can no longer be characterized as a fight against terrorism. Europe at least displayed some sense of moral outrage by criticizing Turkish atrocities, but the State Department continued "understanding" the need to slaughter innocent masses of civilians. Not surprisingly, a *Wall Street Journal* editorial called for more Kurdish blood, under the pretext of helping "a friend in need." The friend, of course, is Turkey. And of course with the racist and despotic government of Turkey as a friend, the US does not need any enemies in the region to tarnish its image. Indeed, too much "understanding" of Turkey's bloody actions can only breed further terrorism, as evidenced recently in a rash of Kurdish attacks on Turkish targets in Germany.

4. The U.S. government has already pledged its support to the plan which would make Yumurtalik, the Turkish port on the Mediterranean, a terminal for Azeri oil. Turkey was delighted with the news, which in its estimation will give her OPEC member status despite the fact that she has no oil reserves of her own. At the same time, Washington seems to have convinced Ankara to agree routing Azeri oil through Armenia.

Assuredly, in exchange for these compromises the US has demanded more lenient treatment of the Universal Greek Orthodox Patriarchate in Istanbul, at no cost to Turkey.

Washington has also convinced Ankara that it is not in the interests of the West, and certainly not in the interests of Turkey, that Russia should consolidate its permanent military presence in Armenia. The Armenian leaders in Yerevan would be wise not to trust all their political eggs to the Russian basket, and they are well aware of that.

The Humanitarian Corridor Act, which has gained some momentum in the US Congress, has really frightened the leaders in Ankara. At least that is what one gathers from the angry reaction of Nuzhet Kandemir, Turkey's Ambassador to Washington.

The US, then, is using a carrot-and-stick policy to guide Turkey along the path of its own interests.

The blockade of Armenia may also have proven to be counterproductive to Turkey, besides failing to bring Armenia to her knees. Indeed, voices of resentment that the blockade has also hurt Eastern Turkey, whose economy remains shaky at best, were first heard from the Mayor of the city of Kars and were later amplified in the Turkish media and Ankara political circles.

Before giving in to US pressure, Turkey had to be reassured on certain issues.

1. The genocide issue has haunted and will continue to haunt Turkey until she decides to come to terms with her own bloody past. Libaridian seems to have indicated that it is up to historians to determine the facts of that issue, which is what Turkish leaders wish to hear.

No matter how much we, as Armenians, hate the Turks for the genocide, we have to take a very objective view if we are to see our way clear. Armenia is in no position today to force Turkey to make an admission of guilt and immediately restore Armenia's historic territories. Should we press these issues, we would have to wage a full-scale war against Turkey, the outcome of which is all too obvious. As the French saying goes, vengeance is a dish that can only be eaten cold.

The leaders in Yerevan realize that they have a responsibility towards an Armenia which is in existence and lives today, and that its existence cannot be put at risk for the sake of a dream which is all too elusive at this point. This does not mean that Yerevan is selling the Western Armenian cause short, as suggested by some parties in the diaspora. Sometimes disturbing announcements have been made in Armenia. But those announcements must be understood in their political context.

The Turks are reading too much into President Ter Petrossian's decree banning the ARF in Armenia. They claim that the President took that action to please and appease Turkey, because Turkish leaders believe that the ARF is the political group which hates the Turks most. Given their history, the Turks cannot be blamed for having a short historical memory. In fact, when Armenia's First Republic fell under the full control of the ARF it leaned more towards Turkey and less towards Russia, so much so that after a visit to Istanbul Foreign Minister Alexander Khatissian publicly expressed his dismay that Western Armenians could not get along with "the gentleman Turks." In 1920, when the Turkish army advanced to Gumri (Alexandropol), the ARF-dominated government signed the Treaty of Alexandropol with General Kazim Karabekir, virtually disowning Wilsonian Armenia, at the very moment they were turning over the reins of government to the Soviets.[2] Even after the February, 1921 revolt, Vratzian directed his first appeal for help to Turkey; of course, the Turkish leaders did not lift a finger, allowing the internecine fight to claim 20,000 young Armenian lives.

It is abundantly clear, then, that should the opportunity arise, the ARF can be more pro-Turkish in the name of realpolitik than any other party.

2. Another issue which has strained Turkish-Armenian relations is the conflict in Karabagh. Until recently, the leaders in Ankara were in full support of the Baku position on the issue: that is, no deal until the Armenians relinquish all of the captured territories, including the Lachin corridor and Shushi. After Libaridian's visit to Turkey, some nuances in the respective positions of the two countries surfaced, and at one point Turkish officials blamed Baku for holding Turkish foreign policy hostage.

---

2. *See the two essays in the previous section of this collection "Armenia's Independence "Day" (p. 108) and "The Murderous Duplicity Continues..." (p. 137).*

As the occupying power in Cyprus, Turkey realizes that in any given negotiation 90% of the argument remains in the hands of the party which controls the territory; therefore, they do not expect Karabagh Armenians to give up any territory against vague promises of future good behavior. And every time Azerbaijan has tried to find a military solution to the conflict, it has lost more territory. At this point negotiations are progressing at a snail's pace, but at least a tenuous cease-fire is still holding, giving the Karabagh Armenians a breathing space.

The Turks have gone to great lengths to improve their relations with Armenia. They have allowed Alpaslan Turkes, the most violent representative of the Turkish right, to meet with President Ter Petrossian in an official capacity, knowing full well that the strongest reaction to a Turkish-Armenian rapprochement could come from Turkey's nationalist right.

Armenia needs to survive in order one day to achieve its ultimate historic goals. In order to survive today, some accommodations with her neighbors, including Turkey, are necessary.

Why did Germany acknowledge its guilt in the extermination of six million Jews? Because a) it was defeated and was weak; and b) because Germany is a civilized nation. Therefore, either we help Turkey attain European standards of civilization whereby she might come to realize the dimensions of the genocide perpetrated by the Young Turks, or Armenia may, in time develop into a regional superpower, which will be able to force Turkey to admit its guilt.

Neither option may seem very realistic, but we must keep both options open for possible historic developments.

Meanwhile, Armenia's frozen relations with Turkey seem to be thawing.

April 8, 1995

Part Three

CHURCH IN POLITICS & POLITICS IN CHURCH

Opposite page, the author with:
1. *His Holiness Vasken I.*
2. *His Holiness Karekin I.*
3. *Archbishop Khajak Barsamian.*
4. *Archbishop Shnork Kalousdian.*
5. *Archbishop Vatche Hovsepian.*
6. *His Holiness John Gregory Kasparian.*
7. *Archbishop Karekin Nercessian.*
8. *Reverend Krikoris Manian, Abbot.*
9. *Archbishop Kude Naccashian.*

The history of our Church in this century could have been described as spectacular, were it not so tragic. The following pages discuss decisive steps in that history. The criticism therein is recorded without malice, but with sincere pain.

Catholicos Karekin II of the Holy See of Cilicia, today Karekin I, Supreme Patriarch and Catholicos of All Armenians, has played a major role in the momentous events of the last forty years, and the essays in this book reflect that role, albeit not always under a positive spotlight.

A deep commitment to, and love of our Church history and traditions have been the guiding force behind the criticism. On a personal level, I have held the intellectual qualities of His Holiness in very high esteem. The crux of the matter has been Karekin II's struggle against the supreme authority of Holy Etchmiadzin. His election to the throne of the Supreme Patriarch is one of the most dramatic events in his own life and a unique and ironic reversal of our entire history. That change also upset all the equations of moral and legal principles.

In a personal letter not meant for publication, I discussed these dramatic events with His Holiness. The underlying theme of that communication was the role that His Holiness had played in recent years of our Church history. He had played that role with sincere conviction that he was acting in the best interest of the Armenian Church. He did not repent for those actions before or after his ascension to the throne of Etchmiadzin.

My criticism of those actions was equally sincere and based on the same principles of defending the Church; therefore, they should be entitled to the privilege of not requiring a retraction.

Following that letter, which His Holiness valued highly, a personal audience with him helped to turn a new page in our relations.

Edmond Y. Azadian

THE ARMENIAN APOSTOLIC CHURCH:

A Political Perspective

Religion and politics go hand in hand. They have always complemented each other and they have been used alternately to achieve the same objectives. Islam fueled the expansion of the Arab empire towards domination of most of the ancient world, just as Christianity was used to provide a noble guise to the crusaders, who intended to return to the Middle East as the ruling force. Inside the Christian world, the Inquisition provided the most effective tool any totalitarian regime has yet been able to devise for the subjugation of the individual to the absolute authority of the ruling class.

The Church and religion have played a more benign role among Armenians. If anything, the Church, at times, has substituted for the national government, but most of the time it has championed the preservation of the Armenian heritage. Over many long centuries, the Church has also served as the prime creator and preserver of Armenian literature and the arts.

Foreign rulers and enemies of the Armenian people have better understood and used the Church's political role than we have been able to comprehend and appreciate; thus, following his occupation of Constantinople in AD 1453, Ottoman ruler Fatih Sultan Mehmet encouraged and was actually instrumental in founding the Armenian Patriarchate of Constantinople, which played a prominent role in Armenian history for over half a millennium. Armenians did, indeed, enjoy the benefits of such an institution, but the primary goal of the Ottoman ruler was to create a competing Christian center which would weaken or overshadow the Universal Patriarchate of the Greek Orthodox Church in Constantinople.

Similarly, during World War I, when Armenians were deported from their ancestral land to the deserts of the Middle East and the last Catholicos of the House of Cilicia was exiled to Jerusalem from his historic See of Sis, Jemal Pasha forced Catholicos Sahak Khabayan to declare himself Patriarch of Jerusalem and Catholicos of All Armenians. He had a dual political purpose in mind for the move: to sever the umbilical cord which connected Armenians to the cradle of their Christian faith, and furthermore to prevent Eastern Armenians, and for that matter Russians who could work through Eastern Armenians, from influencing their brethren living in the Ottoman empire. Jemal Pasha was fully aware that most of the political movements and national liberation aspirations had originated in Eastern Armenia.

We could cite many other instances and examples where Church and religion have been used by foreign rulers to influence Armenian life politically.

Therefore, it would be naive to assume that the present state of affairs in the Armenian Church is not the direct result of the political undercurrents which influence our lives today. Indeed, the Armenian Church has become a casualty of the Cold War, and yet many factions have waved its ideological banners in passionate defense of their own positions.

The superpowers, in their overall onslaught to outwit and outdo each other, left no stone unturned. And the Armenian Church fell prey to that superpower rivalry. An already fragmented diaspora failed to demonstrate a collective national will to guard the Armenian Church from the spill-over of the Cold War. The only wise course would have been to stand united against outside pressures and rally around the Mother See of Etchmiadzin, in order to defend her from the encroachments of foreign totalitarian rule and to allow her to continue her inspirational historic mission in the lives of diaspora Armenians. Instead, battle lines were drawn and vehemently opposed groups clashed with each other, with catastrophic results for all.

Just as World War I was sparked by the assassination of an Austro-Hungarian archduke in Sarajevo, the war to dominate the Armenian Church broke out when the ARF (Armenian Revolutionary Federation) decided to assassinate Archbishop Ghevont Tourian in the Cathedral in New York in 1933. Of course, dissension within the Church had been long brewing, but that spark was sufficient to bring it to the surface. Today many people call for reconciliation; they advise magnanimity: to forgive and forget. Only the culprit remains unrepentant: no ARF leader has implored forgiveness. On the contrary, the assassination continues to be glorified as a "heroic act."

When a reconciliation is sought, the parties involved must recognize that a serious error lies behind all the quarrels and that unless historic wrongdoings are corrected with mutual cooperation and understanding, no real peace can be achieved or endure.

Today the prelacy in the US contends that its succession to the American-Armenian See is legitimate, and indeed there is superficial evidence to substantiate that claim. Following the assassination of Archbishop Tourian, the ARF took over the diocese through violence, and the original defenders of the Church had to hold their diocesan assembly at Hotel Martinique in New York in order to continue the mission of the Armenian Church in the United States.

The ensuing antagonism raged with consuming ferocity and the opposing factions sometimes resorted to extreme measures. Groups opposed to the ARF takeover reacted violently, and in fact some exaggerations were committed on this side of the fence as well. But that does not alter the fact that Armenians were divided into two major opposing camps as the ARF tried to dominate the Church and consequently Armenian life in the diaspora, and the majority of Armenians defended the Church against a political take-over. The Armenian Democratic Liberal Organization has been at the forefront of that defense force and has valiantly conducted the struggle against the political ambitions of the Dashnak Party (ARF). It is a fact, albeit one that is seldom recognized, that had it not been for the vigilance and leadership of the ADL in the United States, the ARF would have completed the take-over of the Armenian church in the 1930s. Thanks to the courageous leadership of people like Dr. H. Dzovickian and his fellow ADL delegates, the Armenian church in the United States was converted into an impregnable fortress. And no frontal assault was able to weaken or break the resolve of those who defended the primacy of the Mother See of Etchmiadzin.

The unrelenting Cold War did not spare the Armenians in Lebanon, and the ARF, taking advantage of the critical situation, moved forward to expand its hegemony over diaspora Armenians.

In 1956 no force could legally over-run the resistance of the Armenian masses who defended the Church. But tanks moved into the Antelias monastery compound and a sham election took place under the turrets of machine-guns: bullets spoke more loudly than ballots. Today, Karekin II embodies the perpetuation of that illegal act by Antelias. As of today, Catholicos Karekin II and his political patrons have not demonstrated any sign of national reconciliation, nor have they admitted to any wrongdoing. On the contrary, the Catholicos in Antelias is so intoxicated with his successful expansion that he dares declare himself co-equal to the Catholicos of All Armenians.

Once again the ADL leadership stood steadfastly with the forces of Etchmiadzin and aroused the masses to stop the flagrant acts of illegality. In the heat of the conflict, people were willing to throw themselves against the advancing tanks in defense of the Church. But bullets proved more persuasive than human flesh, and the Dashnak party took over Antelias.

Immediately following the "election" of Catholicos Zareh I in 1956, the dissident church in the United States linked up with Antelias, extending the illegality throughout the diaspora.

In addition to the political aims behind its design to take over the Church, the ARF leadership was taking out its frustration on the diaspora Armenians. In fact, that leadership was not able to maintain power in Armenia and tried instead to exercise its totalitarian policies through the Church, by reducing the clergy to a subservient group which would be ready to execute the orders of its political leaders. They were also required to use the Church as a conduit for funds to fill the coffers of the ARF.

While paying lip service to Etchmiadzin and to unity talks, the rulers in Antelias have not yet shown any desire to return to legality, nor have they given up their designs to expand into Canada, South America, and elsewhere.

In the legitimate camp of the Mother Church, the beneficiaries of the successful resistance to the Dashnak take-over were the clergy. They were spared the humiliating destiny of the clergy ruled by Antelias. Their freedom was maintained and they enjoyed decent family incomes, unlike the servants of the dissident church. But an ironic turn of events soured the situation. The ADL, which deserved only recognition for its organized defense of the Church and the clergy, suddenly became a target of attack by the same clergy, whose freedom had been saved from aggression. Suddenly, theories were developed which equated all political parties to each other. A number of spiritual leaders found ADL participation in the Church as reprehensible as the Dashnak designs for a takeover. A campaign was orchestrated to undercut the ADL presence in the Church. The same treatment was meted out to both the culprit and the defender of the Church, unmindful of the fact that only an organized and politically motivated force might serve as a counterweight to such a highly motivated group, which has mobilized a militant lay and religious following. The religious leaders were successful in undercutting the ADL involvement in the Church, to their own detriment. History will record that this ill-conceived philosophy was the brainchild of a brilliant clergyman, Archbishop Tiran Nersoyan. It would make an interesting study to research and analyze the life of this, most erudite spiritual leader of his time, a life which nevertheless proved to be a series of tragic failures. His philosophy continues to gain momentum within the Church, demobilizing the clergy and resulting in utter confusion. The lay and clerical followers of that philosophy are not strong enough to defend the Church, but they are strong enough to keep the defenders away. Our clergy do not seem to possess either the resolve or the motivation to use the pen or pulpit in order to educate their parishes concerning the historic causes of the current disunity within the Church. This complacency has already born bitter fruit, encouraging people with a limited knowledge of historical facts to act on behalf of our Church and shortsell it to a highly motivated camp which has not yet abandoned its political plans for the Church. From primates to parish priests, few clergymen are willing and able to conduct the defense of the Mother Church.

It was a welcome breath of fresh air to see a young, talented, and knowledgeable clergyman, in the person of Rev. Yeznik Balian, take up the challenge and expose, through historic perspective and legal dialectics, the fallacy behind the concept of the "Two Catholicoi."

Where does the Church stand at this historic juncture? Unfortunately, our future seems darker than our past. The restoration of democratic rule in Armenia has encouraged all sorts of sects to penetrate the spiritual substrata of the Armenian people's conscience. Antelias has also taken advantage of the situation: hand in hand with the ARF, Antelias has been bribing its way into Armenia. This state of affairs will reverse the situation completely: the challenge will no longer be to defend the diaspora churches for Etchmiadzin, but the unity and sanity of the entire Armenian Church around the world.

It is incumbent upon our clergy to recognize the gravity of the situation and to act vigilantly and courageously. They must be prepared to fight with the very same weapons which their regimented antagonists have been using in their unholy war, or they must seek the advice and cooperation of groups that have demonstrated their competence.

And this can be done by our clergy without any inhibition.

November 2, 1991

CATHOLICOS VAZKEN I

Discusses Church Unity and the Role of Religion in Armenia

The following is an interview with His Holiness Vazken I, Catholicos of All Armenians, conducted at Holy Etchmiadzin on January 10, 1991

Q. *How would Your Holiness describe relations between the State and the Holy See now that Armenia enjoys new statehood and our country is on the threshold of democratic change?*

A. Relations between the new independent government of Armenia and the Holy See of Etchmiadzin are very normal and cordial, full of mutual respect and understanding. We are consoled by the fact that those who now occupy the highest positions in the government are faithful members of the Apostolic Church and have great respect for the spiritual and moral principles of Christianity.

Q. *Armenia is now experiencing a spiritual reawakening. What is the Holy See doing in this respect?*

A. Indeed our people, including the youth and the intelligentsia, are experiencing an amazing spiritual reawakening. They are thirsty for the eternal truth of the Holy Bible; people truly worship the Mother Church. Under these circumstances, it is up to our Church and our clergymen to meet the spiritual needs of our faithful children.

Although there are not very many clergy at present, we do our best to give spiritual guidance to our people. The primates as well as all our priests are working hard and with dedication. Under the auspices of the Mother See, a Christian Mission Center has been opened in the diocesan center of St. Sarkis Church, in Yerevan. Most of the operating churches now have Sunday schools, and women's guilds and Christian youth associations are being formed. Religion is now being taught in the elementary schools. Armenian television broadcasts religious programs every Sunday, prepared under the supervision of the Holy See, and a one-hour religious program is offered every month.

Q. *Do you have similar plans for the Soviet diaspora[1] and has there been progress in this sphere?*

A. The same situation can be found in the Soviet diaspora-- Georgia, the Northern Caucasus, and Russia. In scores of cities and villages with Armenian populations there are now active community and cultural associations which are striving to reopen churches or build new ones. In the Soviet diaspora, which comprises more than 1.5 million Armenians, the national-religious reawakening is robust. We are currently planning the creation of two or three new dioceses there.

Q. *The demand for ordained priests is great. How is the seminary of the Holy See coping with it?*

A. The training and preparation of priests are our number-one priorities. We have placed our hopes in the Seminary of Holy Etchmiadzin, where 120 seminarians are currently enrolled. Preparatory classes have also been established in the monasteries of Sevan and Haghpad, with a total of 30 enrollments. We hope that the number of students will increase and that in the near future we will have new generations of clergymen. It is most encouraging for us to note that a great many high school graduates are eager to enroll in the Seminary.

Q. *Has there been any progress in the preparation of a constitution for the Armenian Church?*

A. Work on a structural constitution for the Armenian Church began years ago. Committees of bishops, headed by the late Archbishop Tiran Nersoyan, have worked on it for the past ten years and have come up with more than one outline. We believe that work on this project will continue, and that a final draft will be ready in the near future. In the meantime, we need a set of canon laws to regulate religious life and activity in the Republic of Armenia and the Soviet diaspora. Under the prevailing new and favorable conditions in the country, we have the opportunity to prepare such a set of canons. Moreover, a draft has already been prepared and the Supreme Ecclesiastical Council of the Holy See has examined it. We hope that in the coming few months we will have a final set of canons and regulations.

Q. *Have you ever thought of a co-adjutor Catholicos?*

---

1. *I.e, Armenians living in other parts of the former Soviet Union.*

A. The Catholicosate of Holy Etchmiadzin does not have a tradition of co-adjutor Catholicoi.

Q. *What is the current status of relations between Holy
Etchmiadzin and Antelias?*[2]

A. It is well known that at present the Mother See of Etchmiadzin
has fraternal and cordial relations with the See of Cilicia in Antelias.
Those relations, on the level of Catholicoi, proceed on a normal course.

Q. *Taking into consideration that unexpected and public meetings
and announcements have caused considerable confusion among the leadership and the faithful in the diaspora, whose dioceses are in the jurisdiction
of Etchmiadzin, what steps are being planned to dispel that confusion and
to prevent future misunderstandings? Moreover, has Antelias expressed any
willingness to return to Holy Etchmiadzin the dioceses it unjustly usurped?
If yes, which dioceses and under what conditions? If no, how can Church
unity be achieved and maintained?*

A. We are aware of the existence of such confusing sentiments in
the diaspora, especially in America, and are truly concerned about it; yet at
the same time we believe that it is a temporary and passing phase. The
faithful and clergy of both Holy Etchmiadzin and the Cilician See must
exert every effort to dispel such confusing thoughts. We believe the reason
for this confusion is that some people view Etchmiadzin-Antelias relations
in the light of old presumptions and therefore do not realize that the
objective situation has now basically changed. Beginning in 1956, the
Cilician See adopted its well-known tactics and spread its influence over
certain dioceses, as a result of the political reservations it had towards Soviet
rule in Armenia. But with the proclamation of independent statehood and
the establishment of a multi-party system, everything has basically
changed. All three political parties of the diaspora are now present here and
function freely. There are no political reservations. Therefore, there is now
no basis for the old misunderstandings and the relations between
Etchmiadzin and Antelias need to be viewed under new conditions.

The political parties no longer need the Church as a support;
their support is now Armenia. And, of course, the Armenian people. The
Church does not side with one, single political party; it sides with all,
because it believes that the members of all parties equally are the children
of our nation and of the Mother Church.

In a democratic and multi-party society, the Church functions

---

2. *The Holy See of Cilicia is headquartered in Antelias, Lebanon.*

on the religious-spiritual level and performs its unifying mission, loyal to the popularly elected government of a sovereign state. The Armenian people as a whole have one Mother Armenia acceptable to all, and one, indivisible Armenian Apostolic Church. The See of Cilicia is a historical and local see within this indivisible Church structure and within the confines of its historic jurisdiction; clergymen anywhere in our Church can function with the blessing of Holy Etchmiadzin, while maintaining their membership in the brotherhood of the Cilician See.

We are confident that the time has come for the elimination of the confusing and complicated conditions now prevailing in regard to the diaspora dioceses, on the basis of the principle of one indivisible Church. There are at present no political or other reasons for the continuation of separations from the Holy See such as those witnessed during the past decades, especially in Iran and Greece. The situation is, of course, more complicated in North America. We believe that the unity committees there must continue their negotiations, while we and the head of the Cilician See work together for the restoration of the canonical unity of the Church, with a formula acceptable to both sides. But above all, it is necessary that all of us discard, completely and for good, our old habits of thinking and acting.

Q. *Can Your Holiness tell us about the meeting in Belgium and the consequent developments?*

A. Our meeting in Belgium with Karekin II, Catholicos of the See of Cilicia, on the occasion of the consecration of a church, strengthened our brotherly cooperation, which is based on the principle of one indivisible Church.

Q. *We in the diaspora have the impression that Holy Etchmiadzin is not reacting forcefully to the activities of various sects.*

A. We are of course concerned that with the establishment of democratic rule various sects have found in Armenia a fertile ground for their activities. We find this to be an unhealthy situation for religious and national unity. These sects have been introduced into Armenia from abroad and are financed from there. Our clergymen actively proclaim the truth to the faithful and call on them to be wary of alien influences. We personally have made similar appeals in the Armenian Parliament and on Yerevan television. It is necessary to continue this work seriously and with patience.

February 2, 1991

Beware of the Bear Hug

Armenia has been in turmoil since its independence; old structures have been falling apart, yet no new structures are in sight. A sorry state of confusion has been reigning in all areas. And since the diaspora traditionally takes its cue from Armenia, the same confusion has also been influencing our lives.

With the end of the Cold War, our divided Church has also been subjected to pressure for realignment. Yet before any internal issue is addressed, the Church in Armenia is faced with new challenges: a wide assortment of sects, religions, and denominations has invaded Armenia, and the general state of chaos has served as a fertile breeding ground for all brands of "saviors" who claim to have the prescription for our people's redemption. The Armenian Church is ill-prepared to deal effectively with this onslaught.

For more than seventy years it was very convenient for Soviet authorities to deal with the Church through a single authoritarian ruler, reducing all institutions to symbols. And before those institutions could reorganize to assert themselves, our octogenarian supreme spiritual leader is faced with a host of pressing problems, which have overtaxed his energies.

Thus, all kinds of external and internal challengers have been taking advantage of the sorry state of affairs to gain a foothold in Armenia's spiritual life.

As if the Armenian Republic and Holy Etchmiadzin did not have enough problems, a Patriarchal encyclical has been released by the Armenian Catholic Patriarch, Hovhannes Bedros XVIII Kasparian, denouncing the Armenian Apostolic faith as an unorthodox brand of Christianity and announcing a "return of Armenia" to his Church, promising to bring back the "true light" of Christianity to the Armenian people, who, for all practical purposes, would prefer a few loaves of bread in these dreary times to any brand of Christianity.

To force a religious war upon Armenia in this most crucial period is the most insensitive and reckless act that anyone could conceive! The Catholic battle cry could not have come at a worse time.

A reaction by the Holy See at Etchmiadzin had to be expected as the most natural response. The Holy See had to mobilize its flock and defend itself. Thus, an appeal was issued warning all Armenians of the many dangers threatening their faith. The appeal condemns religious intrusions of all sorts, but focuses mainly on the intentions of the Catholic Church.

Unfortunately, the appeal is as awkward and inappropriate as the challenge itself. Indeed, it raises more questions than it solves, and in fact opens a can of worms.

A more restrained response and behind-the-scenes quiet diplomacy would certainly have achieved better results than this ill-prepared response, which was pressed upon His Holiness Vazken I by Catholicos Karekin II of Antelias, whose signature is also superfluously appended to that of His Holiness Vazken I.

One wonders: why the rush to react, and to react unprepared? Following the release of that appeal, a superficial editorial also appeared in the official publication of the Holy See, *Etchmiadzin* (it was also faxed to all Armenian papers for reprinting), and a cable was dispatched to the Vatican, declaring the Armenian Catholic Church "unwelcome in Armenia."

On the face of it, one is at a loss to comprehend this haste and the confrontational posture, at a time when our Church has not yet been able to put her own house in order. Representatives of all kinds of esoteric religions had been invading Armenia for four years, yet Etchmiadzin had been slow to react.

The participation of Catholicos Karekin II in the crusade sheds some light on the motivation behind this conduct. This imprudent reaction promotes the ulterior motives of Antelias. Unfortunately, His Holiness Vazken I chose to depend mainly on the judgment of Karekin II, who has his own agenda, notwithstanding Armenia's tragic situation.

Karekin II ensnared Holy Etchmiadzin for a number of reasons:

1. To lock Etchmiadzin into a conflict with the Catholic Church, thus diverting attention from the internal divisions of our Church, which are long overdue for a solution;

2. By affixing his signature on the appeal next to that of His Holiness Vazken I, Karekin II achieves de facto status in our Church, impressing upon her followers that the Church is run by two co-equal heads: a status for which he has been clamoring for a long time, ever since he declared Antelias to be an autocephalous church.

The fact that the two signatures appear together is, however, far from denoting or inspiring unity. In fact, it rather perpetuates the duality in leadership which has plagued our Church for far too long.

Ironically, the issue in question concerns a problem in Armenia

proper, where Antelias has no business even to intervene. It is not surprising that several high-ranking clergymen have protested Karekin II's
signing of the appeal, some of them publicly.

3. This swift and unthoughtful reaction has also brought to the
surface the rivalry which exists between Karekin II and Armenian Catholic
Patriarch Kasparian, who, quite apart from his ill-advised encyclical, stood
tall during the Lebanese civil war, protecting the Armenian community
from several attempts at mass slaughter. He has also been instrumental in
obtaining the release of kidnapped Armenians through his connections
and political clout, which Antelias and Karekin II lack.

Above all, throughout the crisis in the Church, the Armenian
Catholic clergy in general have leaned towards Antelias more often than
not, based on a shared policy against Soviet rule in Armenia. But
Catholic Patriarch Kasparian has put the national interest above political expediency and has steered his Patriarchate away from the influence
of Antelias, pursuing a rather independent course, and this has touched
a raw nerve at the Cilician See.

Today, in his Byzantine scheme of politics, Karekin II is trying to
settle scores with the Catholic Patriarchate at the expense of Etchmiadzin,
regardless of the consequences to the Armenian Church as a whole.

Unfortunately, decisions are still made in Etchmiadzin at the
personal rather than the institutional level, and they are therefore vulnerable to outside pressure. It seems that through flattery and cunning
Karekin II has been able to paralyze the decision-making process and
impose his will on Etchmiadzin, driving the latter into a confrontation
course with the Catholic Church, all under the guise of "brotherly cooperation" and unity between the heads of the Armenian Church, when a
single head would be amply sufficient.

If Antelias and Catholicos Karekin II are seriously interested in
the unity of the Church, all they have to do is demonstrate a measure of
tolerance towards the communities in the diaspora which have so far
refused their dominance, promote the concept of a single Church
authority, and discontinue their challenges to that authority within the
framework of the World Council of Churches.

While our Church is direly in need of unity and reform to be able
to withstand all outside onslaughts, Catholicos Karekin II seems to be on
an ego trip, riding his Trojan Horse into the Etchmiadzin compound.

The young leadership of the Armenian Church has become
increasingly alarmed at the influence which Antelias has lately been
exerting on His Holiness Vazken I, to the detriment of the Holy See at

Etchmiadzin. That is why that young leadership took upon itself the responsibility of mending fences with the Vatican and shifting our Church's course from confrontation to conciliation. And they have done a masterful job.

Archbishops Vatché Hovsepian and Khajak Barsamian, the Primates of the Armenian Church in America; Bishop Hovnan Derderian, Primate of the Armenian Church in Canada; and Bishop Mesrob Mutafian, representing the Armenian Patriarchate in Istanbul, undertook a peace mission to the Vatican. The message they carried was the most dignified and scholarly anyone has seen in recent years. It addressed the core issue of the conflict with an analytical approach which placed the historic and theological differences between the two Churches in perspective and suggested that they could be bridged in today's ecumenical spirit. In context and style, this document elevated the position of the Armenian Church to that of statesman-like bargaining. Would that all of the recent polemical communications released by Etchmiadzin had been conducted on the same thoughtful level!

The delegation was cordially received by Pope John Paul II, who distanced the Vatican from the controversy, expressed his regret over the incident, and promised to take up the issue at a forthcoming conference with the hierarchy of the Armenian Catholic Church.

From the beginning, the entire purpose of the commotion had been to reach just such a solution, but what could not be achieved through confrontation was made possible through diplomacy.

Always overly concerned with Antelias' partisan interests, Catholicos Karekin II tried to either jump on the bandwagon or else derail the mission, by pressuring His Holiness Vazken I to include Antelias in the delegation. But fortunately, thanks to our vigilant clergy, it was too late for Antelias either to destroy the chance of a reconciliation or to take credit for it. This accomplishment brought home the fact that our clergy is eminently qualified to defend our Church, without any help from Antelias.

The leadership of the Armenian Church is at a crossroads. Recent events demonstrate that the younger generation of our Church leadership must make a determined and assertive effort to institutionalize the decision-making process at the highest levels of the Church and to prevent Etchmiadzin from falling victim to the selfish interests of over-ambitious adversaries disguised as "brothers in Christ."

Beware the bear hug.

November 21, 1992

Assistant to the Supreme Spiritual Leader

Since 1955 the Armenian Church has experienced turbulent times, through which our young and dynamic supreme spiritual leader, His Holiness Vazken I, has steered our Church skillfully and with the utmost dedication.

But in recent years turmoil and uncertainty have hit our homeland, creating an extremely complex situation for our Church. Suddenly, the challenges became overwhelming: in addition to the problem of the division within the Church, a spiritual revival in Armenia called for the full attention of the leadership at Etchmiadzin. Additionally, the need for a Church constitution, the shortage of clergy, the reorientation of the Church under a democratic rule, and many crying needs overtaxed the energies of our aging Catholicos, whose deteriorating health became a national concern.

Although still alert and in full control of his mental abilities, His Holiness realizes that he is too overburdened to carry out the responsibilities facing him. Therefore, he has demonstrated his wisdom by looking for assistance. To be more specific, for some time now he has been considering the appointment of a vicar general to oversee day-to-day operations at Etchmiadzin. This would also smooth the leadership transition which our Church will ultimately face.

A host of Church problems needs to be addressed immediately, since they have been waiting for a solution for a long time and creating a sense of desperation in the ranks of the clergy.

The recent convocation of bishops in Etchmiadzin has seriously studied this issue; however, no nomination was put forward, allowing more precious time to lapse before the Church gets back to its business seriously.

Competition among the clergy, jealousies, and pre-election posturing may all delay the long-overdue resolution of this problem. But His Holiness has to make up his mind before things get out of hand.

And the sooner the better.

October, 1993

As the Curtain Falls

After a long and agonizing illness, His Holiness Vazken I last week entered into his eternal rest, leaving behind a remarkable forty-year legacy which will have an impact on our religious life for many years to come.

He had a meteoric rise on the troubled horizon of our Church history. He was a young, inexperienced, and unknown celibate priest from Romania, who took his historic mission seriously and served the Church well, guiding it unscathed through the most turbulent of times. It will be some time before scholars gauge his place in history, but that place will certainly be prominent. Many articles, stories, memoirs, and accounts will no doubt flood the Armenian press, all eulogizing the Patriarch and trying to assess his valuable contributions to our Church. As I ponder on his illustrious life, I find my thoughts turning to the first year of his forty-year tenure, when he rushed to Beirut, Lebanon to put out a brush fire which threatened the life of our entire Church. The Holy Muron still fresh, glistening on his forehead, in the aftermath of his elevation to the throne of St. Gregory the Illuminator, *Vehapar*[1] arrived in Antelias to pacify passions and to find an equitable solution to a debate raging around the Cilician See, which was threatened by a political takeover. The Lebanese police and army, complete with tanks and armored cars, had taken positions around the Cathedral, where a so-called "democratic election" was to take place and a candidate hand-picked by a political party was to be thrust on the Armenian Church. The young *Vehapar* could hardly realize that the political tentacles which imposed an unwanted Catholicos reached far beyond Lebanon. As he negotiated a compromise solution, he believed that he was talking to Armenians of good faith, who had the best interests of our Church at heart. His voice was most inspiring and convincing. But the die was cast, and Vazken *Vehapar* was to experience the first shocking disappointment of his career.

He had been received in Lebanon like royalty, but within a week he left the country like a defeated general.

I remember his first sermon from the pulpit of the Cathedral in Antelias, which was jam-packed. Loudspeakers blasted his trembling voice

---

1. *His Holiness.*

to the flock gathered in the courtyard. That day I was covering my first journalistic assignment: to record *Vehapar's* sermon. With no dictaphone, without even a decent pen in my hand, I placed my note-pad on the grave of Catholicos Karekin I and tried to capture the sermon verbatim. My editor was satisfied. The sermon appeared in the next issue of the *Zartonk²* daily, together with an emotional welcoming article under my byline. I felt so flattered and overwhelmed when, months later, I found my article reprinted in *Etchmiadzin*, the official monthly of the Holy See. Out of the dozens of journalists who had covered the occasion, I had been the lucky one chosen to have his article reprinted. That was the first encouragement that His Holiness extended to me, albeit indirectly, perhaps believing that he was selecting the piece of an experienced writer.

Since then, our paths have crossed in Cairo, Etchmiadzin, Paris, the US, and all over the globe. I developed a personal fondness for His Holiness which went beyond esteem for him as the supreme spiritual head of our Church.

Vazken *Vehapar* will occupy a unique place in Armenian history. He rose to a thorny throne, during the cruelest years of Soviet rule, and he was able to steer our Church with wisdom and courage. At times he was accused of being a Kremlin lackey and he was unjustly blamed for many misdeeds, but he kept his dignity and went on with his constructive missions. He was able to convince the ruthless Kremlin leaders to have the present Veharan (the official residence of the Catholicos) returned to the Holy See. That building was under construction, through the generosity of a renowned Armenian benefactor, Alexander Mantashef, during World War 1, when it was taken over by the Russian army and converted into a military hospital, and it was used as such until the election of Catholicos Vazken. He was also able to regain control of the Gevorgian Seminary, which was reopened for the training of young clergy under the strictest government control.

Vazken *Vehapar* will be remembered in our Church as a great builder. His reign was characterized by a zeal for construction and reconstruction within the Etchmiadzin compound, which became an oasis of serenity, meditation, and religious inspiration amid the chaos of atheism which was rampant in the country. One of his spectacular feats was to find a home for over forty crates of religious artifacts, vestments, and hangings which were saved from Western Armenia during the genocide,

2. *Awakening, revival.*

brought to Etchmiadzin, moved to Moscow for safe-keeping during World War II, and eventually returned to Armenia. His Holiness appealed to another prominent benefactor, namely Alex Manoogian, to build the magnificent Alex and Marie Manoogian Museum, the modern structure which was a perfect match for the centuries-old buildings and Cathedral of Holy Etchmiadzin. In all he built or renovated four museums in the Etchmiadzin compound and undertook the renovation of many historic monasteries and churches throughout Armenia.

He will also be remembered as a peace-maker. Unfortunately, his ascension to the throne of St. Gregory the Illuminator coincided with a schism brought about by the forces of the Cold War. Throughout his rule he went to great lengths to heal the split and reunify the Church. At times he even compromised principles in an attempt to attain his goal, but to no avail. He even traveled to Jerusalem in 1963 for the famous "Jerusalem Embrace" with Catholicos Khoren (appropriately named "The Black Candle" of our Church by the late Patriarch of Constantinople, Archbishop Karekin Khatchadourian) of Antelias--an embrace which bestowed legitimacy on the latter's illegal election--but he failed to gain any concessions in return.

All along, the leaders of the dissident church argued that they had divided the Church in order to fight Communism. And when the division continued even after the collapse of the Soviet Empire, which liberated Armenia from Communist rule, it was hard for our *Vehapar* to understand the persistence of cold-war positions. "There is no Communism any more; why do you keep the occupied dioceses under your control?" he would ask rhetorically in a trembling voice. He undertook many initiatives to bring about a reconciliation with the leaders in Antelias, but it seemed that they were exploiting his good intentions in order to perpetuate the split and thus further the political agenda of their overlords.

His Holiness Karekin II has had a profusion of praise for His Holiness Vazken and the Mother See of Etchmiadzin on many occasions, but he has never shown any intention of giving up his cold-war booty: the churches and dioceses usurped from Etchmiadzin through political machinations.

Many high-ranking clergy were alarmed when Vazken I promoted Karekin II of Antelias in the past few years, even though the promotion was purely symbolic. Nevertheless, no one dared lodge a public criticism, and private expressions of concern led nowhere.

Painful as it was for me, even at the expense of alienating our beloved *Vehapar*, whom I respected and admired, I believed that I had to write an article which would sound the alarm and awaken our Holy Father from the misguided illusions which he was fed.

I knew that he would least expect a dissenting voice from me, who had faithfully admired him for 38 years. Unpalatable as it was, the article served its purpose and encouraged other high-ranking clergy to gather courage and become more vocal in their warnings. The Trojan Horse which Antelias was riding was stopped half-way.

I learned that at first His Holiness had commented bitterly on the article, but as time passed and other voices of caution joined the chorus, he probably realized that the unpopular step was designed for the good of our Church and for real unity and harmony within our Church. I witnessed that change of heart last November, when I visited him in Etchmiadzin. He was a most gracious host and he had a forgiving fatherly smile as he received me.

When I went to Etchmiadzin this past March I did not realize that I would be making my last visit to His Holiness. But he somehow felt that the end was near. After the official visit he invited me to his residence in Yerevan, the Villa as it is called, for an intimate chat over tea. "I have something important to discuss with you," he added mysteriously.

As I sat across from *Vehapar* sipping my tea, the room was illuminated behind him, framing his saintly head almost in a golden halo. He was in a very cheerful mood. He began telling about his life in Romania, where he had been a teacher. "I thought I had been born to be an educator," he continued. But circumstances led him to become a celibate priest--"almost reluctantly," he added with a grin. "Then a few years later I was nominated as a candidate for the Catholicosate of All Armenians. I was not ready for that position; I did not want to become Catholicos. I remember even making a few anti-Soviet criticisms in order to discourage the authorities from considering my candidacy. But somehow they had confidence in me, and I was elected the first servant of our Church." In a few short minutes he reminisced about his entire life, sometimes as if talking to himself or thinking out loud.

After almost forty years, the man who reluctantly became a priest and reluctantly rose to St. Gregory's throne, the man who served his Church and his people with the utmost dedication and distinction, has left behind his "golden footsteps" in the annals of our church.

Today, as the curtain falls on that illustrious life, an entire nation bows in awe to his memory and his cherished legacy.

August 27, 1994

CATHOLICOS KAREKIN II:

An Ironic Twist of Destiny

As debate rages about the election of the Catholicos to the throne of St. Gregory the Illuminator at Etchmiadzin, many questions still remain to be answered before the most deserving clergyman for the office can be determined. Therefore, at this late period in the campaign there is no clear candidate for the office: pros and cons may be cited for each potential candidate.

But it is clear who should not be allowed to rise to that position: His Holiness Karekin II, the Catholicos of the Illustrious See of Cilicia, not because of any lack of talent or for personal misconduct, but because of the ill-conceived policies he has meticulously pursued over the past decades. He is certainly one of the most deserving Armenian clergymen alive: a theologian and a scholar, an administrator and a PR man par excellence. But he has used all of his talents, not to serve the Armenian Church, but to put the Armenian Church at the service of a single political party, causing dissension and division in the Church and within the Armenian communities around the world. All along his contention had been that he was fighting Communism or the Soviet rule of Armenia. But once that rule collapsed he did not exhibit any change of heart or moderation in his conduct. The dioceses which were usurped from the Mother See during the cold-war years were not returned to their rightful jurisdiction, nor were any concessions made to the groups within the Antelias camp which opposed political domination of the Church. All this because the political group with whom he had thrown in his lot was not in power in Armenia. All he did was play up to the weaknesses of the aging and ailing Catholicos Vazken I, making him believe that true concessions and conciliation were forthcoming. That may have added more confusion to an already complex situation within the Armenian Church.

Karekin II has therefore disqualified himself as a candidate. He cannot be elected for a number of reasons:

1. Never in our history has a Cilician Catholicos been elected to the throne of Etchmiadzin;

2. It would be almost a paradox if a clergyman who has cam-

paigned against Etchmiadzin all his life were to ascend to that very same throne;

3. His hypothetical election would not cause him to change or give up his affiliation with the political party with which he has been identified. He would continue to serve the narrow interests of that party and, more importantly, would use the means and the prestige of his office to bring that party to power in Armenia;

4. Some intellectual circles in Armenia, impressed by the eloquence of Karekin II on the TV screen, believe that he would make a good Catholicos and could heal the division in the Church. These naive people are, of course, in for an unpleasant surprise, because the political party which controls the reins at Antelias has more deadly secret weapons in its arsenal: clergy who would promote the party's interests even more vehemently than the incumbent Catholicos, to the detriment of our Church.

Even in this country, there are people who believe that the departure of Karekin II from Antelias might reduce that See to the status of a Patriarchate, and consequently resolve the issue of division in the Church without further conflict. But no one has indicated that such a resolution is indeed being planned, certainly not Catholicos Karekin himself. It would be hard, even impossible, to convince any involved Armenian that such a scenario is plausible.

Although recent events in Armenia have dramatically reduced the chances of Karekin II, one never knows what might happen at election time.

Unfortunately, the situation that has emerged is very similar to that which existed on the eve of the 1956 "election" at Antelias, when clergymen traditionally loyal to Etchmiadzin were engaged in in-fighting, inadvertently paving the way for the single candidate promoted by the Dashnak party. Thus that party, using the illegal ballots in its control and the bullets of then-President Camille Shamoun--who had made this election a linchpin of his Cold War policy--were able to impose a Catholicos on Antelias who was opposed by the majority of the Armenian people and the clergy. Karekin II inherited that imposition and tried very hard to legitimize it. To his credit, he succeeded to a certain degree.

Today the clergy in the Etchmiadzin camp are once again engaged in their perennial power struggle and, with fewer than three months before the election, they have not been able to come up with a single viable candidate, leaving the way open for Karekin II to throw his hat into the ring at the most appropriate psychological moment.

Therefore, wisdom has to dominate and the right candidate must soon appear if a catastrophe is to be avoided.

Catholicos Karekin II has been cultivating his image in Armenia in a most careful and subtle way, waiting in the wings for the right moment. It is not impossible that one or more delegates under his spell may promote his candidacy during the election. After all, nomination to the office is open to all high-ranking clergymen.

On the other hand, it is a sad commentary and an ironic twist of destiny that one of the most deserving clergymen should disqualify himself because of a lifelong pursuit of wrong and misguided policies.

January, 1995

THE ELECTION IN ETCHMIADZIN:

Tempest in a Teapot or Global Political Chess Game?

Those who believe that the uproar following President Ter Petrossian's decision to step into the election process at Etchmiadzin and back a controversial candidate for the position of supreme spiritual head is a storm in a teapot should recall the recent history of those elections. In February 1956 our naive leadership was convinced that the issue of electing a Catholicos at Antelias was an internal community matter, until the turrets of tanks and armored vehicles appeared at the Antelias monastery gate. At that point it dawned on all principals in the drama that a Cold War in miniature was being staged in the Armenian Church, with the involuntary and uninformed participation of our clergy and community leadership. But we had reached the point of no return: things could only deteriorate, and they did.

After almost four decades, and after the collapse of the Soviet Union, the Cold War is supposed to be over, and this new election should not have political ramifications. But as it turns out, a low-intensity Cold War is still simmering: East, in this case Russia, still faces West, by implication the US. Armenia is caught in that tug-of-war.

As we watch events unfold in the Caucasus, we notice the constant ebb and flow of the Russian sphere of influence, as Moscow desperately tries to retain the borders of the former Soviet Empire as its defense parameter and is persistently pushed back by conflagrations in Nagorno Karabagh or Chechnya and by the challenges from Turkey and the Baltic states. Armenia is in the heat of things. Indeed, as Armenia is the most stable former Soviet Republic, Moscow has invested a tremendous amount of military hardware there, making it the vanguard of the Russian strategic configuration. That may give us some comfort in view of perennial Turkish threats, but it may also render our homeland a bone of contention between the warriors of this new confrontation.

Thus far President Ter Petrossian and his government have performed their balancing act admirably; a policy for which Turkey was credited throughout the Cold War era.

Indeed, by allowing a Russian military presence in Armenia, Yerevan must have touched a few raw nerves in Washington and Ankara. Armenia has further angered these two erstwhile allies by trading extensively with Iran. Of necessity and to the chagrin of the US, Teheran has become Armenia's major trading partner.

In view of these developments, Washington had two options, namely, a carrot-and-stick policy: a) to deny assistance to Armenia and encourage Turkey to continue the blockade, thereby pushing Armenia further into Moscow's arms, or b) to lure Armenia away from Russia by offering political rewards. It seems that Washington has opted for the second alternative, expecting Armenia also to play by the rules of the game.

On the other hand, the Armenian leadership was quick to learn the intricacies of the game and take advantage of them, hopefully for the long haul.

Apparently as a result of US arm-twisting, Turkey is about to lift the blockade. It is almost a foregone conclusion that the Azeri oil pipeline will pass through Armenia in order to integrate the latter into the Western economic system and hopefully undermine Russia's position in that stronghold.

In its turn, the Armenian leadership is expected to pay in kind; there are already signs that Western and Turkish demands are being met, albeit tacitly. Senior presidential adviser Girard Libaridian has publicly and understandably downgraded recognition of the genocide from the status of Armenia's historic right to that of a "moral obligation." The decision of Ashot Bleyan (Acting Minister of Education) to ban the teaching of the genocide in schools should not be viewed as simply another example of his characteristically eccentric behavior; it reflects, rather, a well thought-out government policy, despite the fact that it goes against the grain of all Armenians.

The President's policy, which has been fraught with dramatic surprises, may even lead one day to a gradual or total withdrawal from the captured Azeri territories, even before Armenia's public demands are met. That will certainly prove a tougher nut to crack than the election of the Catholicos. By now we should have learned something about our President's *modus operandi.*

To the disbelief of many, the election itself has to be seen in the broader scheme of a political chess game.

In early 1960s, as the crisis in the Church evolved, the then-young celibate priest Karekin Sarkissian confided to this writer that he was engaged in the crisis within the Church in order to combat Communism, the resultant turmoil in the Church notwithstanding. And within that limited framework, he has certainly earned enough credentials to persuade any political power to bet on him.

By singling out Karekin II, President Ter Petrossian is following a pattern of trying to pay political dues to the West. The President does not reveal his true motives for his choice of candidate because he believes that a politician or statesman need not divulge his motives in defending a case. We might argue with his reasoning ad nauseam, but it would be to no avail. He knows better than anyone else that the clergyman who has symbolized the division in the Church is the last person to unite the Church. Also, the Armenian Church has other archbishops in its ranks who can dwarf his candidate in the knowledge of theology, linguistics, scholarship, and diplomacy which the President attributes to him. That he is fully aware of the existence of such deserving candidates to the throne merely adds insult to injury.

The President's decision, in turn, has angered Moscow, which is trying to counteract it. Indeed, how is it that the delegates from Russia doubled in number overnight, from fewer than 50 to 100? Who supplied (or manufactured) the statistics? Archbishop Diran Gureghian of Moscow is the last remaining resistance to the President's strong-arm tactics; the other candidates and primates have been intimidated into submission. Who is backing Archbishop Diran? We have yet to see one other high-ranking clergyman stand up and be counted. Every other clergyman seems stunned by the dramatic turn of events. But we should not give up hope: there is still a chance for a last hurrah on April 3.

Moscow's resentment has also surfaced publicly, so much so that President Ter Petrossian has been summoned to Moscow to face some tough questioning. It has been learned that on his way back from Copenhagen, Armenia's President is scheduled to stop in Moscow for a CIS[1] meeting, and especially to discuss his backing of a Western protégé to the throne of Etchmiadzin.

Therefore, President Ter Petrossian's decision transcends our

---

1. *The Commonwealth of Independent States: the confederation of former Soviet Republics which followed the collapse of the Soviet Union.*

concerns over legalities, the separation of Church and state, tradition, and democratic niceties, and touches on global political games to which Armenia is now a party. We hope that it pays off.

So viewed in its political context, the Presidential decision may not seem so aggravating as it otherwise sounds, and that may temper our anger to a certain degree.

We realize therefore that the election of a Catholicos continues to be part of a global political chess game!

March 25, 1995

A DRAMATIC REVERSAL ON THE EVE
OF THE ELECTION IN ETCHMIADZIN:

An Interview with Edmond Azadian

Upon learning that President Levon Ter Petrossian has decided to push the candidacy of His Holiness Karekin II to the throne of Etchmiadzin, the Los Angeles semi-weekly Nor Or[1] *contacted Edmond Azadian, Chairman of the ADL Central Press Committee, for an interview. Hagop Boghossian, editor of* Nor Or, *had an in-depth discussion with Azadian on this most topical issue. The latter has indicated that the opinions expressed in the interview are purely personal in nature and do not necessarily reflect those of the ADL or of this newspaper.[2]*

Q. *We have learned that in a dramatic reversal the authorities in Yerevan have decided to favor the candidacy of His Holiness Karekin II, Catholicos of the See of Cilicia, to the throne of Etchmiadzin. Have you heard any news regarding this change in position?*

A. The information reaching us from Armenia concurs with what you have just said. I personally am not surprised, after carefully observing, over the past three years, the very special way in which the Armenian authorities deal with issues. The approach they have applied to problems, both in Armenia and abroad, has always been defended as government policy. Of course, it is understandable and justified that any opinion expressed at the higher levels of government should reflect the government position; but it sometimes happens that even government functionaries in lower echelons tend to justify their mistakes or awkward policies when criticized by throwing it in your face that this is state policy.

I am sure you know full well that I have publicly expressed my

---

1. *New day.*
2. *I.e., The Armenian Mirror-Spectator.*

opinion about His Holiness Karekin many times, sometimes touching raw nerves. Indeed, His Holiness is a man of high intellectual qualities, but throughout his career he has always been under political control. That is why people at the higher levels of the Armenian government, up until recently, have indicated that since he is not an independent agent his candidacy is out of the question. This opinion was also personally expressed to me by people at the highest levels of the government.

On the other hand, I am aware of His Holiness Karekin's ambition to reach the highest post in the Church. That, coupled with the very flexible policies of the Armenian government, sometimes even at the expense of being unprincipled, did not rule out this dramatic change, which comes just three or four weeks before the election.

During the first period of Armenia's independence, when the authorities were a honeymoon with the ARF[3] leadership and especially with Mr. Hrayr Maroukhian, President Levon Ter Petrossian exerted every possible pressure on Parliament to force the adoption of the present coat of arms and national anthem, as measures that would please Mr. Maroukhian. Beginning on that day, I have learned that President Ter Petrossian can be extremely flexible and is capable of confronting us with many surprises. If the surprises are in the best interests of the Armenian people, we need not complain. Whenever I find myself confronted with such an unbelievable reversal, I remember Vahan Tekeyan's very appropriate lines on Armenia, which state: "You are not the same as my dream, / But that may be for the better."

I have indicated in one of my articles[4] that the election in Etchmiadzin reminds us very strangely of the eve of the 1956 election at Antelias, when the clergymen loyal to Etchmiadzin were pitted against one another, fighting or undermining each other without being able to rally around a principle or a common candidate. It was therefore apparent, I pointed out, that while our clergy were carried away with in-fighting, Karekin II could position himself to jump over their heads to the throne of Holy Etchmiadzin. Every time I have discussed this possibility with our high-ranking clergy, they have all expressed their concern about the sorry situation of our clergy and have concurred with me that such an election would become a reality if our highranking clergy did

---

3. *Armenian Revolutionary Federation.*
4. *See the previous essay in this section, "The Election in Etchmiadzin: Tempest in a Teapot or Global Political Chess Game?" (p. 216).*

not put their house in order. But they have always expressed their personal inability to bring about any change in this dangerous situation.

Q. *Before Karekin II was elevated to the throne of Antelias, and even after that, there were many embraces between high-ranking clerical representatives of Etchmiadzin and Antelias. But to this day the Church still remains divided. Can the authorities in Armenia, with the support of Karekin II, heal the rift in the Church; or is it their main purpose to further divide the ARF?*

A. I believe they have two goals, and they intend to achieve both at the same time. If indeed that is one of their purposes, it is not worth electing Karekin II as the 131st Catholicos of Etchmiadzin solely to score a tactical advantage over a political party which opposes President Levon Ter Petrossian's policies.

On the other hand, if Karekin II has given assurances that after ascending the throne he will be able to bring an end to the division, we have nothing to say.

I would like to make a brief analysis, based on my own personal experience. In trying to solve certain problems related to the diaspora, government functionaries and even ministers have tried to hide behind the excuse of applying government policy every time they have mishandled an issue.

When we talk to government representatives or intellectuals from Armenia, their position is, "Yes, indeed you are Armenians, but you must not interfere in our internal affairs. We are a government; we are a state; and it is we who must determine the fate of our own people." It is a fair policy, and I have always maintained the position that the leadership of Armenia should come from inside Armenia and that any policy the government applies needs to be derived from the actual situation in Armenia. The diaspora is an addendum, and we should all strive for it to become an addendum that is useful to Armenia. As far as policies which concern Armenia are concerned, we have no right to question the validity of the policies adopted by the government. But when that government or any minister in that government tries to solve a problem which will affect the diaspora, it is our business to express our opinion. The election of a Catholicos is related mainly to diaspora Armenian life, because the people of Armenia, the present leadership included, have been separated from Church life for about seventy years, whereas the Church has been the very life of the diaspora. For the last seventy years, the Church has been identified with the diaspora. We have lived within the Church and for the Church, and in many countries Armenians have been recognized as ethnic minorities through their churches. The division in the Church has deeply affected our lives in the diaspora, and many of our members and political leaders have suffered tremendously. They have literally been stabbed and terrorized and have participated in struggles in order to defend a position in the diaspora, and that position has been loyalty to Holy Etchmiadzin. Therefore, if a dramatic change is contemplated in Armenia, that change must be the result of serious analysis, because it will affect the lives of all of us in the diaspora so deeply. And just as we respect and care for Armenia, we at least hope that the government and people of Armenia would treat diaspora Armenians and their issues with the same care and concern.

Q. *If Karekin II ascends the throne in Etchmiadzin, that will affect the position of the See of Antelias deeply. If the purpose of favoring Karekin II as a candidate is to divide the ARF, the latter can very easily bring another loyal Catholicos to the throne of Antelias and continue the division of the Church as before.*

A. The possibility that Karekin II may rise to the position of supreme spiritual head raises serious questions. We must understand that no political party is there forever: even the almighty Communist Party lasted only seventy years before it collapsed, and the powers which have replaced the Communist Party in Armenia may not survive even that long. I would very much like to know, in a scenario in which the ARF takes over the government in Armenia, what would be the relationship of Karekin II to the party which would have brought him to power, and what his relationship to the ARF, whom he served loyally until very recently.

It would be very interesting to know whether the authorities in Armenia have thought of the possibility that Karekin II might turn out to be a Trojan horse after he ascends the throne in Etchmiadzin, and actually pave the way for the ARF to come to power in Armenia. We have publicly raised this possibility many times, and we do not yet have an adequate response from Armenia.

I would also like to know whether Karekin II, in accepting to be the government's candidate, has given any solid assurances to the government regarding the restoration of unity within the Church. Until now he has not demonstrated that willingness to unite the Church. If he has given secret assurances, we will not be very inquisitive to know exactly what those assurances are, but at least we will be reassured that by pursuing this policy Armenia's government has a firm handle on the future of a united Armenian Church. It has been impossible to create Church unity since 1956, and if the authorities in Armenia can achieve that unity by a magic stroke, my admiration for their ability to actually change the course of our life will be great. But if they fail, my disappointment will be equally bitter.

Q. *We are told that about 400 delegates are participating in the election of the Catholicos. What percentage of those delegates do you think will favor the candidacy of Karekin II? Also, we have just learned that the number of delegates from Moscow has increased. Do you know anything about the change?*

A. Until recently, my information has been that there were fewer than 50 delegates representing Armenians in Moscow. But I understand that just last week that number has doubled. I am not sure exactly how that has happened but, knowing the mathematics applied to the Eastern and Western Dioceses of the United States, I am not surprised that inflated figures are also used by Moscow to elect delegates. I am also interested to know how delegates are elected in Armenia. What bylaws have been used and what rules and regulations have been applied to the election of those delegates?

It would also be interesting to know how informed the delegates are of their role. For many years they have not participated in organized Church life and have not observed any rules or bylaws governing the Church, and now they have come together to elect a Catholicos at this very crucial juncture in Armenian history.

I think there is an overall uncertainty. There has not been an election of a Catholicos in Etchmiadzin since 1955, and those who participated in that election are no longer with us or are on the sidelines of Armenian community life. We have new faces with less experience. This will be an educational process for everyone concerned until we establish laws and regulations to run our Church and to hold elections, crystallize the traditions by which we have been guided in our Church affairs, and bring them up to 21st-century standards.

It would not be right to discuss the legal aspects of the election, because very few participants are aware of the bylaws governing such elections. Just recently we have seen that some people have willfully distorted the bylaws of the Armenian Church to suit their own personal or factional purposes.

Q. *Some political parties in the diaspora, organizations, and many individuals have maintained that Church life should not be subject to political influence. The ADL, the Hunchak Party, the AGBU[5] leadership, and*

---

5. *The Armenian General Benevolent Union.*

many individuals have fought a long and exhausting battle to contain the encroachments of the See of Cilicia over dioceses under the jurisdiction of Holy Etchmiadzin. How now can a person or religious head who has symbolized that division for so long and has claimed to be equal to the head of the Armenian Church at Etchmiadzin ascend the throne of St. Gregory? What repercussions would that entail?

A. The authorities in Armenia are duty-bound to convince the Church and community leaders in the diaspora that what they are proposing today is in the best interests of the Armenian people; if and when that leadership is convinced of this dramatic reversal, it is up to that leadership to go to their constituencies and explain this sudden change and demonstrate to the masses that the position of President Ter Petrossian is indeed in the best interests of the Armenian people. The authorities in Armenia have applied facile policies in resolving issues pertaining to the diaspora, and diaspora Armenians have shown a deep understanding of the situation of the leadership in Armenia, whose hands are full with a border war with Azerbaijan and the blockade which is stifling the Armenian people and who therefore (the diaspora has been convinced), do not have time to treat our problems with equal seriousness and analysis. But if that cavalier attitude in resolving diaspora problems becomes a permanent policy, the diaspora must have a legitimate concern on its hands and has to get its act together in order to defend its own interests. President Ter Petrossian's proposal that Karekin II be elected to the throne of Etchmiadzin is a very, very serious step. He has crossed the Rubicon in dealing with the diaspora, and it is up to the diaspora to stand up and defend its position and its interests.

It is incumbent upon Catholicos Karekin II to dissociate himself publicly from the erroneous policies which he has rigorously pursued in alliance with a single party for the past 40 years. If these two preliminary issues are resolved--i.e., if Karekin II dissociates himself from his previous ties and the government in Armenia explains its position fully--we, as diaspora Armenians, would be facing a dead serious government policy and would have to treat that policy with a high degree of respect. Alternately, if the policy is not well thought-out or defined, we as a nation, both within Armenia and in the diaspora, are up against a catastrophic situation.

As you may remember, almost two years ago I published an article entitled "Church Politics and a Political Church." In it I compared the role of Karekin II to the position of Thomas à Becket who, upon becoming head of the Church of England, did not hesitate to confront the king who had brought him to that throne, his personal friend, when the king tried to trample the interests of the Church. The comparison was very transparent. Catholicos Karekin II has been closely associated with the ARF, but following his elevation to the throne of Holy Etchmiadzin he could indeed have defended the interests of Etchmiadzin and opposed his former friends, i.e., the ARF leadership. If this were to happen, a welcome change indeed would have occurred in our Church life. I would like to judge the situation very objectively and apart from the emotional pressures of the past 40 or 50 years. I would also like to state that if the relations I outlined in my article have changed and if Catholicos Karekin has indeed determined to serve the entire Armenian people, the Armenian homeland, and the entire Armenian Church instead of a single party, that would turn a new page in his life and in the recent history of the Armenian Church.

Q. *Otherwise?*

A. The alternative also has to be studied by the government. After all, when we who are individuals and do not represent a government are seriously concerned with alternative situations, we believe that the government has even more reason to be concerned with that potential. This reversal will have a minimum impact on life in Armenia, where the Church has been re-emerging into prominence only within the past few years, after a long period of hibernation. But the diaspora will be seriously impacted, and we would like to know how serious the Armenian government representatives are in dealing with the destiny of the diaspora.

March 18, 1995

An Uncertain Legacy

As His Holiness Karekin I, the Catholicos of All Armenians, is laid to rest in Armenia, it is early for history to pass a judgment on his life and deeds. Yet there are facts and activities which need to be recorded for posterity.

His Holiness lived and performed during most turbulent times in our history, when it was not difficult for the most prudent leaders to lose their heads and to confuse their way.

Karekin I rose to prominence at the height of church controversy. He was a young priest, serving the Catholicossate of Cilicia in Antelias when that See was taken over by force and used for the political ends by a group which had not demonstrated any interest, in earnest, in church affairs. Therefore, throughout the Cold War period the Catholicossate of Antelias became a component of the Dashnag party's overall strategy. Many clergymen and seminarians left Antelias, in a kind of self exile, because they could not reconcile in their conscience, making a compromise between their religious vow and a political commitment which was being dictated by the new lay rulers of the Catholicossate. Karekin I was among the clergy left behind, which is a telling act about his stand in life, his character and his world outlook in general. He was not even a neutral bystander; in time he became one of the major actors in church controversy, which catapulted him to the supreme position as the young, dynamic, charismatic and knowledgeable Catholicos of the Illustrious House of Cilicia in Antelias.

While the majority of the clergy and the people rallied around the Holy See of Etchmiadzine and its revered pontiff His Holiness Vasken I, Antelias enjoyed better prospects for internal growth and aggressive external posturing. Unfortunately, Soviet rule did not tolerate any internal growth for Etchmiadzine. Yet, at the same time, it encouraged its external role as a rallying point for all Armenians around the world, which was considered in tune with Soviet foreign policy.

Karekin I was an active participant of the church split. The irony is that the schism never healed while he served the church on either side of the fence, which leads many to ponder whether he was an element for resolving the conflict or whether his personality contributed to the perpetuation of the conflict.

While he was at the head of the Antelias church he excelled in such areas as his oratorical skills and his articulation in Christological matters. There is no question that he became one of the religious leaders who thrust the Armenian Church into the mainstream of the world ecumenical movement. He was a respected figure within the ranks of World Council of the Churches, and he likewise commanded respect in Vatican circles. His historic agreement with the Roman Catholic Pontiff was a watershed in the Vatican's drive to bring reconciliation with the Orthodox world, although he was severely criticized by the high ranking clergy in the Armenian Church hierarchy.

His multilingual skills endeared him to many world church and lay leaders. His book on the Council of Chalcedon stands out in our theological literature, otherwise a barren field, because Armenian clergy have not proven themselves as prolific writers. Karekin I's subsequent treatises on theological themes seem to be derivatives of his original work, and the jury is still out on his academic legacy.

Another twist of irony in Karekin I's life is that after dedicating an entire career to fighting Holy Etchmiadzine, in an attempt to undermine its authority, today he comes to rest on the very grounds of that holy religious center.

With the collapse of the Soviet Empire, with the end of the Cold War and with Armenia's accession to independence, the division within the church lost its justification. Yet Karekin I was not able to bring reconciliation, although he seemed sincere in his eagerness to do so. That came to prove, one more time, that deliverance of church unity was beyond his means and the church he seemed to lead was actually controlled by political powers behind the scenes.

With the demise of His Holiness Vasken I, an era ended, and new prospects appeared on the horizon. The church situation was as confused as the political atmosphere in Armenia. In that unstable situation the former President Levon Ter Petrossian thrust Karekin I on the throne of Holy Etchmiadzine, contrary to all church traditions, believing that his political gambit would resolve the church division overnight with a magic stroke.

That tour de force revealed three facts:

A. It proved how pliant our church hierarchy was, as each clergy tried to outdo himself to prove his allegiance to the new pontiff (who, until that period, was considered the antagonist).

B. It demonstrated the shallowness (at least shallowness in church and Diaspora politics) of the political leader who engineered the thoughtless gambit.

C. It was in Karekin I's destiny to be used as a political pawn at every critical juncture of our recent political life.

Yet in Armenia's plight of destitution, all was forgotten and forgiven. That was a healthy stand to take for a people trying to come out of the ruins of the Soviet Union, the ravages of a devastating earthquake, and the dangers of a border war with Azerbaijan.

Even Karekin I's most ardent critics made peace with him, because they wished to see in him the reincarnation of a new Thomas Beckett. Yet his four year reign at Etchmiadzine was replete with tragic, as well as ironic, turns of events.

After his accession to the Etchmiadzine throne, it never occurred to the new pontiff to make amends for his past actions, nor at best to explain them away. While he was alienated from Antelias, he never was able to command full respect in Armenia, especially after the unexpected and expeditious departure of President Ter Petrossian from the political scene. That departure further demonstrated that while Karekin I was competent to function efficiently within an existing infrastructure, it was beyond his abilities to create his own infrastructure. He bitterly complained to close friends about the void he found within the confines of Etchmiadzine. He was frustrated, too, with the high ranking clergy trying to cultivate their own individual feudal turfs in Armenia, at the expense of weakening the overall authority of the Supreme Patriarch of the Church.

Another tragic twist was the political setback suffered in Armenia by the powers controlling Antelias, which led them to appoint a more determined clergyman at the head of the Cilician Catholicosate. Indeed, the most articulate and aggressive Catholicos Aram I did anything and everything to outshine Karekin I and to undermine his authority in world church circles. He was even more aggressive in undermining the Etchmiadzine pontiff's authority than Karekin I was when he was at the helm of Antelias See.

In his desperate struggle to assert himself against all odds, Karekin I discovered that illness had caught up with him. Throughout his bout with cancer, the entire Armenian people empathized and agonized with him, praying for his recovery, but unfortunately to no avail.

It was most heart rending to see such an articulate church leader be condemned to silence, because of his larynx surgery. Today the entire Armenian Church laments his untimely loss.

With the death of Karekin I at a relatively young age, an illustrious church career - with all its contradictions - comes to an end. As the supreme head of the Armenian Church, he will be missed and revered unquestionably. He certainly has carved his place in the history of the Armenian Church. Yet his legacy remains uncertain, waiting to be evaluated by posterity.

June 30, 1999

Part Four

INTERVIEWS

PROSECUTOR THOMPSON VS. DR. KEVORKIAN:

Life or Death?

TWO ARMENIANS CONFRONTING EACH OTHER AT OPPOSITE ENDS OF THE LAW

*Armenians can hardly agree on ordinary matters, let alone on such impor-
tant issues as life and death. Ironically, the controversy over assisted suicide pits two
Armenians against each other. Indeed, every time Dr. Kevorkian helps a patient
take his or her own life, Michigan's Oakland County prosecutor, Richard
Thompson, is compelled to react, taking measures to stop the practice, which he
believes is illegal in Michigan, and for that matter, in the USA. On the other
hand, Dr. Kevorkian insists that there is no law to prevent him from "ending a
patient's suffering," as he puts it.*

*Outside Michigan, perhaps very few people know that Richard Thompson
(Tomassian) comes from a staunch Armenian background. Although their ethnic
origin is not relevant to the issue dividing these two individuals, the coincidence
makes it all the more interesting. Dr. Kevorkian is amazingly fluent in Armenian;
he would even dissect words into their roots in classical Armenian.*

*For a long time I had been intrigued by the arguments on both sides of this
very topical issue, and had wished to interview these two Armenian gentlemen
together. But when I learned that Dr. Kevorkian refused to speak to an "ogre," I
decided to conduct my interviews separately, all the while making each party
aware of what the other had to say about the issue and about him.*

*The controversy over assisted suicide (or euthanasia) has been raging for a
long time. It seems that it has already reached a climax and that society is now
prepared to enact laws either to forbid or to legalize helping a patient take his or
her own life. In either case, neither Thompson nor Kevorkian would emerge as the
winner: the controversy itself would simply be resolved.*

*Each party gives the impression that he realizes that the issue is beyond his
personal opinions or beliefs. It is a public debate on a moral, medical, legal, and/or
ethical issue. Dr. Kevorkian, colorful as he is, does not seem to be after money or
celebrity status. He is driven by a missionary zeal to prove a point. On the other*

hand, Prosecutor Richard Thompson is a reluctant enforcer of the law ("a concentration camp commander," to Dr. Kevorkian). Perhaps he wishes that the law would determine the fate of the controversy, or that Dr. Kevorkian would perform his humane or grisly acts (depending on one's own stance on the issue) outside the parameters of Oakland County, thus getting him off the hook. Thompson will be relieved no matter what the outcome is. But it looks as if Dr. Kevorkian is prepared to spend the rest of his life in jail to carry the issue to its dead end, should a law banning assisted suicide be enacted. Only an Armenian could be that stubborn; but Dr. Kevorkian has the inner conviction that time is on his side.

AN INTERVIEW WITH DR. JACK KEVORKIAN

EA - *I would like to begin by asking some questions about your Armenian background. Could you give me your family story, your educational background, your relationship with your Armenian heritage?*

JK - I was born in Pontiac, Michigan in 1928. I have two sisters: one, who was two years older, is now deceased, and the other is two years younger. My mother is Satenik Kechigian from the village of Govdoun in Sebastia. My father is Levon Kevorkian. I think he's from Erzurum, in Eastern Turkey. My mother came to this country, I think in 1924 or 1925. My father came in 1912. They got married here. I was born, raised, and went to school in Pontiac. I went to the University of Michigan, pre-med and medical school, and when I graduated I served an internship for one year and then went into the army for two years, just at the end of the Korean War. Then I came back and trained in pathology at the University of Michigan for two years and at Pontiac General Hospital for another two years.

EA - *What is your Armenian name?*

JK - Well, they call me Mourad. My mother named me Mourad for the village hero, Mourad Pasha, in the old country. My father would sometimes call me Hagop, but my main name was generally Mourad. The name on my birth certificate was American; it was Jack.

EA - *When, and under what circumstances, did you decide that ending the life or, as you say, the suffering of a patient is a charitable act?*

JK - Well, I always felt that. While I was in training in medical school I felt that there were always some cases where it was better that the suffering be ended by ending a life than by continuation, especially when the patient wanted it or demanded it. But I didn't do anything actively in it until the David Rivlin case, locally here, in 1989, when this young man of 37, who at the age of 20 broke his neck in a swimming accident in California, and was on a respirator and paralyzed from the neck down for 17 years and in a nursing home, decided that this was the end. I read in a newspaper that he wanted a doctor to come forward to take him off the respirator. They wouldn't allow that in the nursing home. No doctor came forward, so I said I would go and talk to him. I talked to him and his nearest relative there. He was really a tragic case. His arms were swollen, face swollen, he could hardly move even his head. He could just sit there with a respirator in his throat. I felt sorry for the man and I said I would help him, but to end his suffering he wanted to die. I couldn't do it myself because by law that was a crime, but I told him that he could end it himself if I could find some way to help him. That's when I got the idea of making the device, so that the patient could do it himself or herself. I didn't make the device to be sensational or different. I had to do it because it's the only legal way to do it.

EA - *You think that not administering any kind of medicine or treatment to end a life and inventing the machine or device gets you off the legal hook?*

JK - Yes, but that's the wrong reason to do it. Whenever you do something, you should do it right. That's the definition of morality or ethics, to do and say what's right--and think what's right too, if you stretch it. But actually it is the best way. In a rare case someone would have to do the actual injecting or do the actual so-called killing because the patient can't move, can't even swallow, can't do anything, can't even move the head. So that there's nothing the patient can do to help himself or herself. But that's a rare case. Even if a person could do the injecting, in my mind it is less immoral if the patient does it himself or herself than if the doctor does it. The farther away the physician is from this, the better it is for the physician. The doctor makes everything available. You don't even need a doctor for this, but it's better to have someone there who's an expert. The patients feel better. So if the doctor can supply everything and then just stay away, now he didn't do anything. If the patient doesn't hit the switch, nothing happens. But if the patient hits the switch, then it's the patient's will and the patient's action that actually causes death. That makes it less immoral for the physician from a medical standpoint. So if you can do that, to give an injection would be more culpable morally.

EA - *Then why do they accuse you of murder when your participation in a suicide is limited?*

JK - Well, that's one way of intimidation. There is so much intimidation. That's why they do it. They feel that the stronger the punishment--the more fear they throw into you--the more you might refrain from doing something. There was no law when I did that, that's why I wasn't afraid. I even went back over the records; I even called the prosecutor's office a year before, because someone told me there was a case in Michigan in which someone had helped someone else commit suicide and he was freed by the appeals court because the court said there was no such law in Michigan and they said it's not a crime to help someone commit suicide. That was called to my attention. When I saw that, I read it myself. Then I knew that that was the way to do it, and when I told the prosecutor's office they said "you do that and we'll charge you with murder." See, they intimidate. There was no basis for that, and they did charge me with murder, but it didn't work, because I knew there was no way they could make that stick. When they passed the law, the law itself was unconstitutional and you can't legislate away a right. They didn't learn anything from prohibition.

EA - *So as it stands now, there is no law against what you are doing in Michigan?*

JK - Well, the Supreme Court said that there's a common law that has always been in effect. But if that's true, why didn't they mention it earlier?

EA - *In Michigan?*

JK - Everywhere.

EA - *The Michigan Supreme Court?*

JK - Yeah, the Michigan Supreme Court. The Federal Supreme Court refused to hear our appeal. They want to stay away from this.

Actually, it doesn't belong in the courts. The sign of a corrupt society is when things like this get to the courts, like abortion. No medical service is regulated by law except abortion, and that's not even a law, it's a court decision. It's the same with what I'm doing. These two things are regulated by court decisions, whereas no other medical service is. There's no court that says a heart transplant has to be done a certain way, or a kidney dialysis has to be done a certain way, even though it's a life-or-death decision. They picked these two cases because the religious insanity of our society is very firm on these two points. They have made it a religious thing instead of medical.

EA - *Are you a religious person? Do you have any religious justification for what you are doing? Or do you have a neutral stand on religion?*

JK - Well, I'm neutral on religion for other people. For myself,

I don't practice religion: I'm not religious. Maybe I am religious, but I don't call it religion and I don't adhere to any dogma or any one person as god. There may be a god: who knows?

All religions are mythological anyway. They are all made up. If there is a divine revelation, how come I'm not aware of it? I mean, it's just a story that's told to me and it's written in books: it's made up. But people believe it fervently and then they commit crimes because of it. There have been many crimes because of religion. But you see, this is a medical problem.

People cite the Hippocratic Oath, but the Hippocratic Oath is not medical, it's religious. The Pythagoreans and this pagan sect in ancient Greece made these rules, and they were the smallest sect in Greece and they were the most strict, like today's Fundamentalist Christians. In fact, many of their principals were taken over by Christianity. Now Christianity is not new; there's nothing new in Christianity. Zoroastrianism had almost everything that Christianity has. So the Pythagoreans put down these rules that we don't want suicide, we're against it. Whereas the rest of Greek society said it's OK. And in those days, when someone was very old or very sick and wanted to end the suffering, they would go to the doctor and the doctor would evaluate it with the patient and the family and, if they thought it was justified, would give the person pills to take to end his life. That was done all over Greece in those days, that's nothing new. It was a medical problem, not a religious one in Greece. Today they have made it a religious issue because Christianity took over the principles of Pythagoreanism.

EA - *Have you ever been asked to administer a lethal injection to a death-row inmate and, if you haven't, would you consider doing it?*

JK - No, I haven't been asked to give a lethal injection, but I would only give it if I were the only one around that could give it. But many people can give it. You don't need a doctor for that, although a medical technologist may do a better job than a lay person. But I wouldn't do it, because others could do it. You don't need a doctor. To me, a lethal injection is just a waste anyway. Many condemned men want to donate organs, and lethal injection is not the best way. You can maybe get the kidneys and the liver, but to do it correctly--to get all the organs--you've got to do it a different way. But I have not been asked to do that, and I wouldn't do it, because anybody can do that.

EA - *There was a program on TV yesterday or the day before--you may have watched it--"The Fight to Die" by Judy Woodruff--on euthanasia in Holland and the rest of Europe. They said they asked you for an interview and you turned it down. Why?*

JK - I don't know. Yesterday?

EA - *Yesterday or the day before.*

JK - That was probably the repetition of a program. I was asked maybe two years ago. I haven't been asked recently. If I turned it down I think I had a good reason. If I turned it down it's because they had a debate on it and they had the opposition side there and I won't debate nonsense. Because everything they say is nonsense. There is no debate on this question. They make it a debate. They make it philosophical: they split hairs. You can always back them into a corner. When you get to religion as the basis of your objection, the discussion ends, because you can't argue religion.

EA - *In that program, which I watched from beginning to end, I found out that in Europe there are many Dr. Kevorkians except that they have other names, especially in Holland. Do you think that that will gradually extend here and that one day it will be legally permissible to do what they have been harassing you for?*

JK -First of all, it isn't just in Holland. In Holland it's technically illegal, but they permit it. In Germany it's widely performed: thousands a year. People don't know that, but the Germans think nothing about it. It's taken as a fact, even though it's technically illegal. The only place it's really legal is in the state of Oregon, which passed a law, and then the Federal Court blocked it because of the religious idiots. The northern territory of Australia has just legalized it. That's the only place where it's legal and in force. So, many doctors do it, even here, but secretly. Whether or not it will become acceptable here--that will happen only if you do it, because you can't make this illegal with law.

EA - *Why do you perform all these assisted suicides in Oakland County?*

JK - No: I don't perform all of them in Oakland County. But I prefer it there. First of all, it's closer for me, and all the court proceedings are closer. I don't want to drive to downtown Detroit all the time if I can avoid it, and we don't mind bothering Prosecutor Richard Thompson.

EA - *I have also asked Thompson for an interview. I will publish this interview and his together. Is Thompson bothering you? Is he exceeding his legal responsibilities?*

JK - He always has. Of course. I mean, Thompson would make a nice concentration camp commander. Thompson was born too late. I can imagine him with a Nazi uniform on, as the commander of a camp. He'd be terrible; he'd be worse than Hitler. It's his nature: he's a cruel man but he doesn't know it. That's what makes him dangerous: he's cruel. He may be using religion as a basis, but he's cruel.

EA - *Isn't he Armenian? Is he a member of the Armenian Church?*

JK - He may be part of the Armenian Church, but it's the religion in back of the Republican Right that's doing it. They run the Republican Party. In fact, they're running the country now. The trouble with all this is, our laws are still based on religion. There's nothing wrong with religion, but you can't make it a secular law basis. Jefferson, Madison, Monroe, Washington--all these great men in this country-- were Christians, but they were deists, who said religion is fine, but it can't be the basis of government. But we are rapidly getting away from that basic concept, and now they're trying to make this an outright bureaucracy in this country, with this religious right: Robertson and all these other idiots. When they get in to write your laws, your constitution will go down the drain. Jefferson would not approve of any of this. When they put the words "under God" in the pledge to the flag, Jefferson would have decried that. He would have condemned it. You know that. But we don't care anymore.

EA - *Do you believe in God?*

JK - No: I don't believe and I don't disbelieve. I don't know. I'm a scientist. I don't know. I'm honest. I don't know.

EA - *Let me ask you this. The Armenian Church does not condone suicide. You know that.*

JK - I don't know that. I don't care.

EA - *Why don't you care?*

JK - Because that's a personal decision. If the Armenian Church doesn't condone suicide, did they blaspheme, all those Armenian women that jumped into the Euphrates River [during the genocide] instead of going with the Turks?

EA - *That wasn't suicide. Maybe we need a new definition for that act.*

JK - What wasn't? They jumped in the water themselves. They killed themselves. Were they all sinful?

EA - *Perhaps that might better be described as martyrdom.*

JK- Oh, that's what you call it! Maybe it's just personal martyrdom if you do it yourself. Martyrdom to nature. You see, the trouble with all this is you're using mythology to run life, and that's not always consonant with nature. You know that. Much of your religion is contrary to nature. You call the body sacred; therefore you perform all kinds of atrocities on the body because you call it sacred; whereas an animal-- which, luckily, you don't call sacred--you make sure it doesn't suffer. But you make sure a human suffers because you made this mythology up that it's sacred. You don't even know what you're talking about when you say it's sacred. You don't even know what you're talking about. The body is sacred? Really? Is all of it sacred? You see, you don't question further, like a scientist does. Is the whole body sacred? Is it? Answer!

EA - *No.*

JK - What part isn't sacred?

EA - *I don't know.*

JK - Tell me: this is a good discussion. Is the entire body sacred? You say the human body is sacred, right?

EA - *Yes.*

JK - All of it? Answer my question. See my point? If you can cut the body into parts of sanctity, tell me what parts you can't cut.

EA - *It's the principle....*

JK - No, no: that's ducking the issue. That's why you get away with it: because nobody questions you.

EA - *Do you talk to Thompson in Armenian?*

JK - I never talk to Thompson.

EA - *You never talk to him?*

JK - I don't talk to animals [laughs].

EA - *Do you want that statement to be published as it is? Aren't you concerned about the legal consequences?*

JK - Oh sure, sure. I'm sorry I said animals, because many of them are humane and compassionate. Thompson isn't. I don't talk to ogres: put it that way. You know what an ogre is?

EA - *Yeah. Why do you think he is so much against you?*

JK - I don't know: maybe he's got this image of being tough on everybody that he wants to prosecute no matter what the circumstances, and that's his mistake. He shows no discretion.

EA - *Is this a political game?*

JK - I'm sure it is.

EA - *Is it helping him or hurting him politically?*

JK - I have no idea if it's hurting him or helping him. From what I've heard, it's not helping him much.

EA - *Are you doing this because you're a scientist or are you doing it for publicity?*

JK - Because I'm a physician. What's a physician supposed to do? Cure disease and relieve suffering. Everyone forgets the "relieve suffering." Now, if doctors today cure disease only.... Today it is "extend life at all costs." I took the other side. They ignored my side entirely, so I will ignore their side entirely and say "end suffering entirely." Why am I to be condemned? A good doctor takes both sides.

EA - *Do you get paid for what you do?*

JK - No.

EA - *How do you make your living?*

JK - Well, I have Social Security and I have a little pension from the hospital.

EA - *Did they take away your license?*

JK - They suspended it.

EA - *You can't use it now.*

JK - Well, I can't get the drugs, but they wouldn't sell me the drugs when I had a license, because they were frightened: the pharmacists were frightened. See, the legal people have frightened everybody. Fear is how you control. This country is controlled by fear, but it's subtle. If you don't do right you get fired; if you don't do right you won't get this promotion; so they use fear to control you in this country.

EA - *Are there any groups in this country that are backing you?*

JK - Not that I know of.

EA - *How about the insurance companies?*

JK - They say they do, but they don't back us.

EA - *Are the insurance companies in favor of what you are doing?*

JK - Well, they should make money. There would be fewer hospital bills to pay and fewer drugs to pay for.

EA - *Are you helping the insurance companies?*

JK - Yeah, but they won't say it. But we are hurting the nursing home industry, they think. We're hurting doctors' incomes; we're hurting hospitals' incomes; and that's what they're afraid of. I'm sure money is involved in this, but that's because you're a crazy society. In medical matters, money shouldn't enter at all; a doctor should never worry about money.

EA - *But you are not personally benefiting from it.*

JK - No, I don't think so. Why?

EA - *I'm just asking.*

JK - I could, I guess, but I'm not. Why should I want to benefit? I have enough income. Why should I want to benefit from it? I mean, if I wanted a yacht, maybe I would, but I don't want a yacht.

EA - *Therefore, this is a philosophical and moral issue for you.*

JK - No, it's a medical issue, period. This is the thing everyone mistakes. It's a medical issue.

Look, if you've got a pain in your stomach, you don't go to a priest, do you? You may, but you're probably crazy if you do. They may help you even, make you feel better, talk to you and all that. To go to a priest with a medical complaint is nonsense, right? Who would you go to? A doctor! What's religion got to do with this? Nothing, see? But they've made it that, unfortunately.

EA - *If a healthy but desperate man came to you and said he wanted to die, would you help him?*

JK - Why would I? There is nothing wrong with him medically. I'm a doctor. I'm not an executioner; I'm a doctor. If a healthy man came to me and asked me to remove his gall bladder, do you think I'd do it? No. Some doctors would [laughs]!

EA - *Since you don't need the money and you have so many legal hassles, why do you continue to do this?*

JK - Should I stop?

EA - *I'm just asking why you continue.*

JK - The question I asked is just as good. Should I stop? What's your answer?

EA - *Just to get peace of mind?*

JK - Whose mind is upset? Your peace of mind?

EA - *No, yours.*

JK - Do I look like I've lost my peace of mind?

EA - *No.*

JK - Then why should I stop?

EA - *What do you gain by doing this? Are you performing a humanitarian act?*

JK - For each patient, I am.

EA - *What is your motivation?*

JK - That's like asking what a doctor's motivation is for giving his patient penicillin.

EA - *But they get money.*

JK - Wait a minute, that's not his motivation. We assume that's not his motivation. We are talking ideally now. He does it because that patient needs help, period.

EA - *And in return he gets money.*

JK - The money has been added on, but the doctor doesn't do it because he wants the money: he does it because he is trained to help a patient. The money, unfortunately, in some cases becomes paramount. But not all: some doctors will do it even without the money.

EA - *You realize that, whether you like it or not, you're a celebrity. Do you think you have a place in history or medical history?*

JK - I don't know, and really it's irrelevant. Should one care? I don't care. It is ego-satisfying to think that once in a while, until you're there. When you're there, it isn't so ego-satisfying. So-called celebrity status is not always nice, you know that? But that's not the point. The point is: do what's right when you can do it, and whatever happens, who cares? But personally I don't think it is going to be such a historical thing as people think it is; I really don't.

EA - *So are you going to continue to perform assisted suicides?*

JK - I've always said publicly that I will help a patient when and if a patient needs it. You've heard me say that publicly; I've always said that.

EA - *Don't you care about the legal consequences?*

JK - They're all illegal. There's no such thing as a really legal act on the other side. When it was first done, there was no law. The law that was passed was unconstitutional; the common law they now say exists is a fraud: there is no such thing. They are doing that because it's the last thing they've got, and the Supreme Court, no matter what it rules, doesn't mean anything. If they rule it's constitutional, there's still no law: it's a court decision. Are they passing laws in the Supreme Court now? That's the way it is with abortion. The Supreme Court has passed a law.

EA - *Can they put you in jail?*

JK - They'd do anything to stop you.

EA - *Why?*

JK - Trying to stop you!

EA - *How could the courts be that unjust?*

JK - It isn't the courts: it's the Medical Society. They're the most crooked of all.

EA - *Do they have the right to do that?*

JK - Does it matter if they have the right or not?

EA - *Yes, of course.*

JK - Why? They don't need the right: they have the power.

EA - *There are the courts.*

JK - The courts are corrupt. Don't you understand what I'm saying?

EA - *No.*

JK - There's no law. The Appeals Court that overturned everything and said that this is a crime, in 1983, in a similar case, said there's no such crime. The same judges did the reverse. Now tell me that that's a competent court! They either don't know the law, or they're going crazy. The Supreme Court is absolutely crazy when it says there's a common law. There is no such thing in common law, and even if there were, who cares? We don't live under common law--our laws have got to be passed--because then you could make anything common law by saying it's illegal. We pass laws in this state: so-called. That's what this country was founded on. England had common law. They came over here to be free of that. But the whole system is corrupt--the whole society is cor-rupt--and the higher up you go, the more corrupt it gets. The medical profession at the top, the judiciary at the top: the US Supreme Court and the Michigan Supreme Court are the two most corrupt courts in the nation. And all state courts are corrupt because they run on the basis of religious philosophy, the laws. We're a bureaucracy; we're not really a democracy.

EA - *One last question. Are you involved in the Armenian community?*

JK - Not very much, no; not actively, no.

EA - *Would you like to be?*

JK - Well, I don't think I'd like to be; I don't think I'd be a good role model in it. I think every Armenian should be an Armenian for himself. I'd like to see every Armenian be able to read and write Armenian. That to me would be a good sign. I'm not active, but by doing that, maybe I'm fooling myself by saying I'm at least a fair Armenian.

EA - *Do you think the language is important?*

JK - It's the only thing. Name something else you've got that is pure Armenian. Name one thing.

EA - *The important thing for the preservation of the Armenian heritage is to keep the language alive?*

JK - Name something else that is pure Armenian that you've got, that you covet so much, that you love so much. Name something that's pure Armenian. Sure, you've got your religion. Your religion, I said, not your Church. You think your Church is Armenian? It's based on something not Armenian, entirely not Armenian, not solid. Give me one Armenian name from Christianity. You don't have one. Not one. I am not denigrating anything--I am not putting down--I am only stating fact, bluntly, and that's what people don't like. I said I'm a scientist; I don't live by myths and I don't believe in something that's not entirely to my liking inside. Name something that's purely Armenian other than your language.

EA - *So the only thing is the language?*

JK - What else? I'm asking you.

EA - *Do you read and write Armenian?*

JK - Yeah: I don't speak it fluently, but I read and write it fluently. Handwriting is difficult, but the printed newspaper I read as fluently as English.

> EA - *Where did you learn?*

> JK - By myself. That's right: you don't need a teacher; you need a dictionary and some effort. You don't even need a school. You can learn the language, you can learn all the grammar you need, from the newspaper. Any Armenian who says he is Armenian has to read an Armenian paper.

> EA - *OK. Thank you. Any other statements?*

> JK - No, isn't that plenty?

> EA - *It is indeed plenty. Thank you.*

September, 1996

AN INTERVIEW WITH
OAKLAND COUNTY PROSECUTOR
RICHARD THOMPSON

EA - *Could you please give some information about your family, your background, and your Armenian connection?*

RT - First of all, my father came to this country in the 1917-1920 era, from Van. His mother and three brothers were killed in the Turkish massacres at that time. Later on, in the 1930s, he corresponded with my mother, who was living in Lebanon at that time, in the Beirut area. It might have been under Syrian control, I'm not sure. He went over there and married her, brought her back, and I was born a year later, in 1937. I have a sister, who was born 15 months after me.

We grew up in the Dearborn area, and I went to military school in Virginia. After getting out of the military school, which was really a high school, I went to the University of Michigan. From there I joined the United States Army and reached the rank of Captain in Army Intelligence. After my stint in the army I went to Wayne State University and obtained my law degree, and then practiced private law for about seven years with a large law firm in Detroit and also with my own firm, before going into the Prosecutor's Office in 1973 as Chief Assistant Prosecutor, which was second-in-command in the office. I've been in the Prosecutor's Office ever since, and when L. Brooks Patterson left I ran for the office. I was first elected in 1988, and took office in January of 1989, was re-elected in 1992, and am now serving my second term.

I am married to my wife Marilyn and have three sons: Richard, age 4; Matthew, age 3; and Andrew, age 1.

EA - *I understand your father was very active in the Armenian community.*

RT - Yes: he was very active in the Armenian community.

EA - *What was his first name?*

RT - Well, his legal name was Albert Thompson. He had his name changed when he became a citizen. A federal judge told him, "Mr. Tomassian, if you want to be an American citizen you should make your name easily spelled and easily pronounced." So the judge gave him the name Albert Thompson, but he still kept his Armenian name, Hapet Tomassian, in the Armenian community.

He was very active in the Church. We lived in the Dearborn area and went to St. Sarkis Armenian Church. He contributed a lot of money: built a church in Lebanon at one point, which I assume was destroyed during the war which occurred there a few years back.

EA - *Dr. Jack Kevorkian and Prosecutor Richard Thompson are household names in the news media here in Michigan, and probably nationally. Who do you think has helped the other most to obtain celebrity status? Richard Thompson, by prosecuting a maverick doctor, or Dr. Kevorkian, by continuing to practice his trade on your turf, in Oakland County?*

RT - I don't think I've gained any celebrity status. I think the name Kevorkian has celebrity status, not only in the United States, but internationally. Everyone knows about Dr. Kevorkian. By the issue that he has advocated: I think he got celebrity status when he took an intellectual exercise--that is, discussion of whether we should assist people to die--and then started to act upon that and actually started to assist people to die through his suicide machine, and now he uses carbon monoxide. So in our prosecution of him, I think he has gained celebrity status, but I'm far below what I would consider a celebrity.

EA - *Do you personally believe Dr. Kevorkian is wrong, or do you just think that you are upholding the law?*

RT - Well, both. As a prosecuting attorney my job is to enforce the law, and in our country we take pride in saying that we are a nation of laws. Whether one believes in the wisdom of a law or not, as a law enforcement officer (and I have taken an oath to enforce the law), I enforce that law. If they changed the law or eliminated the law, then I wouldn't be involved in enforcing that law. For instance, until the 1970s it was illegal for doctors to commit abortions. When that law was on the books and when we had the facts, we would charge doctors with that. Once it was eliminated, we no longer had those trials. When someone looks at what I do as a prosecutor, they must look at the fact that I have taken an oath of office to enforce the law: not just the laws I agree with, but all the laws. That's my job; that's what I do. On the other side, the question is, do you believe in the law? Yes, I do. The more I study the issue, the greater my belief that Dr. Kevorkian is doing something that's not only illegal, but that's not good public policy and is also immoral.

EA - *Dr. Kevorkian contends that there is no law forbidding him to perform physician-assisted suicide. Is that correct, or is he taking advantage of a fuzzy area in the law?*

RT - He is totally incorrect. If he were correct he would not be facing prosecution. He took his case all the way to the United States Supreme Court. When this issue first came up in 1990 with the death of Janet Atkins, an Alzheimer's patient, we indicated that it was against the common law for anyone to assist another person to commit suicide, and we initiated prosecution. That case was dismissed, and we told the legislature that, rather than us appealing the judge, even though we think the judge is wrong in his interpretation of the law, why don't you go ahead and enact the particular statutes so that we can decide what the current public policy is? Well, the legislature did not want to tackle that kind of controversial issue, so they didn't take it up. Several months later Dr. Kevorkian assisted in the deaths of Sherry Miller and Marjorie Wantz, in October of 1991. This time we had a citizens' grand jury, and that grand jury indicted Dr. Kevorkian for the deaths of those two individuals. Those two cases went all the way up to the Michigan Supreme Court, and the court told us we were correct. Even though there is no statute on the books, this is a part of our common law, and therefore he is guilty of murder if what he does is a direct cause of death. However, if he is merely involved in the preparation or providing of the means to the person who he knows is going to commit suicide, he is guilty of what is called "assistance to suicide," which is a five-year offense and a $10,000 fine. So it depends on exactly what degree of involvement he has, to determine what the crime will be. But it is either common law murder or assistance to suicide.

That is what the Michigan Supreme Court has said, and they are the highest court in our land. Dr. Kevorkian took his case up to the US Supreme Court, hoping to overturn what the Michigan Supreme Court did on the basis of federal law, and the United States Supreme Court said they would not hear the case, and let the Michigan Supreme Court decision stand. So as far as I am concerned as a prosecuting attorney, the Michigan Supreme Court decision is the last word on this. He is now facing trial. He has four cases that will be tried next year--two in February and two in April--and of course it is up to a jury to determine his guilt or innocence. But there is a law on the books.

EA - *Do you know Dr. Kevorkian personally or have you only confronted him in the courtroom, at opposite ends of the law?*

RT - I don't know him personally. Basically, my office has prosecuted him through various assistant prosecutors. We have 102 assistant prosecutors on our staff, so I don't get into court that often. In these cases, we have had assistant prosecutors present the case.

EA - *So you haven't come face to face with him?*

RT - No.

EA - *He imagines what you are, but he hasn't talked to you.*

RT - We have never talked. I assume he imagines what I am, and after reading the interview, I guess he doesn't think very highly of me. But my job is to enforce the law and that's what I'm doing.

EA - *Why do you think Dr. Kevorkian is so adamant in defying the court? Is he crazy, a fanatic, or very knowledgeable in the intricacies of the legal system?*

RT - I don't know what his motivation is, because I haven't talked to him and I don't know what goes on in his mind. Of course, after 26 assisted suicides, he gets smarter and smarter as time goes on. Originally, when he was committing these assistance-to-suicides, he would leave his machine there; he would tell the public what he actually did. In the last several cases he did not stay at the scene, there is no machinery around, and the only one who talks about what actually happened is his lawyer, because they know that what his lawyer says is not evidence against him. What his lawyer basically says is that Dr. Kevorkian was present at another suicide. Now, being present at a suicide is not a crime. A hundred people can be present at a suicide and there is no crime there. There has to be assistance and there have to be specifics and we have to know where. None of that comes out: Kevorkian doesn't talk; none of the family members who may be there ever talk, because they also hire Feiger, or retain Feiger as their attorney. So what we have is a conspiracy of silence. No one knows where it occurred; no one knows who did what. And these bodies now are dropped off in Kevorkian's van and sometimes in his car, behind the Sheriff's Department or behind the Medical Examiner's office: hardly what I would call a dignified death.

EA - *Then he has to pay the towing fee to get his van back.*

RT - Yes. I understand the last body was dropped off in his vehicle and the Sheriff's Department turned [the fee] back to him and he contributed it to some charitable institution.

EA - *My next question was if you had ever talked to him. You said no, but is your common ethnic background relevant to the issue or to your personal relations with him?*

RT - Not really. My job is to enforce the law, and I enforce the law whether the person is Armenian, Italian, Jewish--whatever the ethic background. It has no relevancy when you are looking at enforcing the law.

We take pride in the fact that we are a nation of laws and we have a statue of Lady Justice, and if you've ever seen it, this is a woman with a blindfold on, holding the scales in one hand and the sword in the other. The blindfold is there, symbolically, to indicate that it doesn't make any difference who you are when you appear before the bar of justice. We're all the same. No one is above the law; no one is below it. Therefore, it really is irrelevant.

Ironically, when Dr. Kevorkian's medical license was in jeopardy, it was an Armenian Assistant Attorney General from the State who prosecuted the case against him. I think his name was Larry Martirossian: I'm not positive of the last name, but he's there, at the Attorney General's level, taking the same oath of office to enforce the law, and he enforces it regardless of ethnic background.

I don't like the idea of hyphenated Americans. When you hear it in this country--you might have an Armenian background, a German background, an Irish background, but we are all Americans, and we ought to be treated that way.

EA - *You don't think the background has any relevance to the law?*

RT - Absolutely not, but some Armenians will confront me and ask how I can do this to Dr. Kevorkian, because he's an Armenian. I tell them that my job is to enforce the law, whether it's against an Armenian or against someone else. That's why I got elected. If we had an Italian prosecutor, is he supposed to treat Italians differently than Armenians? Absolutely not: that would be abhorrent to our idea of justice.

That's on the legal level. On the personal level, it is difficult for me to imagine Armenians supporting what Kevorkian is doing, because Armenians are so intertwined with their religion. I think it would be very difficult to separate Armenians from their Christian heritage. After all, we were the first nation that accepted Christianity as our national religion. So I find it ironic that so many Armenians who do support him are also Christians, since it's against the doctrine of their Church.

EA - *And they hold that against you: why are you prosecuting this poor doctor?*

RT - Yes.

EA - *You said it's in the hands of the courts, but would you like to see a law passed, clearly defining the government's position on euthanasia? Should that law allow assisted suicide? If so, would you still be personally opposed to it?*

RT- There is a clear law against it now; we don't need any more laws. The citizens of Michigan, in 1963, adopted the State Constitution. It's been revised since the 1850s, but in 1963 they re-adopted the Michigan Constitution. A provision of that constitution is that wherever there is no specific law prohibiting a criminal act which was criminal under the common law, then the common law is going to apply. So we do have a vote of the people, in 1963, that said we are going to apply the common law. That's why it's so relevant today. The common law is throughout our system of justice and throughout our legal system in Michigan and most other states. It's a part of the system, so when you throw up your hands and say "that's only the common law," the common law is the heritage of our judicial system.

The only place where a statute might be appropriate and relevant is where it makes clear that the law does make a distinction between intentionally killing someone, which is illegal, and withdrawing medical assistance or refusing medical assistance, or even giving pain-killers knowing that those pain-killers may hasten death, which is legal. I think a lot of people support Kevorkian because they don't really understand what the law is. And there's a fine line that the law has developed, and that is that you have a right as an individual to say you do not want medical treatment. You have a right as an individual to say that you do not want to be treated in the first place; I just want to die. And you have a right, and doctors have a right to give pain medication as long as their intent is to alleviate pain, not kill. Legislation that would specifically say that, I think would make people a lot more comfortable. If you have specific words in a particular act, people could look at that and feel more comfortable about it.

EA - *Europe has been more tolerant about the concept of assisted suicide. Now that we live in a global village, will the European trend affect the decision to be made in this country, or do you think that there already is a law and there is nothing to be done beyond that?*

RT - I think that certainly we look at what is happening in other countries; however, if we look at what's happening in other countries, that ought to convince us we should not ever legalize assisted suicide. For instance, the House of Lords in England, a few years back, debated this issue, and even though the members of the select committee initially started out with saying that it would be a good idea to legalize assisted suicide with controls, after hearing from all the experts they finally decided that no, it would not be a good policy, because there is no way you can control the abuses that would occur. What you are really doing is privatizing killing. The Canadian Supreme Court, again a few years ago, also had this issue up and they also refused to legalize it as a constitutional principle.

In Holland what we have is a situation that has been in existence since the 1970s, where, although it was technically against the law to assist suicide, the court started making exceptions, and over the years they basically have an informal recognition that under certain circumstances doctors can actually kill patients. For the first time in 1992, the

Dutch government did a study on what happened, and they found that this was a system totally out of control. Thousands of Dutch citizens were being put to death when they never made the decision to be put to death. Thousands of others were being given lethal injections that they didn't even know they were being given, and thousands more had life support systems withdrawn when they did not request it. About 11% of the people in the Netherlands who are being killed don't want to die. What we have now is where they are killing babies that are deformed, and they are doing that sometimes without even telling the parents, on the basis that they want to protect the parents from emotional turmoil. But that has no basis in the philosophical premise that what we are really doing is allowing people to make up their own minds, because babies certainly are not making up their own minds.

What we've seen here is the slippery slope. Once you say there is such a thing as a life not worthy to be lived, it's very easy for people to start throwing categories of individuals into that definition. They are doing that in the Netherlands. Last year there was a woman who was assisted in her death by a psychiatrist. There was nothing wrong with her physically. She just didn't want to live anymore because her husband had divorced her, her one son had died, her other son committed suicide, and there was no meaning to life for her. The psychiatrist said OK, I will assist you in your death. So, once you start, how can you have a principle or line that you can draw? If the principle is patient autonomy, then there is no way you can say "you can die, but you can't." If you don't want to live based upon a bad romantic situation, who's going to say that that's not suffering? So there's no principle, way you can stop, and that's the concern that I have.

But even though in a specific case you might think it's a great idea, or this is a compassionate idea, once you make it public policy--in Michigan you have 20-30,000 doctors deciding which lives are going to be snuffed out and which aren't. And another fallacy is: it's not really the patient making the decision, it's Dr. Kevorkian making the decision. All at once he has become a god, deciding who will live and who will die. That's not right, and there's no way you can tell another human being that you have decided that his quality of life is not good enough, therefore, you are going to allow him to die--you are going to use your medical expertise to allow him to die--but someone else is not bad enough yet.

EA - *What does the future hold for this issue? There has been enough exhaustive public debate on the controversy for the legal community to address the issue. Do you think the question is near a legal solution? Do you believe time is with you or with Dr. Kevorkian?*

RT - I think this issue is going to last for a while yet. The reason we have this issue is because our medical technology far out-paced our medical ethics on how to handle that technology. A lot of the blame is on the medical profession, because they view death as the enemy so they did everything they could to stop death. What happened was that there were a lot of futile measures used where they kept the person alive when there was no need to do that. You should at some point realize that we are not going to save this person by just putting a lot of machinery around and hooking them up. We should allow this person to die in a comfortable way. What we ought to be doing is managing their pain, making their life more comfortable, not just hooking up machines. So you have a medical profession that kept on using technology, rather than having the wisdom to know that they should stop.

The other aspect of it is that a lot of doctors don't know anything about pain control. Most terminal patients don't want to die. They want to live. If they're in pain, they want the pain to stop. What the medical profession has to do is determine how to stop the pain. Doctors have to learn that just because someone is going to die, you don't give up on them: you make their life comfortable; you stop the pain. So there's a lot the medical profession has to do. Once they are able to handle those issues--stopping pain, knowing when it is no longer wise to continue treatment--I think this issue will be handled without going to the extent of legalizing assisted suicide.

We can look to Germany and see what happened there. Although it didn't start with the Nazis, Germany started to look at this in the 1920s, and when the Nazi regime came in they really used it to get rid of a lot of people they didn't want. Dr. Leo Alexander, who was on the Nuremberg War Council, wrote a book about it several years later, and he said, "With all the German atrocities we looked at, when you study it very carefully you realize they had their very beginnings in the attitude of the medical profession that there was such a thing as a life not worthy to be lived." And once you have said there is a life not worthy to be lived, we first threw in the disabled, then we threw in the unproductive, then we threw in the racially unwanted. Once you have designed that concept, it's easy for you or the government or whoever is in charge to add more people to it and that's the scary aspect. It's bad public policy. Whether you use a religious basis or not, it's bad public policy.

EA - *And then there is no autonomy. The person whose life is at stake has nothing to say. It is programmed for him to die.*

RT - Right, and the other thing is that there are a lot of subtle pressures that are put on people to say OK, I will die. For instance, if you have an 85-year old grandmother who has a lot of illnesses you have to take care of with medicine, and she's lived a long life, and you go to her and say "You've lived a long life and it's costing us thousands of dollars to give you medicine, and that money could really go for the education of your grandchildren. Wouldn't it be nice if you ended it in a nice dignified way, in bed, with an injection?" How can the grandmother say no? They accept it because they want to sacrifice for their children. These are not voluntary decisions that are made.

You will manipulate people into wanting assisted suicide. For instance, if you start rationing health care. We have an insurance industry that makes billions and billions of dollars; they could make billions and billions of dollars more if they say they will no longer allow people over the age of 60 to have heart operations or dialysis, etc. So once you start limiting the kinds of medical resources that will be used in those cases you have silently manipulated those people into saying that they will die.

The poor people in our communities are the ones that are least able to afford good medical attention, so there will be an almost insidious discrimination that takes place against the poor, the minorities, and against the disabled. If a person doesn't have arms and legs and that person wants to die, we think: that's fine; that's an OK deal to do. If someone has his limbs, but wants to die because of a bad love affair, we think: that's a tragedy. There's a silent message there that says we don't think the disabled person is as good a human being as those with their arms and legs. There's going to be an insidious discrimination that goes on against the disabled community, and they ought to be concerned about what's happening.

EA - *The issue has philosophical, medical, legal, and ethical ramifications, and they must be considered.*

RT - Very profound ramifications. You're right: there are all those areas that you have to look at, and the concern I have right now is that we really haven't had the debate. What we have had are a bunch of slogans: death with dignity, patient autonomy. In our society now there are all these ten-second sound bites. They want to look at the controversial aspect of it. They don't have these philosophers--they don't have the medical ethicists sit down for hours and discuss, like you and I are discussing, all the implications that occur once you legalize assisted suicide. The only thing they throw at you now is if someone is suffering, you're a horrible man for keeping them alive. Certainly I don't want anyone to suffer, but I know that if I start allowing a public policy that says if you are suffering you can die--we will assist you in your death--the unintended consequences are that a lot more people will be suffering and a lot more people will be put to death than we are helping.

EA - *Once you have the mind-set and that translates into public policy, the individual will be lost in the shuffle.*

RT - Absolutely true. And we are not talking about Dr. Kevorkian then; we are talking about 20-30,000 doctors in Michigan, all having that right. How are law enforcement officers going to regulate it? We can't even regulate Kevorkian when there is a ban against it, because we don't get the patient's records. There's physician-patient privilege. And after awhile, when all these deaths occur, we'll become desensitized to it, and there'll be a lot of people who'll be put to death that really don't want to be.

EA - *OK. Thank you for this very interesting discussion.*

September, 1996

U.S. Diplomat Cautiously Pessimistic on Karabagh Conflict

On March 5, 1994, US chief negotiator for the Karabagh conflict, Ambassador John Maresca, was in Michigan to take part in a symposium organized by the Armenian Studies Program of the University of Michigan. During his visit, the State Department official, who had just completed two years of negotiations between the warring factions in the Karabagh conflict, agreed to have an in-depth discussion about the issue with Edmond Y. Azadian. Despite all the diplomatic skills Mr. Maresca exercised, it will not be hard for the reader to detect the inherent pessimism which permeates the conversation.

EA - *Speaking at a forum in Boston recently, you suggested that as a solution to the ongoing problems in the Caucasus Armenia should improve her relations with Turkey. Could you elaborate on that? Hasn't Armenia made enough overtures to Turkey, at the cost of firing its former minister (perceived as unfriendly by Turkey) and alienating its traditional ally, Russia, to accommodate Turkey?*

JM - Turkey is the way West for Armenia, and Armenia will need a door to the West. That's how it's got to be, for Armenia to be able to survive economically. And the other doors that are available on its frontiers just don't look to the West. Now it's true that because of the war at the moment, it looks very difficult to open that particular door, and I would be the first to admit that the Turks have not been 100% helpful in this. I have pressed them continually for more than two years, but ultimately I believe that is the way Armenia has to go. I think one of the best ideas I have ever heard was this idea of developing the Port of Trebizond for Armenia, and I actually talked to the man who was organizing that in Istanbul. I had dinner with him. And he still is very interested in doing it.

EA - *Who are you referring to: Itzhak Alathon?*

JM - Yes: Alathon. He's a Turkish Jew, but a very powerful, rich, and influential man, and he'd brought together a group that was proceeding very swiftly to develop this idea, and then they were told to hold back, basically, because the circumstances were impossible. You may know that up until a year ago there was a regular train back and forth between Yerevan and Kars. And that little train, running perhaps twice a week, was a tremendous economic operation. There were businessmen constantly coming and going, and I think that demonstrates what it would mean if that door were to be open. I haven't found the magic formula for opening that door, and I agree with you and our friend, Gerard Libaridian, who was recently in Ankara, that President Ter Petrossian has done a lot trying to open that door

EA - *Yes. He traveled to Ankara to attend Özal's funeral. The most important issue, which is central to Armenian history, is the Genocide, and the Armenian government was very cautious even there. Before independence, they proclaimed a declaration which outlined Armenia's intention for independence, and in that document they steered clear of the genocide issue. They said, "We will support all efforts towards the recognition of the Genocide." There was no territorial claim, not even any demand that the Genocide be recognized by Turkey. This was in deference to Turkey, to avoid aggravating its leaders. A national debate was raging in Armenia at that time, and there were leaders and intellectuals like Rafael Ishkhanian and a group of the present leaders of the Armenian National Movement who said: "We've tried Russia for too long" and "we're tired of Russia" and "we'll never be able to achieve our national aspirations through our neighbor to the north, so let's try Turkey." And Turkey failed to take advantage of that national debate.*

JM - I've been up against this myself. I don't know how much time we have, but I was the one personally who mediated very urgently between Armenia and Turkey in order to eliminate the last-minute Turkish objections to Armenia's being accepted into the CSCE when I was ambassador to the CSCE, and I spent two days of intensive back-and-forth negotiations trying to get the Turks to drop their insistence and to get the Armenians to ease their position. In the end we were successful, and the Turks dropped their opposition. Raffi Hovanissian will remember this. He even asked me, "How did you do this; how did you manage that?" So I know what the government of Armenia is up against: the Turks are very stubborn people. Right now I do believe, though, that if there is a cease-fire, along the lines that we have been talking about now for a long time with the various components, then the Turks will open the frontier; they will do all the things that they have committed to do. I believe that. Maybe I'm wrong.

EA - *Has Turkey reciprocated in any way that we are not aware of?*

JM - You may be aware of this: most well informed people are. I think the closest we came to something reciprocal in Turkey was when they agreed to provide electricity just over a year ago and they committed themselves to doing it and were ready to do it and that was just the time when Khojalu was overrun by Karabagh Armenian forces.

EA - *During the recent forum at Harvard University you declined to comment on the Armenian Genocide; was that official State Department policy on the Genocide or your own personal position? Does the State Department still insist on inserting the qualification "alleged" before the word* genocide?

JM - On this Genocide question--I'm not being coy here--I know what went on there, but I do believe that in a public forum a United States negotiator has to be careful about the way he deals with this issue. That forum in Cambridge was, I thought, not very well organized, because we were only permitted one minute to introduce our views at the beginning, and our views are rather full, and part of our view--and I explained this--is that we have deliberately decided to be impartial on the issue in order to be able to help find a solution. If you are not impartial, you cannot play the role of the mediator, and we have to have credibility on both sides. So the person who has been the United States negotiator, I think, has to be careful. You ask if this is my personal position; no: it is not my personal position, but I think it is a position which a negotiator needs to be careful of.

EA - *Do you see a contradiction between Turkey's position that it is occupying 38% of Cyprus in the name of defending a Turkish ethnic minority which is only 18% of the population of the island, and its denial of the very same minority right to the Armenians of Karabagh?*

JM - Well, there is no doubt that there are elements of inconsistency in Turkey's position on Cyprus and Karabagh. I've often pointed that out to them. Countries often have inconsistencies in their positions to match their interests. We do too. My feeling is that the UN has some useful guidelines on the subject (and I've used this often). Have you ever seen a thing called "The Secretary-General's Set of Ideas on the Cyprus Solution?"

EA - *Maybe I have.*

JM - It's published; it's a UN document. It's very instructive, as a kind of checklist for the kinds of issues that will ultimately have to be solved in the Karabagh political solution. I'm not suggesting that the solution will be the same; I'm only saying that it's a checklist. Comparing the two issues is instructive.

EA - *Turkey wants to station troops between the warring factions in Karabagh, along with Russia. Yet Turkey is a participant in the war or the conflict. It can't be impartial in order to observe a neutral stand.*

JM - My answer would be that Turkey is clearly supporting one side. Now, the word participant means something a little different. I would not, at this point, say that Turkey is a participant in this conflict. But clearly it is supporting one side, and we have warned the Turks about this: its support for one side is going beyond the limit that is justified. We have told them again and again that there's no justification, for example, for blocking humanitarian assistance, whether you are supporting one side or not.

EA - *The next question is a follow-up, about humanitarian assistance. The Turks have even stopped United States military transport aircraft carrying humanitarian assistance. Why does the US Government tolerate Turkey's ban on humanitarian assistance to Armenia? How can an ally stop US military transport planes carrying relief assistance to an earthquake-ravaged country?*

JM - That's true: they have stopped American planes. In fact, I myself, when shuttling back and forth, had to make huge detours. Sometimes it was very difficult, because you have to go over Russian, even Ukrainian air-space, and that was very difficult. Why does the US government tolerate it? The answer here is a complicated one. You may not like it, but the fact is that we have many things that we're doing with the Turks, some of which are very high priority and in which we need their cooperation. And we find that it's not easy to force the Turks. We tried it once, in fact--I don't know if you're aware of the past history-- after the Cyprus affair, when we cut off all assistance to Turkey for several years, and what they did was turn around and put the squeeze on our bases and made life intolerable for a lot of our people in Turkey. In the end we had to back down. And so we know that the Turks are not easy to force to do anything. But between having issues where we need their co-operation and knowing that they are not easily forced, our approach has been one of persuasion.

EA - *At that time we had the Cold War. Now that the Cold War is over, Turkey is not the same strategic asset that it was. So the balance in the equation is different today.*

JM - Well, the equation is different, but I would not say that it's not the asset that it was. It's an asset in different ways, but it's certainly an asset. Think of the Iraqi war.

EA - *Four resolutions were passed by the UN Security Council (with the US voting for the resolutions) condemning the capture of land by Karabagh Armenians and defending Azerbaijan's territorial integrity. Why does the UN ignore the fact that Karabagh was a legal entity--an autonomous region--under Azeri administration during the Soviet era before Mutalibov unilaterally abolished that status? When speaking of the Palestinians, formal statements always make a distinction whereby the West Bank and Gaza are defined as "Israeli-occupied territories;" why is Karabagh denied such a distinction in UN resolutions? Basically, we see it as a one-sided position, because all these entities (republics or enclaves or autonomous regions), are emerging from the collapse of the Soviet Union and are redefining their status as legal entities; therefore, when there's a resolution condemning the capture of territories, granted we defend the territorial integrity of Azerbaijan. But what happened to the autonomous status of Karabagh? That region had a legal status which was annulled unilaterally. When the United Nations defends the territorial integrity of one side, consideration must be given to the legal rights of the group which is on the other side of the equation. In the Israeli case, where there is no legal definition of the territories occupied, they are still considered "Israeli-occupied territories."*

JM - This is a very big question and it touches on a lot of fundamental issues about the territorial integrity of states and so forth. I'm not sure I can give you a really good short answer, but I'll try. When we recognized Azerbaijan, we recognized their sovereignty and territorial integrity. We are bound under the Charter and by other documents, as are all other states that have recognized Azerbaijan. That doesn't at all have any effect on what might be internal arrangements within Azerbaijan, autonomy being one of those. We have urged the Azeris over the last couple of years to restore that status of autonomy that their parliament simply brushed aside. We have also urged that the Armenian parliament revoke its law, which is still on the books, saying that Karabagh is annexed to Armenia, which is one of the things, the thing, that provoked the Azeri parliament to do its part. We've urged all of these parties, including Karabagh, to go back to the status that was in place after the demise of the USSR, as a way of being able at least to have a starting point for negotiations.

I think, more than that, you have to understand that borders do have status and they do have to be respected. That doesn't mean that borders never change. Obviously: our historical experience is that borders are constantly changing. Even in the last few years there have been many very important border changes. But if you allow, as a general matter, that any border can change, then you're inviting chaos. Our position has been that if there are to be changes in borders, they have to be negotiated peacefully. First of all, because it's an international principle--the UN Charter, and the final act of the Helsinki Accord, etc. Secondly, because otherwise you introduce force as a principle. And thirdly, because borders which are changed by force invite retaliation and revenge in the next generation. So you only have stability if you have agreed changes. That has been our purpose in the kind of negotiations we wanted to see. People say: well, why do you say that they can't change? Well, we haven't. We've specifically said that there should be a conference to decide what the status of Karabagh should be. So the international community has recognized that there may be a change in status there. It has to be discussed. But the very fact that we've specifically designated a conference to deal with it means that the international community has recognized that as a possibility. So that is, I think, a nice balance.

I could talk--and one of the things I carry around with me are articles I've written about this, because I've written a lot on this subject: in 1989, I published an article in the *Herald Tribune* in Paris [saying] that people have a right to choose--which was fixed on the coming break-up of the Soviet Union and what our position would be on that. And it was self-determination--but there have to be limits on it. Every little entity in the world does not have the right, would not have the right, to be an independent state; otherwise, there's chaos.

EA - *It looks as if first comes military force, the fait accompli, then negotiations, as in the Israeli-Arab situation. In Bosnia, the Serbs have occupied 70% of the land. Now they are sitting down to negotiate. It seems that military force always enters first, then negotiations and peace follow.*

JM - This is, unfortunately, the lesson of history. I think it's a very unfortunate lesson and it's one of the things in our time that we have to try to move away from. I'm not saying it's easy, but we have to try to move away from it and find other ways to deal with problems of this kind than by force. You have to remember also, in this particular case, that we of the international community only came into this problem after it was well on its way, because until 1992 it was an internal problem of the Soviet Union and we had nothing to do with it whatsoever. By the time we came in, it was a war. Anyway, it's a complicated issue and I don't pretend that there's a simple answer.

EA - *Maybe the next question is not fair to ask you. President*

Haidar Aliyev of Azerbaijan has been demanding that Karabagh Armenians disarm first, against the promise of treating them as equal Azeri citizens. But in the old system, legally speaking, Armenians were not Azeri citizens: they were Soviet citizens. Everyone was a Soviet citizen. With the collapse of the system, each Republic is defining its own citizenship. Can't the Armenians in Karabagh define their own?

JM - This is a $64,000 question. If Karabagh were an independent state, then of course they would be their own citizens, etc. If they're not, the other extreme--you might say, the ultimate solution--would be that Karabagh is just a province of Azerbaijan. Well, then Karabagh citizens would be citizens of Azerbaijan. There's no question in my mind that the people in Karabagh are simply not going to disarm themselves until their status has been settled, so it's not a real question. Obviously, the other side will make offers. One of the wondrous things about the former Soviet Union--and you know this better than anybody--is that they had all kinds of little statuses, and very different sometimes. The Slavic mentality is not so easy for us to understand.

EA - *And because nobody could use military force to impose his views on others, there was peace, but as soon as these individual entities were allowed to arm themselves, then each one decided to look after its own self-interest.*

JM - What I mean is this. It's a part of the world, and we in the West, I think, are not so comfortable with things that are in between independence and full absorption. But in the former Soviet Union there were many little in-betweens, and maybe there's a lesson for us in the West there also. Maybe we should not be so rigid on the dividing line between independence and non-dependence. There should be a lot of soft, intermediate solutions. This is my view, and I think this is one of these, like I say, one of the wondrous things about the Soviet Union: that it had these things. And maybe we should try to build on that to find solutions for some things: I don't know.

EA - *How does the US view Russia's pretensions of maintaining its military presence in the territories of the former Soviet Union? I understand that there was some concern expressed recently by the White House about Georgia: about the Russian presence in Georgia.*

JM - Well, this is a question that is evolving even as we speak. I think that if you would have asked this question a year ago, the answer would have been very different from what it would be now, because I think anyone can see that there has been an evolution: not just in the Russian attitude toward the "near abroad," but also in the Western, US attitude toward the reaction to that change. And so this is evolving right now.

EA - *Is there a policy to contain Russia? It looks as if there were a tacit or not so tacit understanding that Russia can do anything within the former Soviet borders and the US can do anything outside that sphere.*

JM - No: it's not true that there is any tacit understanding, that's for sure, but I think that people have different views on it. I happen to be one who's probably more hard-line than others on this issue. It's clear that there are security problems on the frontiers, and countries are legitimately concerned when they have security problems on the frontiers. So, many people would give the Russians the benefit of the doubt. At the other extreme, there's certainly no policy of containment of Russia. Nobody has established a policy of containment.

There's another point which needs to be made, and that is a recognition within this administration that the Russians have a legitimate concern about Russian nationals who were left over in these former Soviet Republics. And so there are some legitimate interests which are recognized in Washington and there are varying views on how one should deal with them. I think that the general tendency has been to become more concerned about the movement of Russians into these areas, and probably, more than anything else, because of the Karabagh issue. The Azeris, up until now, have tended to fend them off, so it's a kind of test case. Georgia has been a test case; the Baltics have been a test case, with some success: they are out of Lithuania; there are 600 Russian troops left in Estonia; there are 12,000 left in Latvia, and they are going to leave next week. We believe that they will leave, and so this is an evolving thing, and it's being handled carefully.

EA - *Armenia has an agreement or treaty with Russia to have Russian troops stationed on its territory. Any threat or perceived threat from Turkey will strengthen both the Armenian and the Russian resolve to keep them there and to strengthen their positions. Is it in the interest of the US to restrain Turkey? Because in Özal's time, Turkey threatened hot pursuit of Kurdish rebels all the way into Armenian territory.*

JM - Certainly one of the most worrying things about this whole conflict is the fact that you have Russian and Turkish troops facing each other. Russian troops still guard that frontier. They don't in Azerbaijan, but they do in Armenia, so that's the place where the Russians and the Turks still face each other in somewhat of a hostile frame of mind. That has been one of the most worrying aspects about this whole picture. Just as the Russians are nationalistic and have a kind of a rising feeling of nationalism, so do the Turks. One of the features of the break-up of the

Soviet Union is that the Turks discovered all of these kindred nations, and that has excited a sense of identity in the Turks. And the sense of identity in the Turks has a history of its own. The Turks have suffered, during the Soviet era, in establishing that identity. And we suffered from it too. And these are phenomena that are there: you can't sweep them away. All I can say is that the US government is very aware of the dangers of that confrontation problem.

EA - *You don't think that the United States or the West will ever encourage Turkey to test Russia's resolve to defend its former borders?*

JM - On the contrary, we've been discouraging everybody from getting involved in this thing. The Turks are quite cautious in this respect, despite what they may say.

EA - *But the Turks are now building up a case against Armenia. Their news media and even government officials keep accusing Armenia of harboring Kurdish terrorist camps. This, in their minds, will build up a case against Armenia so that, should they decide to invade Armenia some day, they will have prepared international public opinion for that action.*

JM - Both they and the Russians are trying to put their groundwork in place.

EA - *Now we come to the question of the US Government's position if Karabagh is over-run by Azerbaijan. Do you think the US would have a hands-off policy?*

JM - I can't answer that certainly: that's speculation.

EA - *It is a hypothetical question. But is there any contingency formula for that?*

JM - Most people in government refuse categorically to answer hypothetical questions--for good reasons.

EA - *Has the State Department confirmed news-media reports that Atlanta-based MegaOil has been supplying Azerbaijan with military advisers and trainers? We understand that General Secord was there recently.*

JM - I don't believe that there has been any public confirmation. The last I heard was that all of the rumors were being looked into. There are certain things that would be against the law.

EA - *British laws don't allow them to send mercenaries, but there are persistent reports that Azeris are recruiting mercenaries. The presence of Turkish military advisers is a confirmed fact.*

JM - Even there, if you're asking whether the State Department has confirmed that, I don't believe so. I don't believe there has been a statement confirming it publicly.

EA - *I follow the Turkish press very closely, and they openly admit that the recent Azeri successes can be attributed to Turkish advisers stationed in Azerbaijan.*

JM - I follow the same press articles as you do. That's different from the State Department confirming it.

EA - *I have one last question. You're very much involved and you know all the details of the conflict intimately. What would be an equitable and fair solution to the Karabagh conflict: one that would satisfy all the parties, or one that would satisfy the major powers but settle the issue to the dissatisfaction of the players?*

JM - I'll tell you when I retire. This is what I've stayed away from, but when I retire I may tell you: maybe sooner than you think. By the way, I'm no longer handling the Karabagh conflict.

March 19, 1994

Cautious Optimism on Peace Prospect

President Levon Ter Petrossian's senior political adviser, Dr. Girard Libaridian, recently visited the University of Michigan in Ann Arbor to deliver a lecture on Armenia's foreign policy. Prior to his lecture he met with Edmond Y. Azadian, Chairman of the ADL[1] Press Committee, to discuss many of Armenia's foreign policy issues.

EA - *I would like to take this opportunity to ask you to give us an assessment of President Ter Petrossian's recent visit to the United States on the occasion of the 50th anniversary of the United Nations, above and beyond the protocol: the impact of his meetings with heads of states, and especially his meetings with the Administration of the United States. What returns or dividends will Armenia reap from this visit?*

GL - Well, obviously one cannot discount the significance of the protocol aspect of the visit, considering that this was Armenia's participation in the 50th anniversary of the founding of the United Nations and the first time Armenia had come to and the President of Armenia had participated in those proceedings and celebrations. The non-political and protocol aspects of this visit were quite important in comparison with those of other occasions.

But, as you implied, there was also a political aspect to the visit: consultations with various leaders of states--the Vice President of the United States, Mr. Gore; the President of Turkey, Mr. Demirel; and the President of Azerbaijan, Mr. Aliyev. The political aspect was significant in the sense that not only were the bases for co-operation between the two republics, the United States and Armenia, reconfirmed once more, but each side also confirmed that Armenia had made sufficient progress towards democracy, economic reform, and stability to warrant continued

---

1. *Armenian Democratic Liberal Organization.*

support from the United States. The visit also produced an understanding that there will be an intensification of efforts to resolve the Nagorno Karabagh conflict, and that the parties to the conflict welcome the increased interest of the United States Government in the resolution of that conflict. The last meeting produced specific steps which I personally believe will lead not only to an intensification of the discussions and negotiations, but possibly also to significant progress in the next few months.

EA - *There was a banquet in Washington at the conclusion of the President's visit, following the dedication of the new Embassy building, and the Washington power structure was there. A pretty comprehensive cross-section of the Armenian-American community was represented. The President's speech, by the way, was an excellent one: it was very well organized and it sent the right messages to the right parties: national, domestic, and international. The President raised two major issues: one issue was evaluating the importance of the Armenian-American community or the Armenian diaspora community as a political force, and the other issue, which complements the first, was his concluding observation that the Armenian Assembly should serve as a role model for all Armenian diaspora organizations, meaning that those organizations should lend their support to Armenia without seeking to further their own political ambitions. Would you comment on these issues? How does the President evaluate the political presence of the Armenians in America, which was emphasized and over-emphasized by the speakers, the senators, and the congressmen? Secondly, how will his limitations on the ambitions of Armenian organizations in the United States or the diaspora be applied?*

GL - I think that over the years the President has developed a very deep understanding and appreciation of the role played by Armenians in the various countries where they live, and his assessment is very positive. He particularly appreciates those dimensions in communities which are integrated into the processes of the countries in which they live, as opposed to the ghetto-style politics of some of the organizations or the ghetto mentality, which can become dominant. So, over the years that I have known him, he has always appreciated it when an Armenian community in a country is part of the process in that country and at the same time has a strong feeling for Armenia and the issues in and around Armenia. So in that respect I think there is a much wider context to the issue than he might have been able to express at the banquet.

Secondly, I think he has a very clear understanding of the emotional and historical commitment to Armenia which the Government and people of the United States have manifested since the First World War and its aftermath. I think the most important thing is that he is determined to resist any organization's claim that it has the right to participate in decisions which affect the future of Armenia. After all, democracy does not give special rights to Armenians in general, but rather to the citizens of Armenia--in a specific geographic setting, within clearly-defined borders; and his point would be that the people of Armenia, who must suffer the consequences of their votes and decision-making, are the only ones--through whatever party, association, or organization--who should make decisions for Armenia.

The role of the diaspora communities is to participate in a way that is, first of all, not contrary to international law, not contrary to Armenian law, and not contrary to American law; and the model of the Armenian Assembly is that it works as a group, as an Armenian-American community in Washington: it presents what it sees as the interests of this community. At the same time, it tries to co-ordinate its efforts with the policies of Armenia--without claiming the right to determine those policies for Armenia and without Armenia's having to impose its policies on the Armenian Assembly--since it sees fit to define its role as that of an organization within the community. So I think that in that context the President's comments should be seen not as a criticism of any organization, but rather as a thinking process, after so many upheavals in Armenian life over the past five to seven years--from the independence movement, to the earthquake, to independence itself, to the war in Karabagh--all of which destabilized the situation, not only in Armenia, but also in diaspora community life. It is now necessary to rethink the processes, and since we do now have a structure called the State of Armenia, the Republic of Armenia, which has its own institutions and can articulate its own interests, it is necessary that community organizations articulate their interests and try to co-ordinate them with state policy, to the extent that this is both feasible and possible--without the government of Armenia's trying to regulate life in the diaspora or diaspora organizations' trying to determine policy in Armenia.

EA - *Where do we stand in Armenia's relations with Turkey? For what it is worth, many political observers think that you, personally, are the architect of Armenian-Turkish relations and recent developments in those relations. I refer particularly to the Turkish delegation which visited Armenia during the course of this year, the members of which paid their respects at the Martyrs' Monument. Was that incidental? Was that only lip service, or may we consider it a break-through or the beginning of the end of Genocide denial?*

GL - When an issue is as loaded as Turkish recognition of the

Genocide, it is difficult to believe that the visit could have been incidental. I think that you yourself pointed out in one of your articles that
this event has not been given the significance it deserves. It is obvious
that the President and Prime Minister of Turkey were very well aware of
the delegation's visit to Armenia. It is not just wishful thinking: we
understand the visit to have been a real break-through to the beginning
of possible recognition. One should not exaggerate, but at the same time
one cannot avoid the feeling that this was an important small step in the
right direction and that we are on the right path. There has been slow
progress, hampered by difficulties. The economic interests shared by the
two republics have helped us move onto the right path towards normal-
izing our relations with Turkey. I believe that resolving the conflict in
those relations may take a longer time than we anticipate, but that is
normal. We have too many issues with Turkey--too many difficult steps-
-and if it takes longer, that is fine.

As far as my role is concerned, I think that, at least in the case of
Armenia and the Government of Armenia, policies should not be per-
sonalized. Collective thinking and collective action saved Armenia, in
contrast to some of its neighbors. We work collectively: we work together, we reach a consensus, and we function accordingly. While it may have
fallen upon me to perform certain functions, the policy is that of the
Government of Armenia. And one should not underestimate the political imagination of President Ter Petrossian.

EA - *What price, if any, did Armenia pay for the recent concessions
by Turkey in opening the air corridor? It looks as if it was a one-sided concession, unless there was a deal under the table.*

GL - With regard to the first question, on the price Armenia
may have paid to have the air corridor opened, I think it would be fair
to say that there was no deal made. Just continuing discussions in mul-
tilateral forums and bilateral discussions on steps that would help
improve relations. The main factor in those discussions is the separation
of the two main issues: the improvement of bilateral relations and
progress in the Karabagh peace process. We tend to separate these issues;
Turkey tends to combine them. As the discussions progress, each side
does whatever it feels comfortable doing, but there is no deal, so to
speak. Turkey thought that it could open the air corridor to Armenian
flights over Turkey without losing much. It is expected that Armenia
may do something, there were no immediate steps that we could have
taken to satisfy that expectation. I should add that there are now weekly Armenian flights to Istanbul.

EA - *What are the dividends for both sides in the warming up of relations?*

GL - We always look at those steps not as a trade-off, but as each side's doing something that is beneficial to both. The opening up of air space was something that Turkey should have done a long time ago, because we never closed our air space.

EA - *It is a common belief that the blockade is reciprocal: that Armenia is blockading Azerbaijan as much as Azerbaijan is blockading Armenia.*

GL - Armenia has never blockaded Azerbaijan. The air space has never been closed, either by Azerbaijan or by Armenia. It is land routes and pipelines and railroad tracks that have been closed. We have always told Azerbaijan and everyone concerned that our roads and railroads are open; it is Azerbaijani ideology that the blockade system must be maintained.

But the important thing is that in our opinion the improvement in relations between Armenia and Turkey is not only good for Armenia. It is also good for Turkey. It is in the interests of Turkey, not just of Armenia. Therefore, we are not prepared to say that we are ready to make concessions to Turkey in order to see the borders open. Opening the borders would also be beneficial to Turkey, and eventually to the Central Asian Republics. The main railroad which connects the Caucasus to Russia, Central Asia, Iran, and Turkey runs through Armenia. So this is something that would be useful to Turkey. Whenever they are ready not only to recognize that, but also to act upon that recognition, we are prepared to go along.

EA - *Will you comment on the passage of the Corridor Act? How would that impact on Turkey's behavior vis-a-vis Armenia? Does Turkey now expect reciprocal and corresponding concessions from Armenia? What impact would the passage of the Corridor Act have on Turkey's policy to continue blockading Armenia? Would it help or would it aggravate relations or would it not make any difference, if the land corridor were opened up?*

GL - There are two aspects to that issue. One is that the act is based on principle: that those who get American assistance should not interfere with American interests in neighboring countries. It is very difficult to argue against the Corridor Act, which says that the United States should not support or provide assistance to countries that blockade the transport of US humanitarian assistance to a third or neighboring country. Secondly, I am not sure that the Government of Turkey, involved as it is in so many domestic and foreign policy issues, understands the significance of that. Sometimes countries act on the basis of symbols rather than out of real interests. I personally am not sure what the impact of that Act will be on Turkey.

EA - *The next question is about the conflict in Karabagh. Recently, Deputy Foreign Minister Vartan Oskanian made a statement in an article or a speech which worried many Armenians. It was alarmingly conciliatory concerning the return of captured territories. It looked as if most of the captured territories were being traded away for uncertain guarantees. Even after an announcement like that, the negotiations in Moscow appear to have failed, since Mr. Oskanian came out empty-handed, as he confessed. So, what issue is blocking success when, from all appearances, the Armenian side seems prepared to go the extra mile in order to attain a settlement?*

GL - First, let me point out that while there may be an impression that the Armenian side--meaning both Armenia and Karabagh--are ready to go the extra mile for a settlement, the Azerbaijani delegation thinks exactly the contrary: that the Armenian side is too harsh, too rigid, too uncompromising. Secondly, in regard to withdrawals, there is nothing new in what the Deputy Foreign Minister said. That means that both Armenia and Karabagh have accepted the principle of withdrawals. The principle of withdrawals from territories--but not from territories which have anything to do with the security of Karabagh--has been established, has been accepted, but not as a unilateral action. That, in turn, should bring peace and security to the region. That would also bring an end to the blockades. Should this happen, there could be withdrawals.

There are a few differences between Armenia and Karabagh. Should a determination of the status of Nagorno Karabagh be part of this withdrawal package or not? In this matter Armenia is not basing its actions on any ideology or principle, but on what will work. If we are capable of determining the status of Karabagh at this time, that is all very well. But we believe that if that status should prove difficult to agree upon at this point, we must resolve then not to freeze the situation as it is. It would be possible to conduct the withdrawals after the arrival of peacekeeping forces in the area. The goal then would be to preserve the link from Armenia to Karabagh through the Lachin corridor, and to transform the cease-fire into peace. And then, once we have created a much better environment of trust and confidence, we could negotiate the status of Karabagh. Both of these approaches are acceptable to us. It is a matter of methodology--it is a matter of what will work--rather than of ideology.

So I think that, while the formal negotiations have so far not produced significant results, there has nevertheless been some progress. We have a document--which is a political agreement--of which a good portion of the text has been agreed upon, although I would have to agree with the Deputy Foreign Minister that the progress we have made has not been on the major issues. But we believe that a good half of this problem is attributable to the fact that so far Azerbaijan has refused to negotiate seriously. They have relied, more particularly in the last year, on the influence which they hope and pray that the oil consortium members will exert on Armenia, away from the negotiating table, in order to get concessions from the Armenian side which the Armenian side would not otherwise give. I think that some time very soon Azerbaijan will realize that outside pressure will not influence the Armenian side to make any concessions regarding oil, pipelines, or any other deal, that it would not otherwise make. Whatever concessions we make will be on the merits of the issues which emerge during negotiations, and not because any given country or consortium has blackmailed us or pressured us, or whatever. The security of our people in Karabagh and their right to self-determination is what will determine the concessions, the agreements, that we sign.

EA - *The last question touches on economics. It is about the recommissioning of the nuclear power plant. What kind of impact is it going to make on the economy, the ecology, and regional politics? We have heard that Azerbaijan and Turkey are disturbed by the reactivation of the nuclear power plant. I do not know whether they have made a formal protest, but they are disturbed. First, what is the impact of the reactivation of the power plant on relations with our neighbors? Is it going to aggravate tensions, or will it not make any difference? Second, is it going to help the economy and significantly ease the domestic pressures on the people?*

GL - One should realize that at full capacity the reactivated power plant will produce about 400+ megawatts. That is 25% of the electricity consumed in Armenia. Technically, we should achieve 50% of that capacity in 1998. We will reduce to zero the over-usage of the water in Lake Sevan. Ecologically speaking, this will save Lake Sevan. On a practical level, it will provide additional energy for manufacturing and for homes, which will make Armenia more independent. This is what Azerbaijan in particular and to some extent Turkey are concerned about: that is, to the extent that the Azerbaijani psychology and negotiating position have been based on the blockade of Armenia. The activation of the nuclear plant is obviously one of the methods Armenia has come up with to circumvent the Azerbaijani blockade, so it makes that blockade less effective. It also makes the Turkish embargo less restrictive.

But I also recognize that at least in Turkey some people have very serious concerns about safety and about the fact that they have no knowledge of the safety levels of the nuclear plant. There is a legitimate interest. On the other hand, there has been no formal statement; we have not formally received any protest. There have been informal statements from Turkey concerning matters which they would like the experts to check, but for that there are formal channels to follow and so far I do not believe that we have received anything specifically or directly from Turkey to suggest that they want to come and inspect our plant. True, the absence of diplomatic relations would be a serious obstacle to the implementation of that goal. On the other hand, we would consider it.

EA - *Thank you for your informative and insightful discussion of these most topical issues. Good luck with your endeavors to convert the cease-fire into a permanent peace!*

March 19, 1994

A Challenge to the Deniers of the Armenian Genocide

Professor Raymond Tanter teaches Political Science at the University of Michigan in Ann Arbor. He has served the Reagan Administration as a member of the National Security Council. He is well known in political circles, specializing in Israeli-US relations. On a recent visit to Israel, he stumbled on a topical issue in the Israeli press, in which deniers of the Armenian Genocide had taken up the case with the Israeli Ministry of Education, seeking to exclude an Armenian Genocide segment from Holocaust studies. Professor Tanter published an article in The Jerusalem Post *which suggested that of all the peoples of the world the Jews must take the moral high ground on the issue of genocide. The denial of the Armenian Genocide is being hotly discussed in the Israeli news media these days, and Professor Tanter has taken a very strong position in favor of recognition of the Armenian Genocide. To get further background on Professor Tanter's interest in the issue, a three-way conversation took place with Professor Tanter, Professor Kevork Bardakjian, holder of the Marie Manoogian Chair in Armenian Studies at the University of Michigan, and Edmond Azadian.*

EA - *Professor Tanter, how did you get interested in the Armenian Genocide issue?*

RT - As a scholar I am interested in small countries in turbulent environments; hence I am attracted to states like Israel, Latvia, and Armenia. As the Cold War ended, the West emerged triumphant, yet regional conflicts have escalated and expanded. In contrast, as the hot war in the Gulf ended, the western nations, joined by moderate Arab states and Israel, were the victors over Iraq, and conflicts in the region have diminished in intensity. I also go where the action is. That is, I like to study emerging conflicts. So, Nagorno Karabagh--the regional conflict between Armenia and Azerbaijan--concerns me.

And the issue of the Armenian Genocide emerged for me in Jerusalem, after I had visited Yad Vashem, the Holocaust Memorial to Jews who were victims of the Nazis. With memories of the Jewish

Holocaust in mind, I heard that there was a question of whether the
Armenian Genocide should be incorporated into the high school curriculum in Israel. I wondered how this could be a question, because
Israel itself has the moral high ground on all issues concerning the
Holocaust and genocide. Therefore it has the moral standing to assert
itself. Hence, I began to challenge Israeli Genocide deniers. Jews who say
that the Armenian Genocide never happened are like those who say that
the Jewish Holocaust never happened: both are wrong!

EA - *It is inconceivable that a denial should come from, of all people, Jews, who have suffered so much in similar circumstances.*

RT - I told a friend of mine who is Israeli that Jews have suffered
so much they may have "no right to do wrong." He agreed with me. And
because they know what it means to be wronged, the Jews are the hold-
ers of the moral balance among the people on earth. Thus, Israel can take
on countries like Turkey over moral issues such as the Genocide.

EA - *What were you doing in Jerusalem?*

RT - In Jerusalem, I was writing a book called *Rogue States*. It's
about the US sanctions directed against all the "bad guys" in the world,
such as the leaders of Iran, Iraq and, to a lesser extent, Cuba: because
Castro is a tired guy, you might say! I was staying at a place called
Mishkenot Sha'ananim. It's the mayor's guest house.

EA - *So that's where you came across this discussion or dispute in*
The Jerusalem Post *concerning whether Israel should include the Genocide
in its high school curriculum?*

RT - Yes; I was in Jerusalem reading *The Jerusalem Post*, having just
left the Holocaust Memorial, and discovered in the paper that there was a
debate concerning whether the government of Israel should incorporate
the Armenian and Gypsy genocides into its high school curriculum.

EA - *What is the goal of Professor Kerem in trying to refute you?
First, where does he get his information? Second, does he have a specific agenda in Israeli politics?*

RT - Kerem--who calls himself a professor and a Holocaust
scholar, and may not be either--does not represent Holocaust scholarship
in Israel. I know several people who are Holocaust scholars and he does-
n't have a high reputation with them. At issue between Professor Kerem
and me is whether or not the Armenian Genocide happened. And, to
answer your question, I believe that he obtains his information from
Turkish sources, while my information comes from neutral sources.

I take the position that the Genocide did occur, and Kerem says
that there were killings of Armenians by Ottoman Turks, but he argues

that since these killings did not occur throughout the Ottoman Empire but were only concentrated in certain areas, the casualties were not racial but political. On the other hand, I suggest that the fact that the killings took place only in certain places is indicative that the Ottoman Turks wanted to prevent foreign diplomats from reporting what the Turks had done to the Armenians. As you know, communication was very difficult between Constantinople and towns in Anatolia. The Armenian provinces were isolated from the capital, while massacres occurred in sites such as desert trails, canyons, and other areas where it was unlikely that foreign diplomats would be present. The only persons who could witness what was happening were military personnel or those who were part of military transport units using the Baghdad Railway. As Ottoman citizens, many Jews were in the service of the empire as technical experts, military officers, and soldiers who could move around easily. An Israeli historian, Dr. Yair Auron, has found archival material in the form of the letters, memoirs, and reports of Jewish officers serving in the Ottoman Army between 1914-18. These documents provide evidence that the Genocide against the Armenians occurred, contrary to the claims of the deniers.

Kerem may have an agenda in downplaying the existence of evidence of the occurrence of the Genocide: he contends that Armenians committed atrocities against Jews during the Holocaust. But I cannot substantiate that claim, and I think it is false. I have never heard this charge before. In this respect, I spoke with my colleague here, Professor Bardakjian. Because he directs the Centers for Armenian Studies, the Slavic Languages, and Research on Eastern European Studies, I imagined that Bardakjian would have knowledge of the Kerem allegations. He cannot find any substantiation for this claim. I also spoke with Professor Zvi Gitelman, another Michigan colleague. He is a specialist on European Jewry, and knows of no evidence that Armenians systematically engaged in the killing of Jews.

EA - *But ...*

RT - Kerem suggests that once Armenians began to fight back they were fair game for the Ottoman Turks. I would respond to that by asking: why, on April 24, 1915, did the Ottoman Turks begin the systematic killing of Armenian elites--poets, scholars, humanists? These people had done nothing; they were not engaged in any military uprising. They were the generators of ideas, the carriers of a culture. And when you want to eliminate a group, you first cut off its head: the cultural, spiritual, and political leadership. That's precisely what the Ottoman Turks did.

EA - *Now where do we stand as far as the textbooks are concerned?*

RT - At issue with the textbooks was whether the Government of Israel would incorporate into its high school curriculum the teaching of other tragedies, such as the Armenian Genocide by the Ottoman Turks and what the Nazis did to the Gypsies. Right now, the Government of Israel only teaches about the Jewish Holocaust, and the Education Ministry itself commissioned a study in order to get evidence of other tragedies [that were] like the Jewish Holocaust. It is my understanding that the Education Ministry is reversing its decision but, as you know, in politics "nothing is nailed down unless it's nailed up." And it's not in concrete; therefore, I am personally going back to Jerusalem between July 18 and August 18. One of the reasons for my trip is to pin down this particular decision by the Education Ministry.

EA - *Now we know that in attempting to deny the Armenian Genocide the Turks have manufactured huge lies, and they've been publishing books saying that not only did the Turks not kill Armenians, but that Armenians killed Turks. How that could have happened, I don't know: when you have an enormous empire with a mighty army and a subject people, how that can happen is beyond comprehension. But what Kerem injects here is a very dangerous political game: he accuses Armenians of active terrorism and military despotism in order to overthrow the Ottoman regime. That's one charge; and the other accusation, which is highly explosive politically, is that Armenians participated with the Nazis in the killing of Jews. On the contrary, when the Nazis invaded the Crimea, many Armenians there protected the Jews.*

RT - Well, by criticizing the Armenians for fighting back against the Turks Kerem implicitly condemns the Warsaw uprising by the Jews against the Nazis. If a subject people begins to assert its identity and fight back against oppressors, then people like Kerem come along later and say that this constitutes some kind of terrorism by the oppressed. Kerem has it all wrong: the Jews had a legitimate right to fight off their Nazi oppressors, just as the Armenians had a legitimate right to fight off the Ottoman Turks.

KB - Armenians simply did not want to be killed like sheep. That's the simplest explanation. They knew that they were facing certain death, and hence, some Armenians fought back whenever they could.

RT - Let me develop that point. When I was at Yad Vashem-- one of the things that I learned at the Jewish Holocaust Memorial in Jerusalem was that too many Jews were killed like lambs, passively going to the slaughter. They walked to their deaths. If you recall from reading the book *Schindler's List* or seeing the movie, the Jews acted too passively when confronting their Nazi murderers. So, one of the lessons of the Holocaust is "never again." Never again will Jews go like lambs. The Armenians knew from the beginning that they didn't want to go like lambs, and they fought back. But, in fact, very few fought back.

EA - *Very few, in the very few areas where there was some kind of support, such as in Musa Dagh, where they got on to the mountain and were eventually rescued by a French battleship which was passing by. And in Van they halted the Turkish advance until the Russian army came and saved 250,000. These were very legitimate instances of self defense.*

KB - After the Armenian leadership was decapitated, after they had rounded up all other communities, they knew what was going to happen.

EA - *Yes. The Turks were very tight-lipped and secretive; they isolated different communities so that they could not communicate with each other by telephone, telegraph, etc. But some people who escaped the slaughters and were able to reach the next village or town warned them about what was happening.*

RT - One of the issues between Kerem and me has to do with why the Ottoman Turks only killed in certain areas. And not only was it the case that the Ottoman Turks killed selectively to keep the foreign diplomats from knowing what was going on, but it was also the case that the Turks wanted to keep the Armenian leadership itself divided and uninformed.

EA - *But it isn't true, what Kerem says: that in Syria, Lebanon, and Palestine the local people were not killed. That's not true; it contradicts history. There were mass executions of Christian intellectuals and leaders in Beirut, Lebanon. Even today there is the Martyrs' Plaza, which is the main square in Beirut, where they executed the local leaders. The same thing happened in Syria: the Turks executed the leaders. This contradicts Kerem's theory.*

RT - No, actually it fits Kerem's theory. If Arabs and Armenians were killed, then it's political. If only Armenians were killed, then it could be ...

EA - *It could be racial.*

KB - The Arabs were looking for independence from the Ottoman Turks. That's a separate issue. But what happened was that in the easternmost part of what is known today as Turkey, there were outright massacres. If you check the oral history, we have no survivors from that region. But from the West we do have survivors who were closer to the capital, closer to the diplomatic corps, and thus these survivors had some kind of protection from being killed on the spot.

RT - The closer you get to the diplomatic corps ...

KB - But Armenians near the diplomatic corps were simply deported. They were not killed in place; they were all deported to the final destination, Syria--that's where they were killed.

RT - I think Hitler probably got the idea of deporting the Jews from the way that the Turks killed Armenians, in the sense "don't kill them all in one place; deport first, then kill second."

KB - One of Hitler's closest advisers was the German Consul in Turkey, who himself witnessed the Genocide, wrote reports back to the German Foreign Ministry, and later became Hitler's adviser ...

RT - Was this adviser to Hitler advising him on the killing of Jews?

KB - No; the adviser was active when Hitler started his movement in the early 1920s, i.e., before the Holocaust. He was killed in the Munich Putsch. Hitler uses this story of what happened to the Armenians. Although we have no records of conversations between Hitler and this adviser, it stands to reason that this person told Hitler what happened to the Armenians.

RT - What does Kerem say about American historian Heath Lowry? Lowry says that Ambassador Morgenthau was using forged documents.

KB - This is Heath Lowry's methodology. He finds a small gray area and he builds his case on it. This happened with Professor Richard Hovanissian. In two bulky volumes he found one footnote, one single footnote, about the secondary source information and he built up a whole thesis. Since this footnote was incorrect, Lowry argued that the whole work was incorrect. So what Lowry did was take Morgenthau's memoirs, find some gray areas, then seek to discredit the whole of the memoirs.

EA - *The diaries, which are more factual ...*

RT - Because they're day-to-day accounts, diaries are more valid than memoirs, which are after-the-fact recollections.

EA - *Morgenthau's diaries are in the custody of the State Department, and they're being edited for publication. And there's another set of documents that Susan Blair is editing.*

RT - My understanding is that Israeli historian Yair Auron drew on the State Department collection, but not all the volumes are out.

EA - *There are two things. First, there are Morgenthau's memoirs, which Lowry disputes.*

RT - Kerem also disputes Morgenthau's memoirs.

EA - *Kerem relies on Lowry. Now that the diaries have been dis-*

covered to substantiate those memoirs, they have to devise another way of denying that it was genocide.

RT - My response to Kerem and Lowry is to cite not only the memoirs, but also the diaries of Henry Morgenthau.

EA - *Quoting Heath Lowry, Kerem says that Ambassador Morgenthau's story, meaning his memoirs, is a forgery; he further says that Tanter is also unaware of numerous Armenian forgeries of documents from diplomats and politicians from the United States, Great Britain, Turkey, and Germany.*

RT - I am unaware of those forged documents. I think that Kerem is on very weak grounds when he cites Lowry--for a couple of reasons. One: it seems to me that Morgenthau's memoirs are being reinforced by the diaries. There is a man at the University of Michigan who is publishing the diaries of Ambassador Morgenthau, and I think that Kerem is simply unaware of this particular research, which is ongoing. Secondly, Kerem suggests that I am unaware of the Armenian forgeries and yes, I am unaware of that which doesn't exist.

KB - And Kerem seems to be unaware of a recent article by three scholars, all of them in America, who inadvertently received copies of correspondence from Heath Lowry and the Turkish Ambassador to the United States. No one was supposed to see these but someone at the Turkish embassy mistakenly included these letters, so there is an article which questions Heath Lowry's scholarship and integrity. This is very important.

EA - *Now, taking the broader picture--you are involved in high political circles. What would you advise Armenians to do in terms of networking with other ethnic groups and forcing the Genocide issue into the political arena?*

RT - My view is that Armenia is too important to be left to the Armenians. Just as Israel is too important to be left to the Jews. Armenians need political allies. What this means is that coalitions ought to be formed of like-minded people: people who are concerned with justice, legitimacy, and truth.

The Congressional Black Caucus has ties with the government of Israel and the American Israel Public Affairs Committee. There is an effective linkage between Black American leaders and the Jewish-American political leadership. There is no reason why this couldn't happen with respect to the Armenians as well. But the ties have to be built. Linkages are not accidental; they have to be forged; they have to be created. So I would recommend, on networking, that Armenians reach out to other ethnic groups: the Greeks, for example, because of their common difficulties with respect to Turkey. Reach out to the Jews, because both the Armenians and the Jews have suffered, in the Genocide and the Holocaust respectively.

I am president of Balance Our Future, which is an Ann Arbor non-profit, non-partisan organization devoted to studying regional conflicts and building coalitions among various ethnic groups. Balance Our Future works on issues [such as] Armenia versus Azerbaijan concerning Nagorno Karabagh, and works on issues [such as] the Armenian Genocide in relation to the Jewish Holocaust.

KB - Given political alliances and interests, this is a perennial issue in that in politics the leadership of a given country is led by interests, rather than the truth or historical truth, or whatever. Since you have set up this think-tank organization, do you think in the end such organizations could make some difference, could influence the political elite who may even know or be convinced that the Genocide happened, but...

RT - OK, organizations, as such, are not as important as people. Armenian-Americans already have excellent contacts with the Republican and Democratic leadership at the state level and at the national level. I think effective action is being taken and can be taken in the future. Look: nothing happens on its own, and when you talk about interests, the US has interests in Turkey, but the Greeks lobby hard. Yet the Turks receive American foreign assistance, and the Greeks also get money. The US tries to establish a peace process between Turkey and Greece so that it can avoid having to choose between the two. Similarly, the Saudis have oil; Israel is an ally and friend. You can't say that in the absence of the Cold War the US lost all its interests in Israel. But Israel has legitimacy, and it has the political community fighting for aid to Israel in Congress. Those two things together are what Armenian-Americans could improve upon. There is less of a perception of the legitimacy of the Genocide cause than in the case of the Jewish Holocaust. There is the Holocaust Memorial in Washington, and Armenian-Americans need to be represented better there. How are the Armenians represented in the Holocaust Memorial located in Washington?

EA - *Just one sentence. Hitler's statement ...*

RT - But how are the Armenians represented?

KB - They're not represented as such.

RT - OK: that's one of the points I'm making. The Armenian Genocide has to reach the public through the intellectuals, through the people who write op-ed pieces in newspapers, through letters to the editor. In Michigan there ought to be a concerted effort to get the point across, and not just by ordinary people, but by people who have "Professor" associated with their names. That's important. Your question is a good one. Can a single organization working out of Ann Arbor make a difference? I say yes. You target a specific group and you just start hammering and you see that you too can make a difference.

I don't know why the Israeli Education Ministry began to turn around on the issue of teaching about the Genocide, but I'm not surprised it did. It didn't hurt that I was in there pushing the Armenian agenda. Similarly, with respect to foreign assistance to Armenia, it doesn't hurt for someone to push. There are people pushing for Lithuania, for Latvia--and the foreign-aid pie is getting smaller and smaller. So therefore, active political lobbying is the only way to save the day. The pro-Israel community is the engine that drives the foreign-aid train. Without Israel there would be no foreign aid, because no member of Congress wants to vote for foreign aid. The American public thinks that foreign aid is in the hundreds of billions of dollars, when it is only fifteen billion, which is less than one-half of one percent of the Federal Budget. But the public thinks that it's huge.

King Hussein was recently photographed with 75 presidents of American Jewish organizations. Why do you think he took a picture with them? Because he was trying to get the $250 million ear-marked in the US Foreign Assistance Program for Jordan.

EA - *Thank you.*

August 26, 1995